C000111250

THOMI KELLER

A Life in Sport

THOMI KELLER
A Life in Sport

David Owen

First published in 2018 by Independent Publishing Network

Copyright © David Owen 2018

The moral right of David Owen to be identified as the
author of this work has been asserted in accordance with
the Copyright, Designs and Patents Act 1988.

All rights reserved. No part of this publication may be reproduced or
transmitted in any form or by any means, electronic or mechanical including
photocopying, recording or any information storage or retrieval system,
without prior permission in writing from the publishers.

Every effort has been made to trace copyright holders and to obtain their
permission for the use of copyright material. The publisher apologises
for any errors or omissions and would be grateful to be notified of any
corrections that should be incorporated in future editions of this book.

ISBN 978-1-78808-468-0

Also available as an ebook
ISBN 978-1-78808-467-3

Typeset by Tetragon, London
Cover design by Steve Leard
Printed and bound in Great Britain by Clays Ltd, St Ives plc

FSC
www.fsc.org

MIX
Paper from
responsible sources
FSC® C018072

For Martin, who loved to row

ALSO BY DAVID OWEN

Foinavon:
The Story of the Grand National's Biggest Upset

Rain Starts Play

Contents

Foreword

Like some stranded concrete and glass spaceship, the Palace of Culture and Sports has been part of Varna's cityscape for half a century now. Yet it remains just as distinctive as on the day, towards the end of the Black Sea's 1973 summer-holiday season, when a tall Swiss sports administrator with winning brown eyes took the floor there and announced himself as a figure of global stature.

Thomi Keller was already a commanding force in his own sport of rowing. He had acceded to the presidency of the world governing body fifteen years earlier at the unfeasibly young age of thirty-three. Now a gathering of Olympic top brass in this quiet resort in Communist Bulgaria afforded him an opportunity to make his mark on a bigger stage. With influential members of the international press present in numbers[1] – this was, after all, the first Olympic meeting of its kind for forty-three years – Keller grabbed his chance with both hands. His blunt, hard-hitting speech became the story of the day. From then on when Keller spoke, the sports world listened.

The immediate effect of Keller's blistering address, in which he took the Olympic world to task over the then burning issue of "shamateurism" and criticised some administrators for being vain and out of touch, can best be gauged by the comments of *The Times'* John Hennessy some days later as he tried to sum up the congress's broader significance. "If one man more than any other

has made a special impact during the tenth Olympic Congress...
it is Thomas Keller," he wrote. "He has the air of a born winner"
and had emerged as "a big man with a big future".[2]

There was an alternative view. "Mad dog without a collar" was
how one Belgian journalist reported that an International Olympic
Committee (IOC) member – "and not the least significant one" –
had "baptised" the Swiss boss of international rowing. The journalist went on: "The definition is apt and describes the personality
quite well: dynamic, intelligent, passionate (often too passionate),
but having an annoying propensity to want to impose his will on
everyone."[3] This short clipping was in Keller's own blue "Varna
1973" file, perhaps hinting that he found the headline description
not altogether displeasing.

With his barnstorming performance in Varna, Keller asserted
himself – alongside figures such as the recently installed IOC president Lord Killanin, his soon-to-be-deposed counterpart at the world
football body FIFA, Sir Stanley Rous, and veteran world athletics
head the Marquess of Exeter – as one of the very foremost leaders
in world sport. Combining his rowing duties with other influential roles in the sector (he was already head of a recently formed
umbrella body of international sports federations), Keller would
retain this status, amid growing rumblings of incipient change, for
the rest of the decade.

The sporting world of the 1970s has come to seem very distant
from the preening, cynical, though still occasionally awe-inspiring,
multi-billion-dollar industry that is sport today. In 1973, the sector
was impecunious. It had also just come under mortal threat: the
Varna congress took place only thirteen months after the profound
shock of the Black September attack on the Munich Olympics
that left seventeen people, including eleven Israelis, dead. And, of
course, like any other international activity, sport was obliged to
operate in the surreal, bipolar world of the Cold War.

It was Keller's skill in balancing the concerns of East and West when it came to rowing affairs, as well as his determination to act always with his athletes' interests in mind – he had himself been an international oarsman of the highest calibre – which cemented his unassailable position at the head of his sport. He had seen the aftermath of the 1956 Hungarian Uprising with his own eyes, and he knew how to play the games that Eastern Bloc politics demanded, frequently choreographing conference interventions in advance with delegates living under Communist regimes, so as to protect the outcomes he required while enabling the delegates to save face with their superiors.

The Palace of Culture and Sports, built in 1968, was itself a creature of Cold War-era Bulgaria, whose articulate and persistent IOC member, General Vladimir Stoytchev, had persuaded his colleagues to grace his small country with their presence for this landmark congress. When I visited one snowy afternoon in January 2017, I found that the Palace's imposing central hall had lately been renovated. The only physical evidence that I could see of the Olympic Movement's week-long passage during the fiftieth anniversary of the Bulgarian Olympic Committee was a pale grey plaque secured on one of the building's angular concrete pillars. This included a Bulgarian rendition of the conference's motto, "Sport for a Peaceful World". And while just across the road, the massive, unmistakably Soviet-style "Pantheon of the Perished in the Fight Against Fascism" still stands, looking defiant if neglected, the Palace's immediate surroundings featured a monument to a more contemporary and commercial age: a fairground-type ride for toddlers with little cars painted in bright Spider-Man and Shrek liveries. The world, in short, has moved on.

I have taken on the task of writing this account of Thomi Keller's life because Dominik, his son, has been kind enough to ask me. The true justification for the exercise, though, was brought home to me at another sports industry gathering on the shores of the Black Sea nearly thirty years after a chastened, outmanoeuvred Thomi had departed the scene. The 2015 SportAccord Convention, hosted around 1000 km east of Varna in the Russian Winter Olympic city of Sochi, got off to just as explosive a start as the 1973 Olympic congress. This time the man lobbing verbal grenades was Marius Vizer, president of SportAccord, the organisation that Keller's umbrella body of international sports federations had become. Vizer – also president of the International Judo Federation and hence a successor of one of Keller's closest confidants, Charles Palmer – startled delegates by attacking the IOC while its president Thomas Bach was sitting in the audience.[4]

When I discussed this later with two veterans of the international sports conference circuit, the name on both their lips was Thomi Keller. "Who?" I said. Their explanations prompted me to find out enough about Keller to be able to write an article for Insidethegames. biz, examining to what extent history might be repeating itself.[5] If I, a journalist who had been covering the Olympic Movement for nearly fifteen years, had not previously heard about Keller, then it seemed more than likely that most of those attached to sport in this early part of the twenty-first century – with the exception of rowers – would be just as ignorant. Yet four decades earlier, this man had been the very embodiment of a heavy hitter, a bull elephant among the big beasts of the sporting jungle.

So it is high time, frankly, that an account was written of the very considerable part played by Keller in enabling sport to make a successful transition from the political era in which he cut his teeth as a high-ranking administrator to the commercial era with which, though he could see some benefits, he felt increasingly ill at ease in his later years. That it has fallen to me, a non-rower who never met Keller, to do this is, I'm afraid, just one of those things. I hope those of you who did know him will feel I have done him justice.

CHAPTER 1

Portrait of the Chemist as a Young Man

A painting of a boy hangs on a suburban Zurich landing. He has a pudding-basin haircut, slightly sticky-out ears, and dark rings around his eyes unusual in one so young. I would say he is, at most, eleven. Wearing a white shirt and a plain pink jumper, he rests his right elbow on something out of frame, perhaps a table or windowsill. He gazes pensively over my left shoulder out of liquid brown eyes. If I didn't know how his life had panned out, I would worry about him.

Were it not for those unmistakable eyes, and the artist's signature in the painting's bottom-right corner, I would struggle to connect this skinny, serious youngster with the man whose story I am trying to stitch together. But when I show a photograph of the portrait to those who knew him in later life, the response is invariably: "Ah yes, that's Thomi!" The artist, whose name "Keller" adorns the boy's left arm, was an uncle who lived in Paris and was known as the black sheep of the family.[1] Black sheep or no, it is a captivating piece of work.

What is the boy thinking? I have stared at his image often since visiting his childhood home one afternoon in November 2016 and if I had to guess, I would say his thoughts are of his father, Max Rudolf, whom he had already had the misfortune to lose.

The accident that took Max Rudolf Keller's life occurred before Thomi was seven, thousands of miles away in Arusha, northern Tanzania – or Tanganyika, as it then was – in December 1931. The thirty-eight-year-old company director and cavalry officer was on a hunting trip away from a sisal plantation the family owned. Approaching a seemingly dead lion, Max Rudolf got close enough for the stricken animal to scratch him when it lashed out with its paw. This was before the days of antibiotics, and the resultant blood poisoning proved fatal. His widow, Anny, was left with the mournful task of bringing the coffin back to Thomi and his two older sisters.[2]

The bereaved family settled in an old restaurant above some vineyards at Giesshübel, on the sunny side of Lake Zurich, that Anny had found and bought some time before when her husband was away on a business trip. It was quiet enough there for the children to run free. They kept horses, including a skewbald pony called Gypsy. On clear days, they enjoyed wonderful, fiery sunsets from their green-shuttered sanctuary high on the hill.

Thomi loved this place, where his portrait now hangs, and when exploring its sprawling, homely, dark-wooded interior it is easy to understand why. Two of the cosiest rooms are dominated by large Kachelofen, or wood-burning stoves, one finished with blue and white tiles, the other bright green. The family would heat bags of cherry stones in them to use as hot-water bottles. Much of the furniture – an oval dining table, a large wooden wall cabinet, a handsome black and gilt wall clock – has been there for decades. Still relatively secluded though only a few miles from Zurich city centre, the oldest parts of the building date from the sixteenth century.

Thomi was born on Christmas Eve 1924. He used to say this was why he had "such a good character". I am not altogether sure whether this was some imagined consequence of the symmetry – "24-12-24... like a phone number" – or because, like many festive babies, his birthday would tend to be overlooked in the Christmas rush.[3]

One other episode of note from Thomi's childhood was a trip, aged eleven, with his mother and sisters to the notorious Nazi Olympics in Berlin in 1936. Whether the family made it down to the Langer See to see the medal-winning performances of the Swiss four in both the coxed and coxless events is not known. It is tempting, though, to imagine Thomi finding inspiration for his subsequent life in sport in the celebrated exploits of Jesse Owens, the US sprinter who sensationally won four gold medals at those Games. Perhaps Berlin too was the genesis of his distrust of politicians seeking to use sport for political ends.

Rowing ability ran in the family: a brother of his mother represented Switzerland at the 1920 Olympics in Antwerp. Nonetheless, Thomi came only gradually to prioritise the sport. He had a brief flirtation with football, but "found I'm a hopeless banana".[4] Skiing, though, proved a much more enduring distraction, and this also seems to have been a skill lurking in the Keller genes. The family went to Klosters each winter and both Thomi's sisters exhibited a similar gift. One of them – Lislott – managed the Swiss women's ski team for a time in the 1960s.[5]

"I was very ambitious in skiing," Thomi recalled towards the end of his life.[6] Ski-jumping and cross-country were his specialities, along with a discipline known as the "four-event combined". In 1947, aged twenty-two, he represented Switzerland at the Academic World Games (later to become the Universiade) in Davos.[7] Eventually, he concluded that it was "impossible for someone living in the lowlands to make the overall national team. Then, I concentrated finally on rowing."[8] Skiing remained a lifelong passion, however, and his son Dominik recalls regularly watching New Year's Day ski-jumping with Thomi on television from Germany.

While rowing did not become his top sporting priority until he was into his twenties, the pistes were obviously not an option during the summer. In 1940, at around the time German troops marched into Paris, Thomi began to practise the sport at Zurich's well-known Grasshopper Club, whose green and oxblood boathouse gates give onto the lake a few hundred metres south of the arboretum. The convivial, not over-starchy clubhouse became a regular haunt for almost half a century, offering the sort of comradeship where a man who spent most of his life after the age of thirty as a leader could be just one of the boys. His narrow, pale-blue locker – number forty-four – is still there in the changing-room, in a long line of identical wooden repositories. He took part in his first schoolboys' regatta in Lucerne that same year, and from 1944 to 1946 formed part of a four that achieved a hat-trick of runners-up spots at the Swiss Championships.[9]

For upwards of two years, between mid-1947 and 1949, sport took a back seat in Thomi's affairs. This would happen one more time, to some extent, during a sojourn in the Far East in the 1950s, but never again in the remaining three and a half decades of his life.

First, there was romance: Thomi had met Dorry Bodmer and the couple had planned to get married in 1947. In the event, nuptials were postponed, owing to the death of Dorry's father, until May of the following year. The first of their five children, Dominik, was born in August 1949.

This period also brought the completion of Thomi's formal education. He emerged aged twenty-three from Zurich's Polytechnic in 1948 with a diploma in chemical engineering. The subject does not seem to have been especially close to his heart. He told one interviewer in later life: "Today I understand as much about chemistry as a cow understands about soccer."[10]

Finally, this was the time when Thomi undertook his military service in the Swiss army, rising to the rank of lieutenant. His friend and former sculling partner Hans Frohofer said Thomi didn't much care for it: "He was a sportsman, not a soldier", though he was a good shot.[11] It could have been worse; Thomi spent much of his time with a motorcycle unit. One anecdote frequently told is that he was part of British wartime prime minister Winston Churchill's escort on a visit to Switzerland. "He loved motorbikes," recalls Dominik. "Then they dissolved the motorcycle brigades and he was transferred to tanks." This is thought to have left him with a hearing problem in one ear. "He just lived with it," says Dominik, who strongly suspects that there were times when his father was not above craftily using his disability to his own ends. "He understood exactly what he wanted to."[12]

Rowing returned with a vengeance in 1950, a breakthrough year. A working man now with an infant son, Thomi decided to take up sculling. His progress was so spectacular that he was crowned national single sculling champion in that first season. In September, he travelled to Milan and took third place in the event behind Erijk Larsen of Denmark in the forty-first European Championships. His joie de vivre is said to have impressed everyone present "both on and off the water".[13]

Throughout Thomi's life, even in the traumatic aftermath of his father's death, the wealth generated by the Keller family enterprises ensured that he and his loved ones could lead a comfortable existence. That wealth was also of incalculable benefit to the sport of rowing, since it meant, as he once put it, that "I have the privilege to be part-owner of a company which can afford that one of its owners works very little in the company and spends most of his time on rowing. As long as the company does well, it's no problem."[14]

The business was partly Far East-based and was the legacy of Thomi's grandfather, Eduard Keller, whose name it bore. Thomi joined it after finishing at the Polytechnic. Because of the group's international nature, a convention had been established whereby, when a family member joined the business, he would work overseas for a period. Thus it was that in February 1951 – when he might have been building core strength and honing his sculling technique in preparation for a renewed assault on Larsen's European title – Thomi, his young family and pretty soon his sculling boat Pourquoi Pas, set off for what turned out to be a three-year stint in Hong Kong and the Philippines. As the presence of Pourquoi Pas would indicate, this long excursion did not keep him off the water. After rowing in a regatta in Singapore for the Royal Hong Kong Yacht Club, Thomi joined the Manila Boat Club on the Pasig river which bisects the Filipino capital. By October he was club captain.

His abiding affection for the club, which was founded on Manila Bay in 1895 – the year before the first modern Olympic Games – permeates an extensive foreword he contributed to a history published in 1979.[15] He recalls how Pourquoi Pas was uncrated after the journey from Europe only to find "a big crack in the bow". Undaunted, Anacleto, the club's boatman, set out to repair the damage using "a piece of cedar wood normally used for cigar boxes" – another receptacle close to Thomi's heart. He cut out a piece of shell around the crack and replaced it with the cedar wood "which he bent with steam". Thomi reports that afterwards the repair "could hardly be noticed" so skilfully was the work accomplished.

One trait of Thomi's that is frequently commented on by those who knew or worked with him is his practice of treating everyone he encountered, from the bellboy to the US president, with the same initial level of respect. So it is no surprise that he made himself "very unpopular by introducing the rule that each crew had to wash its shell after an outing and relieve Anacleto from this kind of work".

Ian Purslow, the Englishman who preceded him as club captain, remembers him arriving in Manila as "very much the scion of a very wealthy family". Writing after hearing of Thomi's death, Purslow recalls that the family "occupied a very large house which had been fully air-conditioned – and this was at a time when the most senior executives only had their main bedrooms air-conditioned".[16] Dominik, who was still only four when the family returned to Switzerland, retains a few memories of a "simple life" and "skeletons of burnt-out ships in the harbour". The latter part of their Asian interlude was spent in a house on the sea shore in Pasay. Thomi remembered early-morning excursions in Pourquoi Pas on a calm sea. "At that time of day," he wrote, "it… looked like a mirror. These outings left an unforgettable memory."

Thomi, who was an enthusiastic if messy cook, acquired a life-long love of spicy food from living in the region, but also a health issue: on returning to Europe he was, in his words, "full of amoebas".

Anticipating a return to competitive rowing when he got back to Switzerland, he had maintained a fairly full training regime while in the Philippines. The posting meant he had missed a possible opportunity to represent his country at the 1952 Olympic Games in Helsinki when, at twenty-seven, he might have been at the peak of his powers as an oarsman. But there seemed every reason to think that, if he trained hard, he might still have the 1956 Games to look forward to. After a knife-edge decision, taken in Rome more than seven years ahead of time, these were to be held in far-off Melbourne.[17]

CHAPTER 2

Two Men in a Boat

It is one of the most sought-after credentials in world sport. A piece of sixty-year-old cardboard, folded in half like a miniature greetings card, with royal-blue writing on a blue-green and white background. Inside, a black and white, passport-style mugshot of, in this case, an excited-looking thirty-one-year-old oarsman from Herrliberg in Zurich. On the front and back, prominently displayed, is the famous five-ring logo, flatter and more chain-like than in its modern configuration. Yes, here in my hands, nestles the document that should have granted Thomas Keller, Swiss rowing champion, access to the pinnacle of his sporting career: his carefully preserved identity card for the 1956 Olympic Games in Melbourne.

There is something unusual about card number 5919, however. The detachable "immigration aid" to be used by boarding officers to record details of the holder's arrival and departure remains affixed. This is because the card was never used. For reasons beyond his control, Thomi did not make it to Australia – though, in an ironic twist, the boat in which he and Erich Shriever were to have sculled for Switzerland did.

When he returned from Manila in spring 1954, Thomi initially found the going hard, though he had been back out on Lake

12

Zurich the day after his return.[1] By the following year, however, his performance level had improved. In 1955, he was again national champion, this time in the double sculls, partnered by Hansruedi Vollmer, a Grasshopper Club colleague.

This was also the year when Thomi began his lifelong love affair with Henley. Strapping the boat onto the roof of his big Buick,[2] he must have been quite a sight driving from Zurich to the stretch of the Thames where this highly prestigious regatta, part of the English social season, has taken place since 1839.

It was not a victorious visit, not quite: he and Vollmer lost the final of the Double Sculls Challenge Cup to Zhilin and Emchuk, a Soviet pair from the Burevestnik club in St Petersburg, or Leningrad as it was then. But they went down fighting by just half a length, with the winners clocked at seven minutes and fifty-five seconds over the classic one-mile-and-550-yard Henley course. Newsreel footage exists of the two crews racing upstream towards Henley Bridge while elegant crowds crane necks on the leafy banks.[3] "At Henley, the weather is warm enough to melt the Cold War," proclaims the voiceover. The double sculls was one of three prizes lifted by Soviet crews that year.

Something about the event in the genteel riverside town of Henley-on-Thames struck a chord with Thomi. In spite of his many other responsibilities and duties, he returned often when the first week of July came around and was sincerely honoured to be made a Steward, a member of the self-electing body which organises the regatta, in 1976. "It was the tradition, the history, the colour, the pageantry," former chairman of the regatta Mike Sweeney told me when I asked him what it was that so appealed to Thomi.[4] Beatrice Rothenbach-Seiler, a former personal assistant, remembers the pink Leander Club socks that he would wear for Henley and Henley only.[5]

Yet the regatta was also a much-relished release from the weight of office for Thomi. Baron Pierre de Coubertin, founder of the modern Olympics, famously modelled the composition of the original IOC to an extent on the Stewards at Henley, which he visited in 1888. De Coubertin wrote of "three concentric circles: a small core of earnest and hard-working members; a nursery of willing members ready to be taught; finally a façade of more or less useful people whose presence satisfied national pretensions at the same time as it gave prestige to the committee as a whole".[6] Thomi, who always expected to be delegated his fair share of the banal, even menial tasks that it fell to the Stewards to perform, could be said to inhabit both the first and last of de Coubertin's three circles.

According to Dominik, Thomi continued to stay for many years in modest circumstances with the household who had put him up on that first visit in 1955, referring to them as "my family". Only in later years was he a guest of the Burrough family, of Beefeater Gin fame, in their large Edwardian residence with a bumblebee weathervane on its boathouse.[7] Said Peter Coni, Sweeney's predecessor as regatta chairman: "What he so enjoyed about coming and officiating at the regatta was that it was the one time each year when he was not in charge; when he could resume being one of the team rather than everyone looking to him to answer the questions and take the decisions."[8]

Soon after Thomi's thirty-first birthday, Olympic year began – a year that promised to bring his one and only shot at claiming the ultimate accolade for any amateur athlete. Prospects looked good when he won two titles at the 1956 national championships, in both single and double sculls, the latter with Hans Frohofer.

Frohofer – with whom he retained the double-sculls title the following year on the strength of just ten days' training, before finishing fourth in the European championships in Duisburg – once gave a brief account of the racing style of the friend and rival whom he said he accepted "every time" as leader. "He always beat me," Frohofer said. "He is the warrior type. I am not a loser, but I do not have that winning instinct. I was a fast starter, but he always came through and I couldn't save enough breath to stop him."[9]

Being staged in the southern hemisphere for the first time, the Olympics took place much later in the year than usual. When the European championships were held in picturesque Bled in what was then Yugoslavia in August and September, there were still nearly three months to go before the leading competitors would line up again at Lake Wendouree in Ballarat, a former gold-rush town about 100 km from Melbourne. The Swiss selectors had paired Thomi not with Frohofer but with Shriever, half of the runner-up crew from the national championships. The new Swiss pairing could manage only fourth place – ostensibly disappointing, but a result which still left grounds for hoping that an Olympic medal was within their compass, since Thomi had rowed the final while running a temperature of thirty-nine degrees. Perhaps those Filipino amoebas had come back to haunt him. Having led from start to finish, however, it was already clear that the Soviet crew of Yuri Tiukalov, a gold medallist from the 1952 Olympics, and Alexander Berkutov would take all the beating when the teams reassembled Down Under.

Melbourne was quite an adventurous choice as Olympic host in the middle years of the twentieth century – not unlike the decision, in the early decades of the twenty-first, to take a far bigger, vastly more complex event to Rio de Janeiro. The seven-year build-up had been plagued by frequent problems. The equestrian competition ended up having to be moved to Stockholm because of Australian equine quarantine law. The extent of uncertainties hovering over the Games is underlined by correspondence in the excellent IOC archive over a) offers to stage the equestrian events in either Dublin or Rio de Janeiro and b) moving the entire Games to Philadelphia or Detroit. A letter to Australian officials from IOC president Avery Brundage, dated 28 January 1953, suggests that "from what I have heard… 85% of [National Olympic Committees] would thank you if Melbourne would relinquish the Games".[10]

The blueprint for the Olympic rowing regatta was not exempt from such difficulties. Lake Wendouree was originally chosen in 1950 since neither Melbourne rowing course met Olympic standards. But there was a flip-flop in 1954–55, with the venue first being changed to Lake Learmonth over depth issues, then switched back when organisers realised that this new locale was "completely wanting in shore facilities".[11] Lake Wendouree was determined to have "ample accommodation for boats of the visiting crews in the three main boathouses", only for one of them to be destroyed by fire. Only in November 1956, just a week before the Olympic regatta, was a new boathouse ready for occupation.

By the time the new building opened, however, Thomi's Olympic dream lay in ashes.

Most followers of Olympic sport know about the politically motivated boycotts of the 1970s and 1980s, and how they might easily have brought the Movement to its knees. Fewer realise that the Melbourne 1956 Games were similarly afflicted. Two separate flashpoints became pretexts for boycotts that reduced the number of athletes and nationalities who made their way to distant Victoria. The Suez Crisis kept Egypt, Iraq and Lebanon away. But it was the Hungarian Uprising – and more particularly the brutal Soviet response to it – that cost Thomi his only chance of writing his name as an athlete on the Olympic honours board.

The revolution started on 23 October, but it was not until 4 November that Soviet forces moved to crush it with tanks. A week of fighting produced more than 3000 casualties, mainly Hungarians and mainly in the capital Budapest. It ended with the Cold War order being restored in the shape of a new Soviet-installed government.

The decision by some countries to react to the attempted Soviet clampdown by withdrawing from the Games was swiftly taken. On 6 November, the Dutch Olympic Committee decided unanimously not to go, with a three-minute silence observed in the country two days later. Fascist Spain was also quick off the mark, opting to withdraw "while the liberty of peoples is being trampled on". It took a couple of days longer for the habitually neutral Swiss to reach a verdict, but eventually, on 8 November, it was announced that they too would stay away. While the Swiss Olympic Committee had decided to embark as planned, it had made this decision conditional on all seven of its competing national sports federations agreeing – and gymnastics had opted not to go.

This outcome touched off a heated debate in Switzerland, with public opinion plainly divided. A disappointed Jean Weymann, head of the aborted Swiss delegation, said the committee had received threats, while emphasising that in his view the correct course would be to fly to Melbourne. Others called for the gymnasts to stay behind if they wanted, but for the rest of the team to go.

On the evening of 9 November, the eve of their original scheduled departure date, Thomi was one of twenty-one team members who met in Zurich and signed a resolution urging a rethink. The text expressed the signatories' "very great sympathy for the Hungarian people, who are fighting for their liberty", but argued that withdrawal from Melbourne was not an appropriate way to protest against "Russian aggression".

"For we athletes," the resolution continued, "Melbourne is the place where we could best express our feelings and it is only there, on the spot, that we will be able to protest effectively against Russian participation." It amounts to a dignified and measured plea given the intense frustration they must have been feeling.

Meanwhile, undiplomatically worded telegrams began to wing their way into and out of the IOC in Lausanne, giving a vivid insight into the charged atmosphere and the speed with which events on the ground were moving. On 7 November, the IOC chancellor Otto Mayer cabled a terse message to Melbourne: "Doing utmost urging all hesitating countries to participate stop shall intervene again [sic] Holland." At the same time, organising committee chairman Wilfrid Kent Hughes requested that Dutch athletes already in situ ahead of the opening ceremony on 22 November be allowed to compete. In the wake of the Swiss decision, Mayer again cabled Melbourne: "Did utmost disapprove Switzerland's shameful withdrawal. Spain reconsiders Saturday". In a message to Brundage, meanwhile, the chancellor's language was even more intemperate: "Swiss disgusting decision unfortunately irrevocable stirring revolution in Swiss sport," he wrote. "Mailing you Melbourne press statements".

On 11 November, the pressure told: meeting in Berne, the Swiss Olympic Committee reversed its initial decision, seemingly paving the way for its athletes to fly south. "Thanks our intervention Switzerland participates stop," Mayer proclaimed triumphantly in his missive to Melbourne the following day. "Trying liberate Bulgarian team restrained quarantaine [sic] Karachi." There was bad news from Bilbao, however, with a telegram from Pedro Ybarra y MacMahon, the Spanish IOC member, informing him that the Spaniards had not undergone a Swiss-style change of heart and would stay away.

Even then, there was a twist in the tail. To what must have been the bitter despair of Swiss athletes packing their bags for the second time in a week, team officials found it was no longer possible to track down a suitable aircraft in which to make the journey. Mayer communicated this dolefully to his Australian colleagues on 14 November. "Despite efforts Lebanon don't reconsider and impossible getting plane for Swiss team whose participation is cancelled for that only reason," he wrote. "Am most upset."[12]

Thomi's frustration at the whole episode still comes across as clear as a bell in his comments to an American interviewer more than three decades later. "I was supposed to go to the Olympics, to Melbourne, and the Swiss, those idiots, invented the boycott," he said. "You were not the first ones to invent it. You don't have to be proud... The Swiss, the Dutch and the Spanish decided to boycott – and we got a kick in the pants three days before departure."[13]

In spite of this, it is worth recording that, in a quirk of Olympic history, the largely absent Swiss did capture a bronze medal at the 1956 Summer Games. This was secured by the three-strong dressage team – Gottfried Trachsel on Kursus, Henri Chammartin on Wöhler and Gustav Fischer on Vasello – in Stockholm in June, before the international tensions that impacted Melbourne began to escalate.

At Lake Wendouree, Tiukalov and Berkutov duly took the double-sculls gold medal, going into the lead before the halfway mark and pulling away smoothly to win by more than eight seconds from the United States with Australia third. Arguably the finest performance of the regatta came from the Soviet oarsman Viatcheslav Ivanov in the single sculls. He surged from last to first in the final 500 metres to pip long-time leader Stuart MacKenzie of Australia, a young chicken-sexer who was to become a good friend of Thomi. The bronze medal in this event went to Jack Kelly junior, brother of Monaco's Princess Grace.

A competitive Hungarian team somehow made it to the Games, winning twenty-six medals, including nine golds. One of these came in water polo, a sport which on 6 December afforded the oppressed nation a moment of pure catharsis in the guise of a game against the Soviet Union so rough it became known as the "blood in the water" match.

In his days as a leading official, Thomi was to make it clear that he was no fan of over-gaudy Olympic ostentation. But he would probably have enjoyed the Melbourne closing ceremony on 8 December, with its intermingling of competitors from different countries which led to the 1956 Olympics being labelled the "Friendly Games". About a week before this ceremony, though, he had arrived in Vienna, en route to participating in a programme called Aid to Hungary, along with eight other Swiss Olympic athletes, six of them rowers. It was an immensely commendable alternative by Thomi and his colleagues to sitting around and feeling sorry for themselves. The four-language "Legitimation" issued to him by the International Red Cross bears the self-same black and white mugshot as his unused Olympic identity card.

In years to come, Swiss team members deprived of their Olympic journey by the boycott would hold get-togethers under the aegis of the "Melbourne Club". The gymnasts were not invited and would often be sent a choicely worded postcard from the gathering.[14]

Two decades on, Thomi – by then one of world sport's most influential administrators – would once again become all too wearily familiar with the tactic of the politically inspired Olympic boycott. But as the winter of 1956–57 closed in while he assuaged his disappointment by helping desperate Hungarian refugees, he could not have guessed how soon he would find himself exchanging his berth in his sculling boat for a president's office.

CHAPTER 3

The Young One

It is June 1958. As a flag droops in the breezeless sky, two young rowers stand to attention, bronzed and trim, in white vests and shorts. Facing them, impassive in a thick dark suit, with a programme or perhaps the notes for a speech peeping out of his left pocket, is a distinguished, bespectacled elder statesman type. The rowers are Thomi Keller and Hans Frohofer, the man in the suit Gaston Müllegg, and this – an award presentation at the International Rowing Federation (FISA) Founders' Regatta – might well be their last meeting.

Six weeks later, the sixty-eight-year-old Müllegg, FISA's third president and holder of a pilot's licence obtained at the age of sixty-four, was dead. A light aircraft he was flying nosedived into the Chalet de Bois-Soleil, a clinic just a few hundred yards from the IOC's Lausanne base at Mon Repos. The devastating impact killed Müllegg outright. Two companions, including Louis Patricot, a French rowing official, were hospitalised with serious injuries.

The accident robbed the federation of a diligent and respected leader who pursued the sport's interests with an air of quiet authority. A *Times* obituary penned by G.O. Nickalls, the former international oarsman and Henley Steward, spoke of an "impressive figure, tall and spare", who had "given FISA a unity" and "endowed it with a presence and importance in the counsels of world sport which it had never previously enjoyed".[1]

In his younger days, the Swiss national had been a sportsman of great versatility, practising swimming, skating, bobsleigh, curling, motor-racing and equestrian sports as well as rowing, with Nickalls noting that "his horsemanship in the field of *haute-école* was of a particularly high order". Given that he had acted as the federation's secretary-treasurer for more than twenty years before acceding to the presidency in 1949, it is little surprise that the part-time obituarist felt able to conclude that rowing would be "fortunate indeed if it finds another man with his statesmanlike qualities and social gifts to guide it with such competence and mastery, or serve it with such selfless devotion".

It seems that Müllegg at least was satisfied he had identified such a man. "He wanted me to become his successor in '62," said Thomi, recalling more than three decades later what had happened. "He wanted to retire in 1962."[2]

Thomi would have been just thirty-seven years old when Müllegg had planned for him to take over. While it is hard to overstate how radical a step it would have been to have installed one so young in the president's office of a prominent and rather conservative international sports federation at this time, it is also worth recording that there was a family connection. A relative of Thomi's called Georg Keller worked at the same fuel distribution company as Müllegg and, indeed, delivered a eulogy at the FISA president's funeral.[3]

Clearly, however, Müllegg's accident had administered a wholly unexpected twist to any succession plan. Not only was Thomi a mere thirty-three when Müllegg died, but he was still an active rower. It is hardly surprising that there should have been some hesitation before his elevation was confirmed.

That year's FISA congress, coinciding with the European championships in Poznan, was scheduled for less than four weeks after Müllegg's death. With feelings still raw, the federation would have felt justified in playing for time. From a dais draped in black crepe in the Polish city's municipal council chamber, Jacques Spreux, FISA vice-president, delivered a lengthy tribute to his late colleague. "He could appear distant to some, even abrupt in certain decisions," Spreux acknowledged. "But many of you, who like me were fortunate enough to know him more intimately, will remember a sincere friend, a fundamentally good, welcoming man." After a minute's silence, it was announced that, since "the shadow of our revered president still occupies the president's chair", all business would be held over until an extraordinary congress to be called before the end of the year.[4]

This meeting duly took place on the afternoon of 22 November 1958, just over a month before Thomi's thirty-fourth birthday, in the ornate Rittersaal at the Palais Niederösterreich in Vienna. The intervening three months had evidently featured a lively debate on the leadership issue, with FISA secretary Charles Riolo and West German rowing federation president Walter Wülfing among those in Thomi's corner. "The other gentlemen could not agree on a successor," Thomi remembered years later.[5] Author Christopher Dodd alludes to a letter the future president wrote in October containing the following commentary: "The fight for the presidency of the FISA is going on merrily and I enjoy watching developments. Things do not seem to look too bad as far as my candidacy is concerned."[6]

He was right. Vienna's Rittersaal proved to be the place where his long reign began – but only after a quaint and presumably pre-choreographed *pas de deux* distinctly redolent of the small gentlemen's club FISA was at the time. This little prelude saw Gaston Walbaum, a vice-president from Argentina, nominate Spreux as Müllegg's successor only for the Belgian to decline the honour on the grounds that his other responsibilities left him with insufficient time.[7]

Spreux then asked those present instead to back "the candidate chosen by the board" – Thomi – "who is young, dynamic and who I hope will fulfil his duties with conviction and to our entire satisfaction". Cue warm applause. Finally, but only after four vice-presidents had been re-elected by acclamation, Thomi – who had agreed to quit the Swiss national rowing team – was shown into the room to more applause to make a brief acceptance speech. "I consider the fact that you have elected a candidate who is relatively young and inexperienced in matters of FISA administration as proof of your recognition of the exceptional work of my predecessors," he told them. Thirty years later, he was more blunt. "The first time I attended any meeting about rowing was when I was elected," he told an interviewer. "I didn't have the faintest idea."[8]

The truncation of the Poznan meeting meant that congress still had a meaty agenda to work through, which it duly did, accepting the principle of a world championship commencing (for men only) in 1962. At 6pm, the meeting was closed, with delegates reconvening to mark the new era in a café on the outskirts of town. Few places can match Viennese café culture, and discussions are said to have continued "in lively manner" far into the night. It was an early example of the "work hard, play hard" ethos Thomi would come to epitomise.[9]

The culture of international sports administration he had sacrificed his twilight years as an international oarsman[10] to enter was exclusively male and almost exclusively a generation older than him. At the time of his election to the FISA presidency, the average age of the IOC was 59.8 years. It had recently come down below sixty with the election of twenty-four-year-old Albert of Liège, the future Albert II, king of the Belgians.

Thomi was to acclimatise to this new world to such good effect that he spent the rest of his life there. Nonetheless – and in spite of his business experience – it must at times have felt like a big and intimidating transition. So his first presidential report to a FISA congress, delivered in the French wine country of Mâcon on 18 August 1959, is worth examining.

Reading back through this report nearly six decades later, it is as if a pulse of energy has emanated from the old pages. You can sense the vigour and relish with which Thomi was starting to get to grips with his new responsibilities. Only when the focus switches to a meeting between international sports federations and the IOC executive, which lasted "two entire days", does the tone veer towards frustration.[11]

Already he had paid not one but two inspection visits, in May and July, to the European championship site, setting an example of the hands-on management style that was to become his trademark. He had begun actively seeking a solution to the problem of the athletes' village for the following year's Rome Olympics being 25 km away from the rowing course. "In envisaging the probably enormous volumes of traffic during the Games and seasonal temperatures that are bound to be high, it will be impossible to impose upon rowers the journey from Rome to Castel Gandolfo and vice versa four times a day," he bristled. The Japanese capital Tokyo was only chosen to host the 1964 Summer Olympics three months before Thomi's address. Yet he had already ascertained from the governor of Tokyo, "a former rower", that this part of Japan had only one four-lane regatta course, that this had been constructed for the Games that were to have taken place in 1940 but were then cancelled owing to the war, and that it was therefore hardly likely to meet modern requirements. Not only that, but Thomi sounded peeved that, having promised detailed plans of their rowing installations, the Japanese authorities had apparently not yet provided them. Three national federations had submitted bids to host the inaugural world championships. These included the Australians, who had proposed the Olympic course that Thomi might have rowed on at Ballarat in 1956. On top of all this, the young FISA president had already reintroduced the idea of setting aside a morning for congress delegates to go out rowing together. This was to become a cherished tradition during his long presidency. More than half a century later, the overall impression is that the federation, and the sport, had been caught up in a small whirlwind.

Even that interminable, rather turgid meeting with the IOC turns out to have been somewhat significant. The two sides were starting to talk about an issue that was not going to go away in an era when the amount of cash going into sports was minuscule by twenty-first-century standards: the idea that federations should be granted some sort of direct financial payment from successive Olympic Games.[12]

The International Amateur Athletic Federation had come up with a complicated proposal − according to Thomi, "brilliantly expounded" by its president, the Marquess of Exeter, the 400-metre hurdler now associated with the feature film *Chariots of Fire* − whereby money for the sports would be raised by a surcharge on Olympic ticket sales. This scheme was backed by all the federations but not, crucially, by Avery Brundage, the IOC president. Though the American had accepted the principle that some sort of financial help for the federations was justified, he thought this should come from a different source: broadcasting rights.

Given Brundage's latter-day reputation as a short-tempered dinosaur − certainly on the issue of amateurism that was soon to flare up, but also on other matters − it is surprising to see him apparently well ahead of the curve with regard to the goose that would in time begin to lay sport a seemingly inexhaustible clutch of golden eggs. After all, at a similar meeting four years earlier, he declared: "We in the International Olympic Committee have done well without television for sixty years and will do so for the next sixty years."[13]

Perhaps the old curmudgeon was simply stalling to avoid giving ground to the federations. Or perhaps – despite abhorring the use of Olympic sport as a vehicle to promote brands – the self-made businessman in him was starting to smell a bull market. After all, around a year earlier, in July 1958, organisers of the Rome Games had worked out a plan for submission to the IOC for "negotiating the televising of the Games with Television Companies on a commercial basis".[14] Ultimately, the Italian National Olympic Committee (CONI) was able to negotiate a $394,000 deal for US broadcasting rights with CBS[15] and a further sum from Eurovision. A total of twenty-one countries all told, from Japan to Canada, were linked to TV coverage of the 1960 Games.[16] Four years earlier, a domestic Australian TV transmission had been arranged for a grand total of around 5000 receiving sets.[17] A revolution that was to transform sport during Thomi's long administrative career and beyond was under way.

CHAPTER 4

Thoroughly Modern Thomi

It would be a few years yet before the full force of the TV revolution was felt in the genteel backwater of rowing. As a new, more prosperous and permissive decade dawned, the sport's young leader had other priorities. As he put it in an interview at the end of his career: "We had to remodernize the whole concept of rowing".[1]

The first fruits of this ambitious but indispensable undertaking would at once have been visible to rowing enthusiasts watching the 1960 Olympic regatta. This was staged at Lake Albano, a small, nearly circular crater-lake 20 km outside Rome in the Alban hills, overlooked by Castel Gandolfo, the Papal Palace. This body of water ended up lending its name to the first important innovation of the Keller era.

The Albano system was a method of providing straight, easily followed lane markings on a multi-lane rowing course. It was devised in 1960 partly because of the depth of the lake. Nonetheless, the fact it was introduced at the first Olympics since Thomi's arrival as federation president is emblematic of the high priority he gave to providing the best – and fairest – possible conditions for all competitors from the very start of his long reign. It also illustrated that, while the callow thirty-something might be lacking in political and administrative experience, there were some advantages to putting a recent athlete in charge. Thomi knew first-hand how difficult it could be for rowers to keep their bearings under the more primitive marking systems in use prior to Rome. "You see I competed for about twenty years and I had a lot of experience by then," he explained some years later.[2]

For aficionados of land sports – for whom delineating the playing surface may involve nothing more complex than a whitewash-wheel – the magnitude of the engineering feat represented by the Albano system might not be immediately apparent. So it is worth dwelling for a moment on the infrastructure that made it possible. This consisted of fourteen reinforced concrete piles, seven at either end of the course, sunk into the lake-bed in two lines at thirty-metre intervals. Seven submerged cables, each attached to forty red and white plastic buoys, were stretched from the piles at the start of the course to those near the finish 2000 metres away, with winches providing enough tension to keep the markings of the six lanes thus formed straight.[3]

Compare this fairly rigid geometrical pattern with the more perfunctory lane-marking system deployed four years earlier at Ballarat for the 1956 Melbourne Games. "Although only four crews were started in each event," the official report states, "five lanes were laid down, allowing the International Federation to select the four courses most suitable under the prevailing weather conditions. The lanes were marked by coloured discs – yellow, blue, red, white and green. The discs in the starting bay were placed two feet above the water level at the shore line and in line with discs thirty feet further back on the shore. At 500-metre intervals along the course, discs three-feet in diameter were suspended twelve feet above water level, marking the centre of each lane, with markers placed on shore at the finish."[4]

Altogether there were to be eight Olympic regattas under Thomi's FISA presidency, and Rome was among the least problematic – even if his own feelings may have mingled pride with a hint of regret at having been deprived of his chance to actually compete at the Games four years earlier. The surroundings were beautiful, with steep banks of volcanic rock sloping down to the water's edge. Technical installations were top-notch: in addition to the buoying system, requiring 26,500 metres of supporting cable, both the timing equipment and a large illuminated scoreboard were widely appreciated.[5] The course was fair for all competitors, and spectators included its eminent neighbour Pope John XXIII.[6]

True, Thomi had been unable to secure the desired overnight accommodation for rowers near the lake, but otherwise the only gripe was that the rowing regatta followed immediately on from the canoeing events at the same venue. The lack of an interval meant that training exercises sometimes coincided with competition and prompted the FISA president to push for an early slot for rowing in the 1964 Olympic schedule.[7]

Soviet sculler Viatcheslav Ivanov – smooth as silk at thirty-two strokes per minute – retained the title he had won at Melbourne, but the scene was stolen by the German crews who won the three coxed events,[8] ensuring that the *schwarz-rot-gold* German flag adorned with white Olympic rings was much in demand for victory ceremonies. This trio of triumphs included the eights, the blue-riband event claimed by the United States at the previous eight Olympic regattas, stretching all the way back to Antwerp 1920. This time, as the evening shadows lengthened, a crew from a tranquil island village called Ratzeburg, east of Hamburg, coached by a former student boxing champion, gained a most noteworthy victory. According to Christopher Dodd, "that first German win marked a revolution in rowing... Inside Germany the men of Ratzeburg were regarded as upstarts, anti-establishment oarsmen who bucked the traditions of German rowing... Outside Germany, the only people who had heard of Ratzeburg were the long-deceased poets, Wordsworth and Coleridge."[9]

Of course, the process of "remodernizing" the small, predominantly European gentlemen's club that FISA was in Thomi's early years at the helm extended much further than introducing better lane markings. Other early priorities included moves to improve the standard of umpiring. These began with creation, in 1961, of the umpires' commission. There was also a thorough overhaul of the racing procedure – the *Code des Courses* – which, as Thomi reminded delegates to the 1961 FISA congress in Prague, was still based partly on the Laws of Boat Racing drawn up in 1872. While well aware that the new standards would entail heavy expenditure on improvements at some traditional rowing courses, he justified them, characteristically, in terms of ameliorating the experience of the athlete. "We will be doing the best service for our beautiful sport and its propagation," he maintained, "and we are giving competitors certainty that everything necessary has been done to establish honest, incontestable rules that allow everyone the same chance of victory."[10] Urging the widest possible distribution of the "little yellow book" containing the new statutes in rowing circles, Thomi could not refrain from commenting how often active rowers were ignorant of the rules that bound them. The FISA president found himself returning to these themes again and again as the decade went on, chivvying colleagues into ensuring that the calibre of both umpires and facilities met the new standards.

While no one held the traditions of rowing in greater esteem, Thomi's "remodernization" also included updating FISA's image. A new logo comprising the blades of five oars in the colours of the continents – and the Olympic rings – was introduced. So was a new flag of similar design. As he took pains to explain, this was not a case of change for change's sake. The stars on the old flag had nothing to do with rowing and the constellation was supposed to add a star with each new member FISA attracted. "Only tradition and questions of taste can oppose the execution of this project," he concluded. And when the inaugural men's world championships – a venture already envisaged under Thomi's predecessor Gaston Müllegg – were held in 1962, FISA's traditional medal design, dating from soon after its foundation in the nineteenth century, was replaced.[11]

The Swiss rowing centre of Lucerne had won the right to stage this trailblazing event. This was after an ultimately abortive contest from which both Australia and Denmark had withdrawn, with the Danes successfully using the exercise as a lever to help secure the 1963 men's European championships. So it fell to one of the sport's best-appointed natural amphitheatres – the hill-encircled Rotsee – to host this milestone in rowing's then still tentative globalisation. With calm water all but guaranteed, in spite of sometimes changeable weather, the event was a huge success – a "complete success", as Thomi later proclaimed it. With single-sport world championships starting to proliferate as administrators caught on to their revenue-generating potential, the FISA president had no hesitation in declaring that Lucerne 1962 had demonstrated that there was a "real necessity" for such an event in rowing's calendar. A keenly contested race to host the sport's second world championships, in 1966, was won narrowly by Bled, another popular and picturesque natural venue, in what was then Yugoslavia.[12]

The Rotsee event was a particular triumph for West German crews, who won all bar the two sculling disciplines. This was after each had rowed off successfully against their respective East German rivals on the eve of the championships for the right to fill the sole German slot then permitted on the start-line. Among manufacturers, the Zurich boat-builder Stämpfli achieved even more dominance, its handsome wooden craft winning six of the seven categories.[13]

Most importantly for FISA, its new venture was a commercial and popular success, with a crowd of 45,000 attracted to finals day. This started, innovatively, with races to determine seventh to twelfth places in the various categories. Author Jean-Louis Meuret writes that a "vast number" of TV viewers tuned in, with national networks in "many" countries screening the entire day's programme.[14] Given this coverage, one might perhaps be justified in regarding the "spontaneous payment" of SFr5000[15] made by the Lucerne 1962 organising committee as the first TV rights income to be credited to FISA's account. By today's standards, of course, this is a trifling sum; but in 1962 this was far from the case. Bear in mind, for example, that the cumulative surplus held by FISA at the start of Thomi's first full year as president was a touch under SFr700. This had swelled to well over SFr10,000 by 1962. Yet this was still very much a time when annual subscriptions from the federation's forty-odd members were comfortably its biggest income source, accounting in 1962 for SFr20,000 out of overall revenue of around SFr28,000.

In fact, financial pressures on the organisation were ratcheting up by the summer of 1963 when delegates gathered for that year's congress at Copenhagen's House of Civil Engineers. Even with the surprise Lucerne payment, 1962 produced a small deficit. Thomi now told the assembly that FISA needed to lease a "modest" office space. With only one dependable income source, annual subscriptions would have to rise – by 50%. After nearly five years at the helm, however, the FISA president was becoming an accomplished congressional performer. He sought to balance the bad news with good. From the following year, he said, FISA had "the promise of receiving 10% of the income resulting from the sale of television rights for our championships". With plans also in hand to demand a percentage on ticket sales, he hoped that the increase in fees would be temporary.

To be fair, the higher subscription rate did only apply for a single year, although it was hiked again very substantially for larger federations before the end of the decade. However, the ticketing plan did not materialise and the federation seriously overestimated what its TV rights would yield. Instead of SFr12,000 budgeted for 1965, less than SFr3000 was received, with the time-lag between broadcast and payment also far longer than originally anticipated.[16] Luckily for FISA, forecasts of a rapid escalation in the value of Olympic TV rights turned out to be more accurate, with the federation receiving marginally more from the Tokyo 1964 Games than the SFr10,000 it had expected.

In other respects, Tokyo foreshadowed a number of Olympic regattas to come on Thomi's watch, absorbing disproportionate time and attention often with less than ideal results. The nub of the problem was that, unlike FISA's own championships, Olympic events might easily be staged in countries with little or no experience of putting on elite rowing events. At the same time, the sport's technical requirements – for a straight, calm body of water more than two kilometres long, and ideally wide enough to accommodate six boats rowing abreast – were particularly onerous.

In the case of Tokyo, two alternative venues remained in the frame until late in the day. These were the Toda course, where the regatta finally took place, which required widening at a cost of ¥192 million[17] and – like Lake Albano – was judged further from the Olympic Village than was ideal, and the canoeing venue at fish-rich Lake Sagami. This was further away from the Village at the foot of Mount Fuji, but had lakeside accommodation for crews. Thomi appeared satisfied enough with the venue choice ahead of the Games, observing in 1963 that Toda was "probably the best Olympic rowing course yet", though even then he pinpointed a potential problem with crosswinds. After the event, he found more fault, commenting on the "charmless" landscape, poor air quality and steep artificial banks.[18]

As it was, the FISA president's initial misgivings proved well founded, with the feared crosswinds striking at the worst possible moment to play havoc with finals day. In a considered post mortem nearly a year after the event, Thomi explained that it had not been possible to move the showpiece occasion back by a day or two because the forecast suggested that the weather was set to get worse.[19] He said that while breakwaters on the north side of the course had proved ineffective, deployment of hessian along one bank had been helpful. But he acknowledged that conditions had not only caused delays but "influenced the results of some races". As a former rower, he admitted "this distressed me very much".

There were two delays: the first of an hour and a half, the second about thirty minutes. This had the unfortunate consequence that the regatta's grand finale, the eights final, took place as night was falling at around 5.30pm. Part-illuminated in the gloom by a motley assortment of flares and car headlights, the US crew regained the crown in the closest the Olympics has come to a nocturnal rowing event. Before that, the uncooperative weather had proved no barrier to the irresistible Ivanov, who was able to complete his Olympic hat-trick. According to the correspondent from *The Times*, the wind had veered to "nearly dead ahead" at the time of this final just after 4pm.[20] The Soviet sculler's winning time, 8 mins 22.51 secs, was over 50 seconds slower than he had managed in the repechage three days earlier, well over a minute slower than when he triumphed on Lake Albano, and was the slowest Olympic gold medal-winning time in this event since 1908.

Olympic problems notwithstanding, FISA's young president had by this time, six years into the job, achieved a position of unassailable authority inside his sport. By Christopher Dodd's analysis,

"Keller found support among rowers and his member federations because his principles were clear from the moment he took office. He separated politics from sports events, and he developed facilities for sportsmen by always asking, 'What is the best for the athlete?' He learned the business from the bottom up."[21]

But of course, while the Cold War raged, Thomi was never going to be able to keep politics out of the equation entirely, much as – given his Melbourne disappointment – he might have liked to.

CHAPTER 5

Flags of Inconvenience

"Germany remains Germany," chanted crowds on the western side of the barriers erected the previous night. "There is only one Germany," they shouted. "Think of Hungary!"[1] Given his personal experience in 1956, there is every likelihood that this is exactly what Thomi did when he first heard the news about the Berlin Wall.

It was August 1961. The fiftieth men's European championships – a major landmark for rowing, underlining the sport's long history – were set to start behind the Iron Curtain in Prague in ten days' time, and the young FISA president, ever more self-confident and assured in his handling of the federation's affairs, had lately been fighting a small Cold War battle of his own.

The Czechoslovak authorities had refused an entry visa to a rower called George Justicz who was Czech-born but held a British passport and had represented Great Britain at the previous year's Rome Olympics. When told about this by Britain's Amateur Rowing Association, Thomi fired off a cable to Prague threatening to move the event to Duisburg if Justicz were not granted his visa and a guarantee of safety. This sort of instant, no-nonsense reaction would be all but unthinkable for an international sports federation president today who would be bound to take into account the interests of commercial partners such as broadcasters and sponsors.

In the tense atmosphere then prevailing, though, the threat proved very effective: on 11 August it was reported that Justicz had been guaranteed "unmolested arrival and departure".[2]

The brief stand-off over Justicz turned out to be just the start of Thomi's trial of strength with Eastern-Bloc officialdom. For Thomi, as for Europe, August 1961 was one of those months when Cold War politics lumbered out of the background – where it could be consigned most of the time for those going about their daily affairs – and demanded to be reckoned with.

Sandwiched between the women's and the men's championships on 22 August was the FISA congress, Thomi's third as president. It was almost as if the Warsaw Pact countries had decided that, after a decent honeymoon, the moment had come to test the new man's mettle. First on the offensive was Evgeny Kabanov, one of the three-member Soviet delegation and a man with whom Thomi was eventually to forge a mutually satisfactory working relationship. For a couple of years, the Soviet Union had been pushing for a reform of the IOC that would see it expanded to include all National Olympic Committee (NOC) and affiliated international sports federation presidents in addition to its current members. This would significantly have increased the USSR's influence over world sporting affairs. The proposal had, however, been rejected at the 1961 IOC session in Athens in June.[3] Kabanov now told FISA colleagues that the USSR would continue to promote the idea, claiming that the current organisation of the IOC left much to be desired and that a reorganisation was necessary. Would FISA and the national rowing federations be so kind as to back them up?[4] Thomi was not going to fall for that one, though, observing correctly that the position of the international sports federations vis-à-vis the IOC was much stronger under the current conditions than if their leaders were inducted into a reformed Olympic body.

Next it was the turn of the German Democratic Republic, East Germany. Since 1955, it had been a member of FISA on condition that a) at Olympic regattas and European championships Germany would be represented by only one team and b) if the country were reunited politically only one federation would be recognised.[5] It was now calling for the right to enter its own teams in FISA championships, which were soon to be augmented by the inaugural men's world championships the following year.

Karl Nagel, speaking for the proposal, argued that all-German championships between the East and West German federations had been halted in 1958. This had forced the introduction of pre-championship eliminators to select the German team. These were difficult to organise and took a lot out of the rowers. Britain's Guy Nickalls was among those who added their support for the East German position.

The debate became more heated when West Germany's Walter Wülfing, an ally of Thomi's, announced that his federation would abstain. "Above all, you must not mix sport and politics," Wülfing said, immediately making the supremely political assertion that "there only exists one Germany". Nagel professed his "astonishment" at Wülfing's comments, while an Austrian delegate – fretting that the discussion risked poisoning the "sporting and friendly spirit" that had always reigned among FISA members – proposed moving straight to the vote. This secret ballot came out in favour of retaining the status quo, though by the far-from-overwhelming margin of thirty-two votes to twenty, with seven blank voting slips.[6]

According to Klaus Filter – then a young boat-builder for the German women's team, who had encountered the FISA president for the first time in the boathouse some days before – Thomi and Wülfing had spent the farewell party for the women's championships which preceded the congress with two German medallists as their table partners. Says Filter, the oarswomen "had the order to use their female influence", while he, Filter, "had the order to keep an eye on the girls". He remembers the night ending "nearly in the morning when the waiters put the chairs on the tables and we were the last five there. I will never forget this because the two guests of honour were taken by car to their hotel while I had to walk with the girls to ours." Thomi's relationship with the East German women was always good, Filter concludes, adding: "He respected first and foremost their rowing performance, but also their ability to drink."[7]

Still the examination of Thomi's leadership qualities wasn't over: with the men's European championships poised to begin, the Czechs hoisted the East German flag – the same tricolour we are familiar with, but with the country's studiedly proletarian emblem of hammer and compass surrounded by a ring of rye. Thomi demanded it be taken down and, when this was refused, threatened to call off the entire championship just an hour before the opening ceremony. Once again, his boldness paid off and the hosts relented. On the last day of racing, on 27 August, Justicz and his partner took silver in the double sculls.[8]

Emboldened perhaps by the ease with which they had batted back these Eastern Bloc efforts to politicise their sport in 1961, Thomi and his colleagues tried to seize the initiative. It was decided to use the world championships to introduce a new type of medals ceremony, stripped of nationalism in the form of flags and anthems. It was nearly a step too far.

Scarcely had opening formalities of the 1962 FISA congress concluded, in the regular meeting-place of Lucerne's Grand Cantonal Council, than Kabanov demanded the floor. He had done this, so he said, to express his "astonishment" – that word again – at the course FISA had taken, and to lodge a protest. Only three months earlier, in Moscow, the IOC had rejected a similar motion. Why would FISA want to do things differently from other international sports federations and the IOC? The logical conclusion of FISA's line that it was important to highlight the exploits of the successful athletes rather than the support of their countries, would be to abolish national colours and emblems on the oarsmen's blades. Flags and anthems represented the honour and pride of the countries and people who created the champions. The Soviet federation did not think FISA should be indifferent to them.[9]

Thomi stuck to his guns, while characterising 1962 as a trial and promising to reassess matters the following year. "Countries do not win regattas," was one of his more resonant phrases. While FISA's stand against nationalism will seem surprising and refreshing to many today, let alone in those politically charged times, it is tempting to see it in part as a reaction to the way in which politics had wrecked Thomi's Olympic career as an oarsman in 1956. Yes, the rules would apply to all, but it was more than likely that the noses of the Warsaw Pact countries would be those put most out of joint. Sport, after all, was already acquiring its status as a soft power extension of the Cold War, capable of offering objective proof of the supposed superiority of the Communist system. Thomi's message appeared to be: you deprive athletes like me of our sporting dreams and I will stop you flaunting your national symbols at events under my control.

Kabanov backed off for the time being, declaring pointedly that he knew very well what being a champion meant since he had taken great pains to become one himself, while emphasising that he had not changed his mind. It was plain both that the ground for making the change could and should have been better prepared and that this would not be the final word on the matter.

And so it proved. A year later when FISA gathered in Copenhagen, some seven weeks after JFK's famous "Ich bin ein Berliner" speech in the divided city, both the East Germans and the flag/anthem issue were back. FISA, arguing once more for the status quo, won the vote on the German question more comfortably than two years previously, by thirty-nine votes to seventeen. This was in spite of East German rowing federation president Alfred Neumann's claim that "this common team has become a fiction".[10] Thomi used the occasion to strike a practical note, remarking that at least then-current arrangements enabled East German rowers to take part in events held in NATO countries. East German athletes trying to go to world skiing and shooting championships in France and Norway respectively had, he said, been unable to get visas.[11]

Then it was on to the de-nationalised medals ceremonies. Thomi said he thought the world championship presentations, featuring a specially composed FISA fanfare, had been widely appreciated by sports people all over the world. "Omitting to use flags and national anthems stops national chauvinism," he argued. Kabanov was strangely quiet; he plainly knew the result was in the bag.

Passing to the vote, delegates decided by a convincing thirty-seven votes to fifteen to keep the traditional ceremony featuring flags and anthems. A victorious Kabanov then found his tongue in order to chastise FISA for shortcomings in its handling of women's rowing. It was a not invalid point, even if the Soviet delegate's timing seemed odd.

In 1964 in Amsterdam, the by-now-ritual East German call to be allowed to enter its own teams was once again voted down, this time by forty-one votes to twenty-two. However, with Thomi claiming merely that the now near-decade-old system "presented the fewest inconveniences", there was a sense of tectonic plates shifting.[12] Sure enough, in 1965, when the inevitable East German proposal was again raised, Thomi acknowledged that "new aspects" had appeared, while asking that formal consideration await an extraordinary congress later in the year.[13]

By the time FISA again gathered in Vienna on 13 November, the IOC had moved to resolve the German conundrum. Meeting in

Madrid that October, it had decided to permit two German teams at the next Olympic Games, due to be held in 1968 in France (winter) and Mexico (summer). However, the two teams would march under the same banner, and use the same hymn and emblem. Tellingly, the original motion – drafted after long debate and a break to allow members to sleep on the problem – referred to East Germany not as a country but a "geographical area".[14]

The East Germans must have realised from the moment the Madrid motion was passed that FISA would probably follow suit.[15] But Thomi had skilfully prepared an additional surprise for them and their Warsaw Pact allies. Taking advantage of his ever-closer relations with other international sports federations, he had used the weeks running up to Vienna to contact them, as well as the East German rowing federation, to ask under what specific conditions participation by East German athletes had been possible at events staged in NATO countries. Armed with their replies, and presumably judging it better not to try and ambush delegates in the Austrian capital during the congress itself, the FISA leadership had drafted a letter detailing its proposals. This was sent to all national rowing federations on 2 November.

The replies, it turned out, had revealed a degree of variance on certain details. On two questions, however, it seems responses had been unequivocal: the flags of competing nations were not to be hoisted; and there were no flags or anthems at medal ceremonies. The letter notified national federations that the leadership would propose accordingly that only the host nation's flag be displayed and that medal ceremonies be held without flags or national anthems. Moreover, rowing outfits and the colour of blades would be determined by the FISA board, in agreement with interested federations. Whereas, when FISA had moved before to rewrite protocol for its ceremonies, this had been for "idealistic" reasons, the letter argued, this time it was being guided by "practical considerations".

The missive also allowed itself a small pop at the IOC, describing its recently adopted solution as having "a provisional character".[16]

It was a masterstroke, reminiscent in some ways of the procedural skills manifested in later years by Juan Antonio Samaranch, the IOC president who turned out to be Thomi's nemesis. By linking the medals ceremony question explicitly to FISA's ability to grant the East Germans what they most wanted, Thomi ensured the reversal of the rout he had suffered two years earlier. He had shown those who sought to use sport for political ends that he was not a man to be trifled with.

The formality of the votes was completed swiftly, with both motions – for the protocol changes and then annulment of the 1955 measure insisting that there be only one German team – carried by the same wide margin: forty-six votes in favour, four abstentions and no one against. Only the West Germans, responsible presumably for three of the abstentions, raised their voice to insist that abandonment of the one-team solution was unjustified. A certain Herr Ziel of Rudersport, the lone press representative in the room, had quite a scoop on his hands.

Nearly nine months later, the first explicitly East German crews made their debut at the 1966 women's European championships in Amsterdam. They won three of the five events.

CHAPTER 6

A Kind of Association

If rowing remained the centre of Thomi's sporting universe, by the mid-1960s he was also actively engaged in efforts to boost the influence and profile of the international sports federations.

For Thomi, it was the responsibility of the federations to run their sports on a day-to-day basis. And yet, when it came to crunch topics such as where the line between amateurism and professionalism should be drawn, it was the IOC – which Thomi tended to regard as a jumped-up event organiser – who called most of the shots. The more money that flowed into sport as a result of the escalating value of TV rights, the more important it became to get such judgements right. This, in turn, provided a strong incentive for federations to organise themselves, and coordinate their views and actions, more effectively.

The quantity and delicacy of the big political issues of the era – the Cold War and persistent Eastern Bloc efforts to use sport as an instrument of soft power; China/Taiwan; what to do about apartheid South Africa – also provided the motivation, along with money, for NOCs to find better ways of pulling together on matters of common interest.

Both groups, the federations and the NOCs, were further encouraged to act by what they perceived as IOC president Avery

Brundage's condescending attitude towards them.[1] According to journalist and historian David Miller, "For a man of business it was strange that Brundage was never able to understand how essential collaboration was between the three arms of the Movement, how the IOC could never hope to stand in isolation, how the Games were ultimately or even more financially dependent in practical terms upon the individual sports bodies and those who provided the competitors than upon the IOC as rights holders".[2]

It was the NOCs – more numerous but also more disparate than the federations – who moved first, under the ambitious, energetic leadership of Giulio Onesti, head of the Italian National Olympic Committee that had negotiated the breakthrough TV deals for the 1960 Rome Olympics. In October 1963, on the day when the United States and the USSR in effect agreed not to place nuclear weapons in outer space, the NOCs made the seemingly modest request for an annual meeting with the IOC's ruling executive board. Onesti's election to the IOC the following year failed to take the wind out of the NOCs' sails as Brundage may have hoped that it would. In 1965 a first general assembly of NOCs was staged over three days in Rome, and in 1968 a permanent general assembly of NOCs was created.[3]

By this time the international sports federations, though slower off the mark, had already formed their own permanent collaborative body, the General Assembly of International Sports Federations (GAIF).[4] At an IOC session in April 1966 at the Hotel Excelsior in Rome, agreement had been reached on the distribution around the various constituent parts of the sports movement of the sums arising from the sale of broadcasting rights to the 1972 Summer and Winter Olympics. The formula would ensure that federations whose sports were included in those Games would secure a far bigger slice of the revenues than they had got up until that point. However, it would leave them well short of the one-third share they had been asking for since 1963. How far short would only become clear with the final reckoning some years later. The formula entitled them to around 12.5% of the $26.3 million that the events in Sapporo and Munich actually generated. The NOCs succeeded in negotiating an identical share of the spoils, after a process that had started with appointment of an IOC committee chaired by Onesti.[5]

While the federations approved the Rome formula by what the minutes of the meeting describe as "a large majority", the arrangement left some of them far from thrilled. This was hardly surprising. An announcement ten days before the session of a $4.5 million deal for US rights to the 1968 Games made it obvious how fast broadcasting rights values were escalating. Yet, under the new formula, federations stood to get only one-ninth of the income generated by the 1972 Summer Games beyond the first $2 million. Of this initial tranche, admittedly, they would garner $555,555 – or nearly 28%.

Reporting back to FISA colleagues some months later, Thomi made it clear that while the accord meant that "large sums" would in due course be paid to the federations, relations with the IOC still left much to be desired. "In this collaboration, [the federations] have a dominant position from which, up until now, they have only profited to a very modest degree," he told them.[6]

By January 1967, plans were being laid for the meeting at which GAIF would be created.[7] Not all federations were in favour of the growing militancy being exhibited by colleagues such as Thomi. In particular, the International Amateur Athletic Federation (IAAF) – whose president, the Marquess of Exeter, was also a senior IOC member – remained broadly comfortable with existing conduits for dialogue between Lausanne and the international sports federations. Accordingly, when federation representatives gathered on 21 April at the Continental hotel opposite Lausanne railway station, the IAAF, FIFA, the football governing body, and AIBA, the international amateur boxing association, were all missing.

At 9.30am sharp, the French president of the international amateur wrestling federation Roger Coulon, who had convened the meeting, called delegates to order and over the next three days the foundations of the new umbrella body GAIF were laid.[8] Even within the confines of this gathering there was disagreement about the need for a new organisation. Bunny Ahearne from the sport of ice hockey spoke out against a "super body" of the federations.[9] Marc Hodler – the president of the international ski federation who was also, like the Marquess of Exeter, an IOC member – criticised the move two weeks later at an IOC session in Tehran.[10]

On the morning of 23 April, William Berge Phillips, Australian president of the international swimming federation, was elected president of GAIF for the new body's first year of existence. Thomi was one of two unsuccessful nominees for the post, along with basketball's R. William Jones. Already, though, the rowing leader was emerging along with Coulon as the organisation's main driving force, taking the lead role in drafting a six-page letter to Brundage that stands as a comprehensive but succinct summary of the federations' aims and demands.

Thomi's draft was revised by other delegates, in line with the collaborative spirit of the new venture, and the tone betrays this, fluctuating between outright audacity and transparent concern that they would continue to be ignored. Of its many "requests", the most eye-catching are perhaps a) a reiteration of the call for one-third of the TV money raised by the Games; b) a proposal for an Olympic congress (an event, last held in 1930, bringing together the constituent parts of the movement) every four years; and c) a call for the federations, under the guise of GAIF, to play a much more prominent part in the selection of Olympic Games host cities. (Concerns were running high at this point over the state of preparedness of Mexico City for the 1968 Summer Games that were less than eighteen months away.)

Brundage, predictably, was less than impressed. Welcoming delegates to the sixty-fifth IOC session in the Shah's capital on 6 May, he told them that "several" international sports federations had recently formed "a kind of association". They had sent a letter dealing with matters that were "not of their competence and only the concern of the IOC".[11] Back in Lausanne on 22 May, he wrote a short reply to Phillips that, while somewhat more measured, underlined this same jurisdictional concern. "We were astonished," he noted, "to see among the subjects suggested for discussion, several which are the exclusive concern of the IOC".[12] It is tempting, in the circumstances, to think that the salutation "Dear President Phillips" with which he begins his reply is steeped in irony, particularly since GAIF's original letter was addressed plain "Dear Mr Brundage".

Thomi, however, fully appreciated the potential significance of the new body, telling his colleagues in rowing that he was convinced GAIF would "develop in coming years for the good of the international sports federations and that in the end it will be the athletes who will profit from it".[13]

Two months on from the birth of this new sporting body, Thomi was in Italy fêting the achievements of a considerably older one: FISA. The federation's seventy-fifth anniversary was celebrated in Turin – the city where it was founded – with much joyful pomp and circumstance, including a nautical parade on the river Po in which representatives of the body's founding nations wore period costume. Thomi proclaimed the event, reverting to a favoured phrase, "from every point of view a complete success".[14]

The organisers enhanced their chances of a rave review from the FISA president by staging a firework display on the riverbank on the first evening. All his life, Thomi loved fireworks, the louder the better. On Swiss National Day on 1 August, firework parties were an annual event at the Keller family home, with many guests invited. Thomi would bring back the fireworks from a supplier in eastern Switzerland and often light the blue touch-paper with his cigar.[15]

The history and traditions of rowing which the anniversary was celebrating also meant a great deal to him. Right up until the end of his life, he took mischievous pleasure in pointing out that FISA, founded in 1892, was two years older than the IOC.[16] But it was also typical of Thomi that he should take advantage of the anniversary to look forward as well as back, using it as a pretext to organise the first FISA regatta for juniors. Originally intended for Turin, this inaugural event was moved ultimately to Ratzeburg. Thomi described the friendship between participants as "remarkable", declaring "we tried to do something new".[17] This was a comment that might equally have been applied to the notion of staging an elite international rowing event in Mexico City.

CHAPTER 7

A Long Sprint

On the evening of Friday 18 October 1963 in Baden-Baden's Belle Epoque-style Kurhaus, the IOC chose Mexico City to host the 1968 Summer Games. The Central American metropolis won comfortably on just one round of voting, securing thirty of fifty-eight ballots cast, in spite of concerns about the effect on athletes of its altitude of over 7000 feet. Detroit, hub of the US car industry, came second; Lyon, capital of French gastronomy, third. So began four years of high anxiety for Thomi.

He spelt out the reasons for this in another elegant German-speaking city, Klagenfurt, in 1969 after a particularly successful Olympic regatta had finally been staged, and after paying ten visits (and counting) to the 1972 host Munich.[1] "Much more work is required for Olympic regattas than for a FISA championship regatta," he told international rowing federation colleagues gathered in Austria for their last congress of the decade. He went on: "It was necessary to insist first of all on the construction of an artificial course... After the consent of the responsible authorities had finally been obtained came all the detailed planning. The building of the structures followed the building of the course and only then came the setting up of the organisation. In the case of a FISA championship regatta, our work usually begins at this point since we normally only hold our regattas on well-tried courses."[2]

He concluded: "If we had not given the organisers... the alternative of either putting perfect courses at our disposal or not holding an Olympic regatta, rowing would again have been the wallflower of the Games. Our races would have been held either on courses which did not fulfil present-day requirements or were situated far from the centre of the Games. Because we stood firm we have created a precedent."[3]

This is a workmanlike summary with a ringing conclusion, but it gives little sense of either the exasperation Thomi often felt as the October 1968 start date drew ever closer with little sign of progress on the ground, or the lengths he threatened to go to in order to ensure a satisfactory outcome.

Four years out from the 1968 Games, everything seemed more or less in order. Thomi told a FISA meeting in Tokyo that an existing course, ten minutes away from the Olympic Village, was to be upgraded. Work had not yet started, but this was because officials were awaiting the entry into office, on New Year's Day 1965, of a new Mexican government. The president-elect had already given an undertaking that a FISA representative would be invited to Mexico to discuss details with local officials later that year. The regatta would last longer than usual to help rowers cope with the effects of competing at high altitude.[4]

On 12 April 1965, Thomi met General José de Jesús Clark Flores, organising committee and senior IOC member, in Lausanne. By that summer, however, the FISA president's patience had run out. In the wake of an address in which he reminded delegates how often conditions for Olympic rowing regattas have been less than ideal – starting with the very first modern Games in 1896, when rough water forced abandonment of the planned competition – he secured congress's permission to send a letter to the organising committee. This told them that if in a year FISA was not satisfied about the state of preparations for 1968, it would ask the IOC to scrap the Olympic regatta. "Many promises have been made to us, but nothing has been done," the record states. "When we know the difficulties that have to be overcome to put on a FISA championship, especially in a country organising one for the first time, the three years remaining is the minimum time necessary to guarantee correct organisation of this regatta."[5]

If the presence at that meeting in Duisburg of a lone Mexican delegate might lead one to wonder whether FISA's rather draconian threat was partly for show, in the hope that the message would get back to organisers that these guys meant business, there can be no doubt as to Thomi's seriousness when the subject again came up in November. In the post-prandial session of the extraordinary congress in Vienna, the FISA president basically let rip. The minutes detailing his broadside cover no fewer than six pages.[6]

There was still no definitive plan, a fuming Thomi informed his colleagues, and the organising committee did not even know where it wanted the venue to be. FISA had had no news. He then read out the letter containing his ultimatum to the organisers, despatched after the Duisburg meeting. That too had gone unanswered. Rather shrewdly he then asked colleagues to publicise in their countries the efforts the FISA leadership had been going to, in the hope that oarsmen would better understand the decisions that may have needed to be taken if the worst came to the worst. In answer to a question about the feasibility of staging an Olympic regatta outside Mexico,[7] Thomi finally disclosed that Avery Brundage, the IOC president, would not consent to this.

The mood began to change as of April 1966. Thomi and FISA's North American representative John Carlin spent four days in the Mexican capital discussing "questions of the utmost importance". Thomi reported back that the regatta would be held on the Cuemanco canal at Xochimilco, literally "the place seeded with flowers". The canal would be dredged, and with banks flat and plenty of free water either side of the course, the "problem of certain lanes having an advantage in the case of a side wind will not exist". Time, though, was "very short" and "great efforts" would be needed to complete installations. A dearth of experienced on-the-spot personnel was a further "serious problem".[8]

Some of these issues were still playing on Thomi's mind a year later when he took a leading role in drafting the federations' letter to Brundage notifying the IOC president that the GAIF had been founded. "In most sports the preparations of the installations are far behind the state in which they should be," the letter warned, going on to express "considerable concern" at the "apparent lack of technical personnel available to conduct the events". In trademark Thomi style, the missive also pulled no punches in championing the athletes' cause. "All over the world athletes are training for the Games of the XIX Olympiad", the document proclaimed, "and in view of the altitude of Mexico City this has to be effected with additional sacrifice of time and money. They are therefore all the more entitled to compete under the best possible conditions only."[9]

In rowing's case, however, Thomi's worries had been partly assuaged, in spite of a further modification of plans, following another visit he made to Mexico City in early February 1967. "I could discuss there the major questions on the spot," he reported. "The construction of a canal which runs parallel to the one previously taken into consideration is now completed. Clean water is pumped into it from a depth of 400 metres." By September, a somewhat contrite Thomi was congratulating the builders for the "rapid completion of this project" in the presence of José Alverde, president of the Mexican rowing federation. Having been the target of so much criticism, the Mexican official, understandably, did not mince words in underlining his country's accomplishment in constructing what would turn out to be an outstanding Olympic facility in exceptionally beautiful surroundings. "It was exactly one year ago, in a very sceptical atmosphere on your part, that we began work on the new course," he recalled. "At the end of July 1967, flooding started. Thanks to very powerful pumps and the considerable efforts of technicians and workers, this course will be ready for the Third International Games [a test event] which will take place in October... We hope that the president of Mexico can inaugurate the course."[10]

Given the efficiency with which the Mexican organisers eventually constructed the venue, was all the tub-thumping in the build-up strictly necessary? Probably not. But Thomi was undoubtedly haunted by the issues that had bedevilled finals day at the Tokyo Olympiad, and communications on the Mexican side in the wake of their selection as hosts do seem to have left plenty to be desired.

Beyond Xochimilco's tranquil, lily-carpeted waterways, 1968 was a particularly turbulent year in world affairs. There were the assassinations of Martin Luther King and Robert F. Kennedy, the Tet Offensive, which dragged on most of the year, and the widely publicised student protests in Paris. The crushing of the Prague Spring in August may have struck a chord with Thomi, with its echoes of Budapest 1956. Then, ten days before the Olympic opening ceremony, scenes of large-scale violence came to Mexico City itself. Perhaps provoked, the authorities moved against protestors in the Plaza de las Tres Culturas. The death toll has been estimated at 150 or more, but the Games went ahead.

In the rowing competition, which took place between 13 and 19 October, there was a good spread of medal-winners, with the East Germans – competing for the first time as a separate team at the Summer Olympics – mustering two golds and one silver. This silver medal came in a coxed fours event in which the New Zealand quintet won their country's first Olympic rowing gold medal and the bronze was secured narrowly (and rather unexpectedly) by a Swiss crew including a twenty-one-year-old oarsman from Neuchâtel called Denis Oswald.

Rather like Thomi, Oswald – whose first really high-level international competition this was – gravitated towards rowing only gradually. At thirteen, when he took up the sport "a little bit by accident" as some friends had started rowing and his family home was next to the rowing club, he regarded himself primarily as an ice-hockey player. "I thought rowing was maybe a good way to improve my physical condition in the summer and to become a better hockey player," he recalls. After a couple of years, however, he gave up the puck and the ice-rink to dedicate himself wholly to rowing. His four became junior Swiss champions. Oswald was the youngest member of the crew.[11]

In 1965, the four broke up when two of them completed their studies and left the local region. Oswald and his remaining crewmate, both law students, decided to try and qualify for Mexico in the coxless pair. In the event, a rival Swiss duo was slightly faster. This might have ended any Olympic ambitions, at least for 1968, but for the problems being encountered by an experienced Swiss coxed fours crew. It was decided that performance might benefit from an injection of youth, in the shape of Oswald and his crewmate, into the squad. As their Olympic bronze medals would testify, this turned out to be a smart move.

Oswald recalls meeting and getting a spot of on-water advice from Thomi during two weeks' altitude training at Saint Moritz before the team's departure for Mexico. Some years earlier he had witnessed a speech delivered by the FISA president at a youth training camp. "We were very impressed," he remembers, not least by the E-type Jaguar Thomi was driving.

Once ensconced in the Olympic city, Oswald says he had "no problem" with altitude, though others did. In a very tight final, he and his crewmates spent much of the race in fourth spot before overhauling the fading US boat in the final 500 metres, while holding off an Italian crew who were hot on their heels almost throughout by just half a second. Oswald describes rowing as an endurance sport that is also a "long sprint". At the start of a race, he says, there was often "a certain anxiety or fear, knowing you were going to suffer". Those six minutes and 49.04 seconds at Xochimilco, gulping in lungfuls of thin Aztec air while straining every fibre to hold the Italians at bay must have seemed like the longest sprint of all for the young Swiss oarsman.

CHAPTER 8

An Opportunity Denied

Just over a month after this race, Thomi reached the milestone of his tenth anniversary as president of FISA. By this time – November 1968 – though still young by the standards of fellow top administrators, he had established himself as master of all he surveyed in the sport to which he had devoted his life. He was respected by athletes for taking their concerns seriously and by officials for his energy and for having the best interests of the sport always at heart, as well as for not playing politics but not being naïve. He had begun his diversification onto a bigger and broader stage by playing an active role in the establishment of GAIF, the umbrella body of international sports federations. But he was also keenly aware that change – and not necessarily positive change – was in the air, with commercial interests beginning to knock ever more loudly on sport's door.

At the FISA congress in Mexico he tried to take stock of this in words reflecting on his decade at the helm and on sport's growing role in modern society. Competitive sport, he warned, had been "partly estranged from its original goal and has become a political and economic instrument". This process had progressed in different types of sport to varying degrees. It might be controlled "to a certain extent", but it could not be stopped.[1]

Thomi had already shown himself perfectly willing to fight on international sports federations' behalf for a generous slice of the broadcasting-rights income which the Olympic Games had started to generate. Clearly he understood how beneficial this new source of money could be for rowers and for rowing. Yet in Mexico, he was still able to prefix the statement "rowing does not lend itself as a spectator sport nor as a medium for advertising" with the adverb "luckily". Though not as hostile to the wall of money then zeroing in on sport as the ageing and largely inflexible IOC president Avery Brundage, Thomi could picture the potential downside of sport's transformation into a business every bit as vividly.

Part of this downside lay in the new temptations that would assail sports officials who, in rowing's case, were at this time exclusively amateur. Thomi accordingly took the opportunity in his speech to make a passionate case for the high standards he would continue to expect of colleagues who, while mostly not fortunate enough to be as wealthy as he was, had benefited just as much from the sport's character-building qualities. "We all feel the temptation sometimes to stray from our true goal and to turn our position to personal ends," he told them. "The kind of administrator for whom growing prestige and perks are more important than sticking up for the competitors is well known. But we will never forget that we owe our sport for the multiple impressions that have decisively marked our personalities. We have learnt to understand the true meaning of words such as comradeship, discipline, self-sacrifice, personal commitment and others besides through having to put them into practice. The exercise of an official function within the extensive network of our sport enables us to pay back our debt of recognition by contributing to helping the next generation to enrich itself as we did... Our aim in the final analysis must be to teach young people to become valuable members of human society." It is a demanding but profoundly humanist creed.

Thomi had no way of knowing while making this speech that the next six to seven months were to be critical in shaping his own career path in sport. On 6 December, Albert Mayer – the seventy-eight-year-old jeweller, former mayor of Montreux, brother of former IOC chancellor Otto, and (most significantly for Thomi) one of the Swiss IOC members – died.[2] This left a possibly once-in-a-generation vacancy at the Olympic body. On 31 January 1969, Thomi attended a meeting with Brundage and was asked if he would be interested in the position.

It is worth pausing to reflect on the context in which this tempting prospect was dangled. Though recently re-elected to another four-year term until 1972, the eighty-one-year-old IOC president was under immense pressure to wake up to reality and recognise that the writing was on the wall for traditional, unadulterated amateurism, a cause he had championed over many years. The Grenoble Winter Games, in February 1968, had enraged him for what he saw as their brazen commercialism: "we had Olympic butter, Olympic sugar, Olympic petrol".[3] So had the formation in Mexico of the permanent general assembly of NOCs, not least one suspects because supporters of the NOCs' Italian leader Giulio Onesti had begun to ponder what one expert has described as "an electoral coup".[4] In the end, the only challenge had come from Comte Jean de Beaumont of France. Part of the price of Brundage's re-election, though, seems to have been that he agree to resign at the end of one final term.[5] He had reluctantly acquiesced too to the idea of holding an Olympic congress, although he started dragging his feet again subsequently.[6]

There was also turbulence within the IOC's administration, with Johann Westerhoff – a multilingual Dutchman who had been secretary general since 1966 – resigning in January 1969, having lost Brundage's support. Westerhoff had formed the view that the new umbrella bodies of NOCs and international sports federations could only help the IOC, an opinion hardly calculated to endear him to his boss, the IOC president.

These frustrations boiled over in a remarkable and "highly confidential" letter written by Brundage to executive board members on 4 March 1969, thirty-two days after his meeting with Thomi. Almost every sentence is quotable, but the unmistakable message was his determination to dig his heels in even further in the face of the mounting clamour for change. "The Olympic Games are not an ordinary sport meeting," he concluded. "They were not created to entertain the public, to make money, or to indicate the national prestige of the participating countries." The Olympic Movement, though "in great danger", has become "the most important social force in the world… We must combat all the nonsense printed about changed times… Olympic is the magic word and it must be kept that way… Without further delay we must organise an active publicity campaign stressing Olympic principles and the reasons for them, in our own defence."[7]

It is clear from this that, while some of Thomi's claims on behalf of the international sports federations would have exasperated him, there is also much common ground in the two mens' outlook. It seems plausible too that Brundage may have come to harbour a grudging admiration for the FISA president's leadership qualities and transparent devotion to his sport. Certainly, he had little or no respect for the leadership qualities of the man who eventually succeeded him as IOC president, Lord Killanin.[8]

This partial convergence of views is probably one of the reasons Brundage approached Thomi at what he saw as a perilous time for the Olympic Movement. But there were quite possibly others. For example, there is also an echo of the tactic he deployed, admittedly to little effect, with Onesti: did he similarly calculate that it would be preferable to bring Thomi inside the tent, rather than stirring things up from outside? Moreover, it must have occurred to the American that if the choice as Mayer's replacement were not Thomi, it was likely to be Raymond Gafner, president of the Swiss Olympic Committee. Not only was Gafner an ally of Onesti but, as a former ice hockey goal-minder and ex-president of the Swiss ice hockey federation, his sympathies would probably lie with the winter sports Brundage saw as posing such a threat to the Olympics' purity.

Thomi's reply, dated 7 February, exactly a week after the original meeting, and addressed to Brundage at Lausanne's Palace hotel, is breathtaking in its audacity. Broken down to its essentials, his response is as follows:

1) It is neither "correct nor advisable" to be an IOC member and president of an international sports federation at the same time (although others did combine the roles);

2) He had planned to remain FISA president for a further ten years and had not even begun to identify and train up a successor;

3) He might well be on the point of election as president of GAIF with a two-year term;

4) Therefore – and this is where it gets really interesting – "Only if I could see a real chance to serve the ideals of sports in the same manner as heretofore or even on an increased scale would I be prepared voluntarily to abandon the FISA presidency in two or three years' time already";

5) "The mere membership of the IOC in its present form does not seem to offer this possibility and in all frankness I would consider such a switch in the near future only if there was a real likelihood to become sooner or later your own successor";

6) "The tasks and duties connected with your position as well as the opportunities to serve our ideals would tempt me very much as I realise the enormous possibilities it offers to influence the future development of sports in general and its role in our society."

Thomi liked to say in later years that he had refused to become a member of the IOC.[9] However, there is one final detail that seems to indicate just how alluring he found the notion of following in Brundage's footsteps. "For good order's sake", he points out that his "financial and business position" would permit him to serve as IOC president, i.e. he was well enough off to volunteer his services. This had been an issue prior to the 1968 IOC presidential election, with Killanin feeling unable to run "until such time as the IOC allowed its president an expense account".[10] Whether by coincidence or not, this matter began to be addressed at the IOC executive board meeting subsequent to Thomi's supremely self-confident missive to Brundage.[11]

We do not know how the IOC president reacted to Thomi's chutzpah. It is doubtful the notion that "mere membership of the IOC" held little appeal would have gone down very well. What we can be fairly sure about is that the other prime candidate for the vacancy was preparing to make his move.

In mid-March, within a few days of Brundage's astonishing six-page *cri de coeur* to members of his executive board, Gafner was re-elected to the presidency of the Swiss Olympic Committee he had held since 1965 for a further four-year term. Within the week, he was able to rub shoulders with Brundage at a Lausanne reception thrown by the Swiss Olympic Committee. There would have been much to talk about with a long, far-from-flattering magazine article by Westerhoff on his time with the IOC having recently been published. But it is hard to imagine that the IOC vacancy would not have cropped up in the conversation at all.

On 2 May, the Swiss Olympic Committee wrote to Brundage, now back in Chicago, making its position plain. If the IOC decided once again to confer the vacant position on a Swiss national, "the Executive Council of the Swiss Olympic Committee would be unanimous in its appreciation if this choice were to fall on its

president, Mr Raymond Gafner". An accompanying career summary mentions his law doctorate and directorship of Vaud canton's
university hospital, but not his mission to Congo in 1967 for the
International Committee of the Red Cross to mediate between
president Mobutu and a group of Belgian mercenaries.

With the IOC session scheduled for early June in Warsaw, this
may have been cutting things a bit fine, especially as Brundage does
not appear to have received the letter until 9 May. Nonetheless,
on 8 June, at an executive board meeting starting at the unusual
hour of 10pm, Gafner was one of four new IOC members nomi-
nated – alongside individuals from New Zealand, Côte d'Ivoire and
Panama – for election during the session.[12] He duly served as an
active, much respected member until 1990, playing a key part in the
channelling of sports development funding to newly independent
nations especially in Africa, and in setting up an Olympic museum.

The minutes of these Warsaw proceedings are, it should be
acknowledged, particularly elliptical. Regarding the new members,
for example, readers are told only that "the many propositions
for new members were carefully studied and discussed in detail".
Had Thomi's name fallen by the wayside by this point or was he
among the "many propositions"? It is impossible to know from
this record.[13]

Before her death in 2015, however, I did have a short discussion
about Thomi with Monique Berlioux. A French former international swimmer and journalist, she took advantage of Westerhoff's
departure to assume control of the IOC's administrative functions,
going on to serve as director for many years. Throughout the
1970s and into the 1980s, she liaised quite closely with Thomi and
was undoubtedly, like him, among the ten most powerful sports
administrators of that era. Berlioux told me that there was an
election – I am presuming among the executive board – and that
Gafner won by one vote. Thomi, she said, was "angry".[14] With eight

board members, including strident GAIF opponent the Marquess of Exeter, present at the key night-time meeting, this suggests a four-to-three margin with one abstention. Most intriguingly, however, the question of new members came up again at another executive board meeting the following afternoon, this time attended by just seven board members. Once again, the minutes are far too brief to give any real idea of the content of the discussion. But they do say this: "A new method of election must be found. The president stated he did not approve of the way in which these elections had been conducted."[15]

Had Brundage tried somehow to intervene on Thomi's behalf? Might his treatment even have been the cause of the IOC president's displeasure? In the absence of a fuller record or a recording, there is no way of knowing. There is, though, something else. Quite a few years later, Gafner told Olympic journalist and historian David Miller that "Brundage proposed to the executive board in 1971 that I and five others should be expelled!"[16] Miller says this was on issues of eligibility and the relaxation of financial restraints imposed on training. However, Guttmann notes that "in 1971, at the executive board meetings in Luxembourg, Brundage expressed his intention of recommending that any IOC member associated with the [permanent general assembly of NOCs] should submit his resignation".[17] Presumably, that would have included the president of the Swiss Olympic Committee too.

Clearly, Brundage's gripes at this time in the final years of his presidency extended far beyond the identity of the IOC members from Switzerland. Yet it is impossible not to wonder whether the veteran Chicagoan had recollected the two-year timeframe outlined by Thomi in his original letter and determined to try and reopen a vacancy that the FISA president might fill.[18] After all, as we have seen, he thought little of his likeliest successor Killanin's leadership credentials.

It wasn't to be. A second bite at the IOC cherry, and a chance of succeeding Brundage, never materialised for Thomi. From that point on it was evident that whatever path he followed in his future career, he was destined to remain outside the IOC citadel. The rejection did, without a doubt, further prejudice Thomi's already not-altogether-complimentary view of the custodians of the Olympic Games, at least in private. In public he tended to stick to the version of events that had him rejecting them. Yet even as the IOC gathered in Communist Poland to seal his fate, Thomi's strategic instincts would have been telling him that, even if his pride were dented, he was quite justified in his bold bid to hold out for a good crack at the IOC presidency. After all, he was about to consolidate his position as one of the most powerful figures in world sport, and this meant, as many already realised, that the IOC needed him more than he needed them.

CHAPTER 9

A Giant Leap

Raymond Gafner had not even taken his oath as a new IOC member when the prediction Thomi had made to Avery Brundage came to pass: Thomi was elected president of GAIF.

Fifty days before the Apollo 11 moon landing, it was a small step for GAIF – Thomi had already chaired at least one top-level federational meeting in William Berge Phillips's absence[1] – but it was a giant leap for Thomi. Rather than become, initially at least, an insignificant pawn in the IOC's chess-set, the unanimous vote by his GAIF colleagues propelled him to the head of a body that he believed perfectly placed to shape the future of sport. This was because he thought the federations, whose common interests he was now charged with pursuing, "entirely independent as far as politics and financial resources are concerned".[2] Supported by secretary general Roger Coulon and his right-hand man from FISA, Charles Riolo, now installed also as GAIF treasurer, Thomi set about working towards the changes he deemed necessary with the same gusto that he had displayed on taking the helm at FISA over a decade earlier.

An experienced businessman by this time, he could well see that change was coming. Sport's position at the end of the 1960s resembled that of an impoverished country that strikes oil, in the form of broadcasting rights. This could end well, with enhanced prosperity improving the lots of sports and athletes alike, or it could end badly, with rapacious business interests manipulating the new situation to their own ends. He must further have realised that with Brundage set to depart as IOC president in 1972, a big brake on the pace of change in the Olympic Movement would disappear in around three years' time.

However, from the work GAIF had previously undertaken, Thomi also knew that if the international federations wanted to defend their own and their athletes' interests in the new environment effectively while avoiding the sort of pitfalls he had already identified, their administrative machinery and communications channels would need a thorough overhaul. Much of Thomi's first two-year term as president of GAIF was accordingly a process of unglamorous, detailed nitty-gritty and under-the-bonnet adjustment and consultation, making ready for when the whirlwind hit.

His first three days in the GAIF president's chair were typical. Sunday and Monday, the first two days of June, were spent in consultations with GAIF colleagues. Coulon's agile, inventive mind was everywhere apparent, voicing ideas for federations to club together to negotiate a 10–15% reduction in air fares and creation of a World Youth Games, but pointing out too that GAIF was strapped for cash: "The GAIF budget was more than a hundred times smaller than the budget of the IOC."[3] There was also an appearance by Philip Noel-Baker, the only person to have won both an Olympic medal and a Nobel prize.[4] The then Labour MP for Derby South and president of the International Council for Sport and Physical Education, an associate body of UNESCO, delivered a speech on international sport.

The other abiding impression from the minutes of this meeting is Thomi's strategic vision. This held that, with political and economic interests already striving to subvert sport's true purpose as he saw it, constructive cooperation between the international sports federations, the IOC and the NOCs was indispensable. Yet efforts in this direction were continually undermined by bickering and petty jealousies. "Instead of openly collaborating in their work," he complains, "mistrust reigns in these organisations. Collaboration is limited to a strict minimum, the competence of the different organisations is not clearly defined and their aims are not coordinated." At one point he alludes to the "feud" with the NOCs, remarking: "I do not quite understand the reasons for the dispute which can only hurt sport". Already, the new GAIF president is advocating formation of a joint commission of the IOC, international sports federations and NOCs to "ensure liaison and cooperation for all problems of common concern".

These two days of intense consultations were followed by a meeting with the IOC executive board, before the latter headed off to Poland for the session at which, among other things, Gafner would be installed as the new Swiss IOC member. Perfectly illustrating the logjam identified by Thomi, this meeting with GAIF would later be characterised privately by the IOC as a "waste of time".[5]

In the past, the GAIF principals would have been reduced at this point to seething away in impotent rage at the IOC's high-handedness. Not any more. As the first month of the new decade dawned, Thomi embarked on a new approach. That year's IOC session in Amsterdam would see the selection of host cities for the 1976 Olympics, Summer and Winter. The IOC had ignored GAIF's request for detailed technical information from the candidates six months in advance. So on 21 January, Thomi wrote to all eight contenders,[6] inviting them to GAIF's general assembly in Munich in March. Explaining the bold tactic later, Thomi said: "Finally we learned that the president of the IOC was of the opinion that it would suffice if this information of fundamental importance were made available to us in Amsterdam. For the sake of our athletes and of our various sports, we simply cannot accept this point of view... I am happy that our invitation has been accepted."[7]

Ten days later, Thomi again thumbed his nose at the IOC, starting the process of repairing the relationship between the international sports federations and the NOCs at a two-day bilateral meeting, featuring five representatives from either camp, in Lausanne.

It was around this time too that Thomi's hand was further strengthened by the decision of FIFA – governing body of the world's most popular sport even if not the overpoweringly cash-rich juggernaut it has since become – to join GAIF. In that first quarter of 1970, in the throes of a first jolt of electricity applied by its vigorous new leader, all the momentum seemed to be going GAIF's way. "GAIF was founded three years ago as a loose association of organisations with a common interest in which each member retains full independence," Thomi recalled, with the merest vestige of self-satisfaction, in Munich. "However, events have moved so fast that there is already close cooperation in various ways."[8]

Brundage, meanwhile, appeared to be growing more reactionary, not less. Having consented to a congress bringing together all arms of the Olympic Movement when re-elected in 1968, he grumbled a year later that he had made this decision "since if the IOC does not do so, somebody else probably will do so". His disillusionment was even plainer in correspondence with IOC vice-president Killanin. "The idea of trying to get any constructive action out of an assembly of 700 or 800 is absurd," he snapped. "No one seems to know what the real objectives of the congress should be... I can think of many better ways to spend money."[9]

Absurd or not, organisation of the great event, pencilled in for Bulgaria in 1971, was going to require establishment, at least on a temporary basis, of the type of joint or tripartite commission evoked by Thomi in the meeting addressed by Noel-Baker but already rejected by the IOC in Mexico. It had been hoped that this body would have been formed early enough to meet during the IOC session in Amsterdam in May 1970. When this did not prove possible, Brundage seized on the opportunity to get the whole affair postponed until 1973 – instantly making it somebody else's problem. He sought to pin the blame for this on the international federations, telling Bulgarian general and IOC member Vladimir Stoytchev that efforts to discuss the matter in Amsterdam had been thwarted by FIFA president Sir Stanley Rous's departure for the 1970 World Cup in Mexico.[10]

If the octogenarian IOC president looked ever more out of touch, however, the eyes of some senior IOC colleagues were proving better able to decipher the writing on the wall.

General José de Jesús Clark Flores was not everyone's idea of a moderniser. But with the burden of the 1968 Games now behind him, the sixty-one-year-old Mexican IOC vice-president chose this moment to stand up and be counted. In the minutes of the IOC executive board meeting held in Lausanne on 21–23 February 1970, his contribution is described impenetrably as a document about "the contradiction of rules 24 and 25 by rule 1". Those taking the trouble to turn to the end of the minutes, where this document is reproduced, however, find a remarkable and passionate plea for his colleagues to start taking the international sports federations and NOCs seriously. If they didn't, he argued, they ran the risk of a breakaway that could sideline the Olympics for good.

"If the IOC is to fulfil satisfactorily its ideals in a harmonious atmosphere," Clark Flores warned, "it must coordinate efforts, with the assistance of the NOCs and the IFs [federations] – which exercise direct control over the athletes – thus avoiding the danger of splitting which exists at present in the world of sport". He went on, in florid but determined style: "I am convinced that there is a strong desire on the part of both NOCs and the IFs to coordinate efforts preferably and exclusively with us, before they try other solutions; but I am fully convinced... that if we do not decide whether or not the IOC is to be, or should be, the ruler of sport in the world, allowing those two forces to join it, in a not so distant future we shall face a break... which will have as final result the weakening of what up to now has been a great success: the Olympic Movement and its Games." The Mexican general then refers specifically to recent meetings both between GAIF and the NOCs and between GAIF and Noel-Baker's International Council for Sport and Physical Education, evidently perceiving in them the seeds of the split he has been warning about. "On the one hand the NOCs and the IFs are trying to find a solution based on their mutual understanding, in view of the fact that the third force, the IOC... has persistently ignored the problem. On the other hand, the IFs are already contemplating the idea of organising, possibly with the support of UNESCO and the respective governments, World Games, both for the youth and open... This would lead to the dangerous position in which sport would no longer be controlled by the autonomous bodies in each area, but by the governmental physical education agencies... It is no longer possible to continue pretending that the IOC is an organisation which must not heed the demands of the other bodies which control sport in the world."[11]

Thomi would have been less long-winded, but he would otherwise have found the content of Clark Flores's rather desperate message hard to fault.

In Amsterdam, where sports leaders assembled for the IOC session from 10 May, the focus switched to more media-friendly topics such as the victories of Montreal and Denver in the two races for the 1976 Games, the future of the Winter Olympics in the face of Brundage's intemperate attacks and, finally, the withdrawal of recognition from the South African Olympic Committee over the country's apartheid policies.

Thomi found himself required briefly to defend his native city, which came under fire from the IOC president for having had the temerity in November to vote against bidding for the 1976 Winter Games in a referendum.[12] It was becoming ever more apparent, however, that the IOC could no longer bury its head in the sand. A new settlement for sport was soon going to have to be drawn up – and, on behalf of the federations, Thomi would have a prominent seat at the negotiating table.

Meanwhile, the pace of change in rowing, the new GAIF president's own sport, had barely slackened. At the end of the European summer of 1969, Thomi had summoned FISA top brass to the scenic Yugoslavian rowing town of Bled to prepare for a congress at which "fundamental" organisational changes were to be proposed. It was basically a matter of settling on a structure that would take account of the federation's transformation from a European men's competitive rowing body into something far more diverse. Thomi explained: "From its foundation until the second world war, FISA dealt almost exclusively with competitive rowing for men. During the Fifties, women's rowing was added and, at the beginning of the Sixties, youth rowing. Now we intend to deal with all aspects of our sport. During the same time we have developed from basically a European organisation into a worldwide body... Our methods of organisation need revision and do not take completely into account the present-day needs of our sport."[13]

Accordingly, FISA's technical commission was entirely revamped; it would be comprised from then on of the chairs of seven specialist commissions. These included Holland's Nely Gambon-de Vos, who, as head of women's rowing, would go on to become the first female member of the federation's council.[14] The umpires' commission was expanded and there were numerous other changes, including to FISA's recently added juniors event. Thomi's long, serious-minded report in Klagenfurt reveals that he was also pondering recreational/ veterans' rowing at this time, as well as programmes to assist the sport's geographic spread. This period also saw the first edition of Thomi's so-called "cook book", a detailed blueprint for running faultless championship regattas. He announced it would be available, in French, English and German, in spring 1970.

A further sign of how sport was changing – and probable stimulus to some of this new thinking – could be found in the body's financial accounts. For the first time, TV rights generated almost as much (SFr33,170.50) as subscriptions (SFr35,637.85). This was a watershed, even if income from sport's new money-fountain remained inconsistent and would be back to zero the following year. Indeed, the delegation from St Catharines, the Ontario town gearing up to stage the first rowing world championships outside Europe in September 1970, bemoaned the "incredible indifference" of US and Canadian television towards the event.[15]

Even so, the trailblazing championship, which ended with a colossal barbecue at a place called Henley Island, was judged a success. Finals day, at which the East German men underlined their strength by finishing first or second in every event, was watched by a crowd of at least 30,000 – including Pierre Trudeau, the super-cool Canadian prime minister, but not Brundage, who had been unable to accept Thomi's invitation.

The event also saw the first of the largely informal get-togethers between rowers, coaches and top administrators, including Thomi, that were to become a valued FISA tradition, facilitating the free exchange of views and ideas and furthering the president's reputation as a man who had his athletes' interests at heart.[16] Mike Sweeney – then an oarsman and later a key FISA official and chairman of Henley Royal Regatta – retains a memory from St Catharines suggesting that Thomi, after almost twelve years in charge, remained as proactive as ever in pursuing what he saw as

74

his presidential duties. "It was windy; we were training," Sweeney recalls in short, matter-of-fact sentences. "A launch came rattling over. I was about to curse. I heard a voice, 'You, British! What do you think about the conditions?' We both put thumbs down. He sped off and racing was postponed."[17] In the semi-finals of the eights, moreover, Australia suffered an injustice when the race got under way even though they were signalling that they were not ready to start. Thomi went out in his launch again to check if there was room on the course for a seventh lane. There was – just. Australia were given the chance to qualify for the final if they could better a certain time in a re-run. Dominik, Thomi's son, says he still remembers Thomi's "huge grin" when the umpire of this race against the clock showed him the stopwatch signifying that they had done what was required with something to spare. The final duly went ahead with seven lanes; the Australians finished fifth.[18]

Almost exactly a month after these incidents, Thomi was back in Lausanne at IOC headquarters for another landmark meeting. With him at the Château de Vidy were two other international sports federation representatives, Sir Stanley Rous and Colonel Rudyard Russell, head of amateur boxing. They were there to see the three IOC vice-presidents, led by Lord Killanin. A succinct five-point record conveys that the six men agreed that an IOC congress should be planned for 1973, "preferably in Varna". There would be no voting. The meeting also agreed that "a committee of nine members under an IOC chairman, consisting of the present three nominees of the IOC and the above three nominees of the international federations, continue and that three representatives of the NOCs should be included".[19]

With these words, the fabled tripartite commission, to be led by Brundage's probable successor, was created. It was another giant leap for Thomi.

CHAPTER 10

Persuasion

The first women's European championships were staged on the Bosbaan course in Amsterdam in August 1954. Yet it took quite some time for it to occur to Thomi that women's rowing ought to be part of the major expansion in FISA's activities he was overseeing.

When the subject of a possible women's world championships was raised by a Hungarian delegate to the 1963 FISA congress – the first since the inaugural men's world championships in Lucerne – Thomi retorted rather curtly that "our statutes do not foresee" such an event. This prompted the Soviet Union's Evgeny Kabanov to launch into one of his periodic tirades, complaining about the second-class status of women's rowing and warning that FISA's statutes were discriminatory and could lead to "annihilation" of the women's sport. "It is no accident that FISA had difficulty finding an organiser for this year's women's European championships," Kabanov grumbled. "Organising a European championship is expensive and the host receives nothing in return."[1] Moscow was about to stage the tenth women's championships on the Khimki artificial lake, so it seems likely the Soviet official had bitter experience of these difficulties.

Kabanov had another crack a year later, when women's rowing was among the subjects discussed at a meeting organised by the

76

international federation in Tokyo in advance of the Olympic regatta. Organising a women's European championships was "inevitably a loss-making proposition", he argued, while proposing that a world championship be staged "on a trial basis". Thomi's closing summary left no reason to suppose such a development was remotely imminent. The point had earlier been made that fully seventy years had elapsed between the first men's European championships and the inaugural world event in 1962.[2] Based on that precedent, women rowers would have been kept waiting until 2024.

It was less than surprising that the Soviet Union should be in the vanguard of this particular push for gender equality. Prior to the emergence of East Germany in the latter part of the 1960s, Soviet oarswomen were utterly dominant. In the decade after the first women's boats sped away under a watery Dutch sun on 20 August 1954, Soviet crews captured forty-two of the fifty titles. What is more, 50% of those that got away were won by the same individual: Jenome Papp, the Hungarian single sculler. On four occasions, either side of Papp's span of invincibility between 1958 and 1961, Soviet crews accomplished the grand slam. In that inaugural 1954 event, they lifted the Silver Dutch Windmill trophy for best overall performance by forty-two points to twenty-five and a half over the next best team, the competition hosts.[3]

This record of success sparked rapid expansion of women's rowing in Eastern Europe. Elsewhere, however, stagnation or even regression was reported. In Canada, that 1964 meeting in Tokyo was brusquely told, an attempt to introduce women's rowing had "failed totally". In Argentina, though fifteen years earlier there had been much women's rowing, competitive regattas had "completely disappeared". The Argentinian delegate expressed the view that the "South American woman is not made for competition and rows only for her health".[4]

If Thomi did little to promote expansion of women's rowing in the early years of his FISA presidency – and is even said to have been against the idea at first – by the late 1960s his attitude had been transformed. And, once convinced, he set about pursuing the cause with typical vigour.

His change of heart coincided with the election to FISA's technical commission of West Germany's Claus Hess. This came at the Mexico congress in October 1968. Hess, then just thirty-five, ran against Kabanov to replace Hans Jacob, from the other side of divided Germany, and won comfortably.[5] Hess and wife Helga were among the closest and most influential confidants of Thomi in his last two decades at the FISA helm. "Is your old man up yet?" Thomi would say, in idiomatic Swiss-German, if Helga happened to answer one of his regular early-morning phone calls. Or: "Is it dark as the inside of a cow there too?" Hess – who competed in the coxless pairs at the 1956 Melbourne Olympics Thomi was deprived of – was from the outset a strong advocate of women's rowing. President of his national federation from 1966 until 1983, his input is thought to have been one of the key factors in changing Thomi's mind.

Within minutes of Hess's election, albeit coincidentally, another Soviet proposal requested that FISA ask the IOC to include three women's sculling events in future Olympic Games. Though hardly effusive, the changed thinking of the FISA top brass is immediately apparent. "The board of management was not against this suggestion," minutes of the meeting record, "but it was of the opinion that such a regatta should include all the FISA categories of boats, that is to say, coxed fours, single sculls, quadruple sculls, double sculls and eights". This counter-proposal was approved by a convincing fifty-four votes to eight, with eleven abstentions.

From that point onwards, things began to move. The following June, Thomi raised the matter with the IOC executive board during a meeting with GAIF, which he now headed. He subsequently expressed surprise that the IOC did not approve the request. The Olympic body was, however, beset by other problems – some real, some of its own making – in IOC president Avery Brundage's twilight years, and engaged on one of its periodic bouts of hand-wringing over the size of the Games. It took just a matter of days to determine that "all requests for admission of new sports were refused on the grounds that the Games are already too large and too costly". Thomi resolved to "take the matter up in more detail", adding: "I believe that in 1976, races for women will be included in the Olympic rowing programme".[6]

Meanwhile, as already discussed, he and federation colleagues were again putting FISA's house in order, preparing a restructuring designed to equip it for a new world in which its span would be genuinely global and its activities cover all categories of rowers, not just elite competitors. The congress at Klagenfurt in September 1969 was where planning turned to action. By the end of that long meeting, the FISA technical commission had more than doubled in size, with each of its seven members given a defined area of responsibility. Hess was to handle competitive rowing and, after the withdrawal of a prospective Hungarian rival on the grounds that it would be "more appropriate" for a woman to head up women's rowing, Nely Gambon-de Vos of the Netherlands was likewise elected for a one-year term. The idea was that each of this septet would chair a specialist commission in their designated area.[7]

1970 was a year for getting this new machinery tuned up and functioning effectively.

In April, Thomi and members of the new sub-commission for women's rowing gathered in Hungary to look over the course for that year's European championships at Tata, seventy kilometres north of Budapest. Besides inspecting sports facilities, commission member Ingrid Dieterle remembers tasty Hungarian food, apricot schnapps and a hotel in the middle of the Danube on Margaret Island. She also recalls Thomi, ever gallant, plundering the hotel flower-bed so he could present her with tulips on her birthday.[8] The championships themselves, in August, were a considerable success, with the East German women winning three of the five titles. This was also the occasion for the new sub-commission's first official meeting, with Hungary's Papp, Daina Šveica, a Latvian represent-ing the Soviet Union, and Magdalena Šarbochová, a Czechoslovak sculler who had taken silver at both the 1964 and 1965 European championships, joining Gambon and Dieterle.[9]

In terms of concrete progress towards new women's events, though, the year was a little disappointing. On 18 March, having previously submitted technical information, Thomi dispatched a business-like two-page letter to Brundage and IOC colleagues, proposing the inclusion of six women's events at the Olympic Games. In our opinion, there is no "valid reason" for rejecting the request, he argued with the zeal of the recent convert. "We would add that the Olympic rowing programme has not been extended since 1924." The English version of the letter signs off: "Yours very sincerely".[10] The IOC executive board had only recently reit-erated, however, that "no more" new sports would be included in the Olympic programme "for the time being" and was not exactly in expansionist mood.[11] The matter was eventually placed in the hands of the commission for the Olympic programme chaired by Árpád Csanádi, an IOC member from Hungary.

Progress towards a women's world championship had been complicated, meanwhile, by deliberations inside FISA over whether to turn the quadrennial men's event into an annual one. Thomi addressed this issue with some sensitivity during the 1970 FISA congress in Canada, where the first men's world championships outside Europe were about to get under way. The two questions – the introduction of world championships for women and of annual men's world championships – were, he said, "closely linked". While he was "certain" that "everyone" would approve the introduction of the women's championships, "many problems, particularly the question of finance, are still unsolved".[12]

Supporters of women's rowing may have harboured mixed feelings when, in September 1971, the IOC approved inclusion of the only men's event Thomi had mentioned in his March 1970 letter – "quadruple sculls without coxswain" – in the programme for the Montreal 1976 Olympic Games.[13] Such a reaction would have been all the more understandable in light of the positive tone of Thomi's latest annual report, which had preceded the IOC meeting in Luxembourg. The FISA president had told the rowing community that he hoped the federation's proposal to introduce six rowing events for women would be successful at that meeting. He also described the introduction of a women's world championships as "the first and most urgent item on our list".[14]

The procurement of that extra men's Olympic event for rowing was, however, a sign of Thomi's growing influence in the world of sport. Through his proliferating roles, he had the ear of those who mattered. And even if they did not always like what he was saying to them, other leading power brokers recognised increasingly that he could not be ignored. The pieces were falling into place for a major step forward in women's rowing.

It was in August 1972, in the busy weeks leading up to the Games of the XX Olympiad in Munich, that the decisive breakthrough was achieved. Ingrid Munneke (née Dusseldorp) recalls that sections of the crowd were very much on her side on 13 August as she sculled her way to a European title. This might be considered surprising, as the championships were taking place behind the Iron Curtain in Brandenburg and she was rowing against East Germany's Anita Kuhlke, a four-time European champion and local heroine. She remembers that she and her Dutch team-mates had collected bananas provided for them in their lodgings and handed them out to schoolchildren in the crowd before racing. Probably unused to such delicacies, they repaid her with their loyalty. "I had a lot of fans shouting my name," she says.[15]

Whether or not Thomi witnessed this spontaneous example of East–West sports diplomacy, it was at Brandenburg that he confirmed a request that had been hinted at before: would Dusseldorp join him and Gambon later that month in Munich to help make the case for women's rowing to join the Olympic programme at a presentation to IOC dignitaries? The Dutch rower had come close to winning the single-sculls title before in Tata in 1970 and was a strong advocate for women's rowing. "The subject meant a lot to me," she told me. According to Dieterle, a lot of thought had been given to how to convince "the old gentlemen of the IOC" that women's rowing would be good for the Games. "We decided to show these important gentlemen the handsome, intelligent and cheerful Ingrid Dusseldorp, the best sculler in Europe," she said. "And it worked! That and Thomi's powers of persuasion."

Dusseldorp – whose husband was set to row in Munich in the Dutch eight and who had opted to stay in a tent near the regatta course at Oberschleissheim rather than accept an invitation to an official hotel – remembers sitting outside the chamber being used by the IOC with Thomi and Gambon waiting to be called in. For the presentation, she "spoke a little bit to say I wanted to have women's rowing in the Olympic Games and they applauded". She had brought her European championship medal and held it in her hand. It all sounds very matter-of-fact. Some observers though – and, who knows, perhaps the IOC – were very taken with her casual, campsite attire. She thinks she was wearing jeans, which would be an unusual garment choice for one addressing the masters of the Olympic universe today, let alone nearly fifty years ago. No matter: the singular combination of Thomi and this be-denimed champion oarswoman from the Netherlands did the trick, and six women's rowing events were accepted for the Montreal Olympics.

It is worth underlining that this outcome was far from a foregone conclusion. A record of the session, at the Maximilianeum, shows that the IOC managed to approve the report of Csanádi's commission while "disagreeing on the introduction of women's cycling, shooting and rhythmic gymnastics in the programme". Only women's handball, besides rowing, got the thumbs-up.[16]

Dusseldorp stayed in Bavaria for the rowing regatta, which concluded on Saturday 2 September. The event was a triumph for the East German men, who took three gold medals, and for New Zealand, who powered to victory in the eights. The Dutch eight were placed ninth.

With the venue superb, thanks in part to Thomi's frequent preparatory visits, and crowds large and enthusiastic, Munich 1972 looked set to be remembered as a great regatta at a thrilling and spiritually uplifting Olympic Games. Then at 4am on Tuesday 5 September, six assailants scaled the wire security fence around the Olympic Village and rendezvoused with two colleagues already inside. The darkest episode in Olympic history was about to begin.

CHAPTER 11

Good Timing

Around two months before those tumultuous and ultimately har-
rowing Munich Games, a partnership was established that would
enable Thomi to expand his growing portfolio of sporting interests
further.

On 3 July 1972, La Société Suisse de Chronométrage Sportif –
Swiss Timing as it at once became known – was founded. Based
in the town of Bienne, at the north-eastern tip of the lake of the
same name, at a point where Francophone and German-speaking
zones of the country meet, it was an alliance of convenience
between watchmakers Omega and Longines. These two groups
saw the value in providing timing services to sports events such
as the Olympics, which juxtaposed their brands with exciting
endeavours and highlighted their products' high-performance
capabilities. The first Olympics that Omega had supplied, indeed,
had been the 1932 Games four decades earlier, when thirty chro-
nometers "of the split-second type" had been loaned to the
organising committee in far-off Los Angeles.[1] But the demands
on official sporting-event timekeepers were ever increasing and
companies had begun to question whether the positive spin-
offs from such exercises were substantial enough to justify the
growing expense.

Omega had been responsible for timekeeping once again at the 1968 Olympics in Mexico City. But then they had – in the words of Denis Oswald, the Mexico bronze medallist who acted as secretary general of Swiss Timing for several years in the 1970s and 1980s – "decided to stop". Omega "came to the conclusion that it was, I think, too expensive for one firm to do it," Oswald told me. "It needed a lot of equipment, a lot of people."[2]

One wonders whether the Swiss company's decision was linked to the last-ditch anti-commercialisation campaign being waged by Avery Brundage, the ageing IOC president in his last term in office. At a meeting of the IOC's executive board in March 1969, not long after the Mexico Games, Brundage drew attention to "the fact that on all photographs taken during Olympic competitions the name 'Omega' is clearly visible". The American thought, moreover, that "the IOC ought to eliminate the trade name 'Omega' and should broach talks with the TV companies in order to control this practice".[3] Obviously, controlling "this practice" in the way suggested would have undercut dramatically the publicity value derived by the timekeeper from offering its services for the Olympic Games. This might well, in turn, have influenced its assessment of whether the game was worth the candle.

Following an intervention by Thomi,[4] Longines stepped in for the 1972 Olympics, along with the German company Junghans, only to draw a similar conclusion, seemingly even before the Games had taken place. With foreign competition thought to be ready to attempt to use top sporting events to muscle in on Switzerland's longstanding supremacy in the market for top-of-the-range timepieces, in spite of the cost, it looked like the Olympics might be lost to Swiss watchmakers.

It was at this point that the trade association, the Fédération Horlogère, headed by a Neuchâtel-born diplomat and politician called Gérard Bauer, stepped in and, according to Oswald, "said we should not let it go" and "we have to think of finding a way to join forces". Swiss Timing was the result. In its initial guise, Omega and Longines each took 20% of the capital, with the remaining 60% in the Fédération's hands. Financial institutions, public authorities and Swissair, as well as the watchmaking industry, all chipped in with contributions to the new body's operating budget for the first four years, underlining the extent to which it was viewed as a project of national interest.

Having created a structure to allow two competing Swiss timekeepers to work together in this way, the right individual was needed to head it. The ideal candidate would require three things: experience of the business world; knowledge of and/or involvement in sport; and neutrality, which translated as no prior direct connection with the watchmaking industry. Thomi ticked all these boxes.[5] From his perspective, this new presidency – which he retained for the better part of two tense and fast-changing decades – brought him closer to the sort of private interests who were starting to identify in sport an opportunity to polish their image and accelerate sales. And, while modern management theorists might perceive a conflict of interest arising from the level of influence Thomi then wielded over the sports bodies who were potential users of Swiss Timing's services, it gave him a chance to deploy his expansive network of sporting contacts for the benefit, as he would see it, both of these sports bodies and his country.

Though he devoted his life to furthering international understanding through sport, Thomi always remained a Swiss patriot and a bred-in-the-bone Zürcher. He was an enthusiastic participant, for example, in the traditional *Sechseläuten* parade usually held in the city on the third Monday in April. A member of the Saffron Guild, one of a number of guilds, or *Zünfte*, which used to organise particular crafts in the city, he would don a dark suit, traditional triangular hat, and blue and yellow tie for the occasion. He would strive mightily to keep his crowded diary empty on the day in question.[6]

Beatrice Rothenbach-Seiler, Thomi's personal assistant in later years, provided an account of his daily routine when in his home city. This usually involved a twenty-minute drive to his light, spacious office in his Mercedes station-wagon. For most of the way, he would have one hand on the wheel, using the other to hold a Dictaphone to compile the day's to-do list. Arriving at 65 Talstrasse at about 9am, he would hand the Dictaphone to his PA for typing up, before embarking on a seemingly endless succession of long-distance phone calls. He had a large wooden desk, with wooden cupboards behind it filled with countless files. In his top drawer, he kept two things: nail clippers and a music box that played "Happy Birthday". Whenever someone in the firm was celebrating their special day, they would be summoned into the seventh-floor office and played the little tune. For lunch, it might be Casa Ferlin, an Italian restaurant, or in summer the so-called "Wurstbunker", a nearby outdoor space where he could enjoy bratwurst. Various books, umbrellas, ties and items of rowing paraphernalia were generally scattered around the office. There were few, if any, of the sort of trinkets international sports federation presidents tend to be given on their many trips, however. These were usually consigned to a cupboard at home referred to as the "horror cabinet".[7]

For all the challenges confronting sport in the immediate post-Munich period, it was the start of a charmed era for Thomi. For the next few years, while the new IOC president Lord Killanin wrestled with the consequences of sport's subjugation to the imperatives of racial and Cold War politics, almost everything Thomi touched seemed to turn to gold.

Still under fifty – and with the very existence of the Olympic Games, and hence the IOC and NOCs, threatened – the head of world rowing looked set to be an important, authoritative voice in the debates and events that would determine whether the Olympics could continue and if so in what form or, if not, what would replace them. When he allowed himself the odd contemplative moment, he must have reflected that his failure in 1969 to secure IOC membership had turned out to be a blessing in disguise.

His increasingly commanding status is best conveyed by the record of meetings of the tripartite commission that was now preparing the ground for the Olympic congress in Bulgaria in the European autumn of 1973. For one thing, he generally got his own way. In one particularly striking episode from a meeting in Munich in the early days of those Games, Killanin – fresh from his victory in the race to succeed Brundage – expressed the view that he could give "a long speech" at the official opening of the event. Thomi, however, disagreed and had no hesitation in saying so. "Lord Killanin's speech at the official opening should not develop the topics for discussion at the Congress," he said. "If he did, it would be difficult for another IOC member to talk on the same subject." As the record makes plain, Killanin "agreed and confirmed that he would only make a short speech".[8]

Equally, it had taken much time and effort to bring the congress about. Now that it was happening, and he was in the command centre helping to organise it, Thomi wanted to be sure the opportunity to focus on necessary change was not wasted. Time and again, he gives short shrift to the formal distractions that etiquette and the sensibilities of the host make inevitable at such occasions. Commenting on the proposed "cultural programme", he is reported to have "hoped that there would be as little as possible arranged in this respect, as they were there primarily to work and not for a holiday". On another occasion, he pointed out that "the reception should be limited as much as possible and to devote all the time to work".[9]

In addition to his preoccupation with the need to update eligibility rules to bring them into line with reality, Thomi was also using his hard-won prominence to punt ideas – some quite radical and forward-thinking – to his fellow sports' decision-makers. At one point, he proposes inviting current athletes to the congress.[10] This foreshadowed a further advance at the subsequent congress in the leafy German spa town of Baden-Baden in 1981, when a selection of athletes including Thomas Bach, rowing's Svetla Otzetova and Sebastian Coe actually addressed assembled dignitaries. This was also the period when he advocated to Killanin that the concept of awarding the Olympic Games to a region rather than a city be studied. This was "above all to allow a better use of existing installations and to ensure the future use of the new constructed ones" and "to maintain the whole programme of the Games without risk of gigantism".[11]

Meanwhile, his proliferation of roles was taking his globe-trotting to new heights. In the year or so before the congress, as well as visits to the USSR in preparation for the 1973 European rowing championships, and to Nottingham to see the first artificial course in "the motherland of our sport", Thomi's schedule included a veritable succession of long-haul journeys.

First came what must have been an emotional trip down memory lane to Hong Kong and Manila, his old Far East stomping ground, as well as to Australia and Ballarat, scene of the Olympic regatta he should have raced in. April saw him in China with Oscar State, then secretary general of both GAIF and the international weight-lifting federation. The transcript of one meeting in Beijing shows Thomi actively advising representatives of the All-China Sports Federation how best to navigate a path back into the international sports community from which the People's Republic had withdrawn in 1958.[12] China was elected a member of FISA that October.[13] A month later, he was in Oklahoma City for the expanding GAIF's seventh annual meeting. The programme reveals an eclectic mix of activities, from a tour of the National Cowboy Hall of Fame to lunch at a McDonald's restaurant and an exhibition softball game. Thomi informed colleagues that "cooperation with the new president of the IOC has developed happily and the same applies to the officials in Lausanne". He added that during his "many journeys... I observed again and again that the name of GAIF is becoming better known and is achieving greater importance". The umbrella body was, however, a "sensitive creation". It was "not easy to achieve satisfactorily the goals we have set ourselves since on the one hand we wish to coordinate common interests and on the other hand we wish to avoid giving the slightest impression of being a super-federation".[14]

The picture in rowing was encouraging too. Though not happy that the sport had lost ground against other activities over the years since FISA's foundation, Thomi could take heart from the recent initiatives he had masterminded in the areas of youth and leisure rowing, as well as from the federation's continued expansion beyond its European heartland. Furthermore, there was money in the till. Thanks to Munich, FISA's income from TV rights (SFr83,369.90) outstripped subscriptions (SFr48,050) for the first time in 1972. The following year, broadcasting proceeds (SFr110,827.95) accounted for well over double the sum received direct from members. All in all, the timing of the first Olympic congress for more than forty years – and the platform it promised to provide for those deemed by mainstream media to have excelled – could not have been better from Thomi's viewpoint.

On 29 August, a month before this gathering of the sports clans in Varna, Monique Berlioux, now cementing her power as IOC director under the body's new president, sent Thomi a short letter.

Signed by hand "I embrace you very affectionately, Monique", it is noteworthy – notwithstanding its adherence to the polite *vous* pronoun – for a strikingly chatty tone, suggesting that not even this formidable administrator was impervious to the FISA president's charm. "I was happy at last to see a friendly face to dine with me and celebrate with champagne in Moscow," she confides.[15] Berlioux also asks Thomi to reply to questions sent to her by Jean-François Brisson, a journalist with *Le Figaro*, the French newspaper. An article on Thomi duly appeared as congress delegates were packing their bags for their jaunt to the Black Sea coast. "Less well-known to the public than Lord Killanin," the article reads, "Mr Thomas Keller will be no less of a star at the Congress of Varna (30 September–4 October)."[16] It was to prove an astute prediction.

CHAPTER 12

Big Man with a Big Future

A few days later than initially proposed, to avoid a clash with the fifteenth World Congress of Philosophy, Thomi and other heavy hitters of the Olympic universe converged on the pleasant Bulgarian Black Sea resort of Varna.

It was the very end of September, still warm enough for the Golden Sands beaches to be crowded with sunbathers, and as he checked into his seaside hotel, the FISA president was in bullish humour. *The Times* journalist John Hennessy was also there, and Thomi – having purchased a supply of the non-refundable coupons that passed for legal tender for westerners, and perhaps digested the news that the two Soyuz 12 cosmonauts had returned to Earth safe and sound – proceeded to put the newspaperman straight on a few things. There was, he asserted, "no such thing" as the Olympic Movement. It was "little more than an organisation for mounting two weeks' sport every fourth summer and every fourth winter". At other times, it was the international sports federations who carried the flag – and the can – for sport. He then rather shrewdly offered his interlocutor a sneak preview of excerpts from his pre-prepared congress speech, which he would deliver about thirty-six hours later. These led Hennessy to expect, as he shared with readers, "if not fireworks, at least a glowing flare". Of Thomi himself, the man from *The Times* observed, "He has that sort of intimidating presence".[1]

The following day, 30 September 1973, at an eve-of-congress meeting of the commission that had planned the event, Thomi's punchy, fired-up mood persisted. He advocated a no-nonsense approach to combating the perennial conference organiser's problem of speakers overrunning their allotted time by sounding a buzzer after five minutes and nine minutes of each speech. He also suggested halving the length of the coffee-break to fifteen minutes and ringing a bell to summon delegates back to their seats.[2] He had to cool his jets during opening formalities attended by Todor Zhivkov, a Communist leader so loyal to the Soviet Union he once said that the two countries breathed with the same lungs. At least the setting in a charming outdoor theatre in the city's tranquil Sea Garden, a park thickly planted with trees if also peppered with brutalist Soviet-style monuments, was agreeable enough. Lord Killanin, the still relatively new IOC president for whom the congress was also a big moment, was plainly moved by the scene. "It is suitable", he proclaimed, "that we should be gathered in the autumn of the year in these beautiful surroundings at the foot of the mountains along the edge of the Black Sea, to plan the springtime and future of the Games". But as Killanin also observed, "We live in a world of knocking and it is easy to knock success".

There was little in the concise, trenchant – and yes, at times, knocking – 3000-word speech which Thomi delivered in the futuristic concrete and glass Palace of Culture and Sports the following day that he had not said before. He had gone over some of the same ground, indeed, in an article published the previous year in IOC director Monique Berlioux's *Olympic Review*. "We thought it would be interesting to give here an outline of his ideas," a short introduction to this piece noted, "even when his statements seem to criticise the IOC".[3] The key distinction was that this time

Thomi's captive audience included representatives of just about all the most influential newspapers of the international press. These pressmen were, moreover, keen for a story, while apprehensive that they might be condemned to sit through an uninspiring three-day marathon of platitudes.

The main thrust of what he had to say was that modern society had evolved in such a way as to make the Olympic Games less important than in former years and the international sports federations more so. Either the IOC must ally itself with "modern competitive sport" and "be ready to face the full consequences", or it should limit the Games to "genuine amateurs". The federations were, of course, ready to cooperate, but expected that this cooperation be "in a spirit of genuine partnership". He ended with a prediction that was at once a warning note and a summation of what he saw as the federations' position of strength: "In society the role of sport will be ever more important, either with Olympism or without, and therefore the role of the international federations will not cease gaining importance."

It was, however, the content of the speech, rather than its conclusion, which excited most interest among the watching reporters. Whether consciously or not, Thomi picked up on Killanin's comment of the previous day to argue that "in spite of, or rather because of, the unbelievable success of the Olympic Games, it seems to be appropriate to make some critical observations". This he went on to do in six specific areas, going well beyond the clichéd diplomatic niceties that the bulk of his audience probably feared and/or expected.

He began with the key issue of eligibility, stating forcefully that "entries for the Olympic Games have largely become an open exhibition of lying". His solution, now that Avery Brundage, high priest of amateurism *pur et dur*, was out of the way: allow international federations to set their own rules governing amateur status which would take reasonable account of the circumstances applying in their particular discipline. This amounted to a characteristically pragmatic stance, but also one that could be portrayed as a potential power grab.

On the Olympic Games programme, he called for a clear definition of what was required for a sport to achieve IOC recognition and for the federations, again, to determine detailed lists of Olympic events, in accordance with guidelines set by the IOC. He also wanted clear definitions of the respective roles and responsibilities of the federations, the IOC and the NOCs, a perennial issue that still flares up periodically even today. And he reiterated his warning over "gigantism" while, interestingly, stopping short of again urging that the Games be awarded to regions rather than individual cities. He was careful to work in a favourite quotation from the Roman poet Juvenal encapsulating, as he saw it, what the whole point of sport should be: "Orandum est ut sit mens sana in corpore sano," he intoned, "the goal should be a sound mind in a sound body".

He saved his most withering rhetoric to attack incompetent sports administrators and the ever-more-elaborate ceremonial appendages spawned by the Games. "Free propaganda for politicians and the gratification of human vanity have become an appreciable part of the Games," he complained. "A football coach whose team wins no matches is dismissed, but this does not hold good in the higher ranks in the hierarchy of sport. An administrative career in sport is often misused to satisfy personal vanity... Everyone holding a leading position in sport should have a thorough knowledge of it and close contact with the athletes themselves."[4]

With his contribution rousing the delegates only to dutiful, formal applause, it is doubtful that Thomi realised, as he made his way back from the podium to the presidential table a few metres to his left, quite the impact his words had made. That realisation would come only when details of the following morning's newspaper headlines started to wend their way out to the sun-blessed corner of the Black Sea where the congress was continuing.

"Olympic Committee Attacked as Hypocritical" said *The New York Herald Tribune*; "Entries for Games are just an open exhibition of lying says Keller" claimed *The Times*; "Honest opening to conference" stated the *Guardian*; and so on. Thomi's speech was almost universally adjudged the toughest and most forthright of a very long, rather tedious day. "I have asked Killanin that he ban the phrase 'Baron de Coubertin, who revived the Olympic Games in 1896,'" revealed a weary John Rodda, the *Guardian*'s man in Varna. An attentive listener, Rodda reckoned this had occurred "in varying and longer forms" in no fewer than eighteen speeches.[5]

By the time Olympic dignitaries had quaffed their last flute of Soviet champagne and flown home to be replaced by the Eighth World Trade Union Congress, Thomi had been labelled by Hennessy "a big man with a big future" and someone who "the IOC should want to have on their side rather than in an enemy camp". This was because he had "the air of a born winner".[6] Coverage like this must have been supremely gratifying for a man who, whether a born winner or not, had lost out in both his quest for an Olympic medal and his apparent attempt to negotiate possible leadership of the IOC itself. More importantly, it ensured that henceforth, whenever Thomi opened his mouth, his audience would extend far beyond the cosy, codified world of sports administrators. With that collection of home truths passionately declaimed, Thomi had rowed irresistibly into the mainstream.

While his plea for a reversion to simpler, more dignified Olympic ceremonies less reminiscent of fashion shows would fall on deaf ears, in other respects his words also produced actions. At the 1974 IOC session in Vienna, an eligibility rule far simpler than the convoluted one that applied at the time of Varna, was introduced.

This avoided use of the dread word "amateur" and allowed the international federations to determine an acceptable period of preparation for competitions in their respective sports. Killanin acknowledged subsequently that whenever he read the pre-Vienna rule, "I realised that it was full of anomalies". He also wrote that the new bye-laws, "without saying so, accepted in the Olympic Games 'broken time'. They permit a competitor... during the period of preparation for actual competition, to accept prizes won in competition within the rules established by each federation".[7] It was a start to addressing the rank insincerity identified by Thomi.

More importantly insofar as the FISA president's personal proximity to the levers of power was concerned, the IOC decided that the tripartite commission – on which he sat and which had been set up specifically to prepare for the Varna congress – would continue to operate albeit with a broader brief. This was to assure him of regular face-time with the IOC president and NOC top brass for the rest of the decade and beyond.

The final cherry came a year later in the form of an invitation from Killanin to sit on a second IOC body: Hungarian IOC member Árpád Csanádi's Olympic programme commission. Here too Thomi could rub shoulders with NOC representatives and make a concrete contribution to the delicate question of defining criteria of an Olympic sport.[8]

It was the latest filament in a web of influence that was now one of the best-placed and most extensive in sport. But other networks were starting to coalesce ahead of a period that would bring great turbulence as well as great opportunity to the sector.

CHAPTER 13

New Friends

The day of Thomi's Varna speech marked a significant milestone for someone else who was in the Bulgarian resort for the congress. Christian Jannette, a Frenchman who had handled protocol at the 1972 Munich Olympics, was spending his first day working for Horst Dassler's Adidas. Ambitious, relentless and astute, the thirty-seven-year-old Dassler had been obsessively building the sporting-goods brand founded by his father Adolf into a global powerhouse ever since being dispatched, aged twenty, to distribute shoes at the 1956 Melbourne Games which Thomi had been so disappointed to miss.[1]

The appointment of Jannette as external relations director and personal attaché to Dassler was a sign that the German businessman had come to appreciate how important decisions taken by the heads of national and international sports bodies were likely to be for his company in years to come. "I am going to create an international relations service," Dassler had explained to Jannette at a meeting in Grenoble earlier that year. The Frenchman's Munich experience had left him with a superlative contacts list. "I knew everyone," he told me.[2] That exclusive address-book was now at the service of one of the main private entities seeking to profit from sport's popularity and the new opportunities that rapidly evolving broadcasting technologies were opening up.

As head of GAIF and FISA, Thomi's details were, of course, already inscribed prominently on page K of Jannette's precious book. The two men had met in Munich, where Jannette helped arrange the 1970 GAIF annual meeting. They had also shared an enjoyable outing together in Paris in 1973, after attending the ceremony at the Racing Club at which Monique Berlioux, the increasingly influential IOC director, was decorated with the *Légion d'Honneur*. In the months subsequent to Varna, it was arranged that Adidas would give a reception and dinner at the annual GAIF get-together in Lucerne from 29 May to 2 June 1974. Prominent members of the Dassler family, including Horst, were in attendance. "It made quite an impact," Jannette recalls.[3]

The epicentre for the charm offensive unleashed by Dassler over the next few years was the inconspicuous goat cheese-producing village of Landersheim in Alsace, eastern France. It was here that the young businessman located his headquarters, beside a former hunting lodge called the Auberge du Kochersberg. This had been converted into a hotel-cum-restaurant where the Adidas clan could – and did – entertain with intimacy but in the grand style. "If Dassler lit a cigar at 11pm, we knew we were sure to be there for another two hours," Jannette remembers, adding that the wine cellar held 80,000 bottles – and, almost superfluously, that "we had an enormous publicity budget at the time".[4] When I asked him why it was seen fit to devote so much money to this activity, Jannette replies with one word: "Power." He then elaborated: "It was so as to be able to use the familiar French pronoun '*tu*' with anybody; so as to be able to pick up the phone to anyone."

At the peak of his powers during the Killanin era at the IOC, Jannette estimates that Thomi would head to Landersheim for discussions a couple of times a year.

Another key figure first invited to Alsace in 1974 was Patrick Nally, a young and extraordinarily energetic marketing man who had been making a name for himself with his work for British and Australian sports bodies. Having tried his hand as a car-washer and second-hand record dealer in west London before leaving school, Nally had found his métier in sports sponsorship, setting up in business with Peter West, a well-known broadcaster.[5] Nally had already encountered Thomi via his links with the British Olympic and rowing establishments, in particular Christopher Davidge, who was to act as *chef de mission* of the Great Britain team at the 1976 Montreal Olympics.[6] Over the next decade and more, the two men were to grow so close as they strove to drum up corporate cash to aid sports development – undergoing various trials and tribulations as well as success stories along the way – that Nally told me the FISA president had been "like my father".[7]

Before becoming a close associate of Thomi, however, Nally became a close associate of Dassler. This was because of something that happened less than two weeks after that initial GAIF dinner in Lucerne. On 11 June in Frankfurt, as the world was waiting for that year's World Cup to kick off in West Germany, the Brazilian João Havelange was elected president of FIFA, the most prominent of all international sports federations. The margin over the incumbent, Sir Stanley Rous, was quite tight: sixty-eight votes to fifty-two. But it was a seismic moment for sport, signalling that the old Anglo-Saxon/North European world could no longer count on having everything its own way in the realm of sports administration.

Havelange's trump card was his unashamedly expansionist platform, which promised a twenty-four-team World Cup and a far bigger emphasis than hitherto on global football development. This appealed to relatively new footballing nations in the Third World.

Having promised a development project, Havelange – who had represented Brazil at the Olympic Games in aquatics and had been an IOC member since 1963[8] – now had to design, deliver and fund it. He struck a deal with Dassler, who had swung behind the Brazilian late in the campaign. In the words of author Barbara Smit: "Havelange would hold the door wide open for Dassler in international football, provided that the German helped him to garner the funds that he needed to make good his costly election promises."[9] Dassler, in turn, looked to Nally, and over more than a year of trailblazing hard graft, the Englishman brokered the creation of the FIFA/Coca-Cola world football development programme, a ground-breaking, genuinely global sports sponsorship. It was at this point, in October 1975, that Thomi provided Longines executive Sepp Blatter with his entrée to FIFA. The future FIFA president still remembers Thomi's words when he got the phone call: "Sepp, I know you are not so happy with the watchmakers. I know that the new president of FIFA, Havelange, is looking for a development officer. What do you think?" Says Blatter: "Immediately I said 'Yes'."[10]

Another critical connection was established a few months after Havelange's day of triumph in Frankfurt. This came in September 1974, when Dassler travelled to Barcelona to meet an up-and-coming Spanish IOC member called Juan Antonio Samaranch. Samaranch had been the IOC's head of protocol since 1968. This meant that in the run-up to the Munich Olympics, he had been the IOC member with whom the new Adidas man Jannette had had the most dealings. A few months into his career with the sportswear company, the Frenchman was contacted by Samaranch to suggest that he and Dassler visit him in his native Barcelona at the time of the city's international boat show. Samaranch was already being spoken of as a possible future IOC president and, according to Jannette, Dassler jumped at the opportunity. The trip included a visit to Camp Nou, home of Barcelona FC. It was this pilgrimage to Catalonia that laid the foundations of a collaboration which, six years later, was to help propel Samaranch into the top job – a position he then used to undermine Thomi.[11]

Immediately post-Varna, however, the FISA president was more influential than ever and juggling a ferociously hectic schedule. At the end of October, after a flying visit to Ratzeburg, he produced a carefully prepared report at the FISA congress, setting out rowing's situation and prospects after fifteen years with him at the helm and advocating the sort of expansionist doctrine that Havelange would have recognised. But whereas football would be seeking to globalise from a position of strength, with rowing it was a question of striving to regain some of its former pre-eminence. The sport's importance, Thomi bemoaned, was "only a small fraction of what it once was".

He went on: "We have failed to recognise the signs of modern times and to take steps to make our sport more popular or even to adapt it at least partially to altered circumstances. The structure of rowing today is like an obelisk with a very high point and a narrow base. It is our duty now to remedy this and transform this obelisk into a pyramid. We have always been – and we still are – proud that competitive rowing is one of the most demanding forms of sport. Our task is to show that rowing is also an ideal physical activity in the open air. We must find additional forms of competition which emphasise pleasure and good fellowship. We must convince more people of the beauties and delights of pleasure rowing and simple outings with friends.

"We need new boats possessing the principle characteristics of racing shells, but not requiring advanced rowing techniques. The cost of these boats and their oars must be moderate. We must aim at standardised mass production. Chemistry has developed basic materials which make the realisation of our goals possible."[12]

A number of boat builders had been invited to the meeting in Lucerne's Palace Hotel, and Thomi had taken pains to welcome them with his very first sentence. It was to take time, however, before these laudable sentiments were to produce positive results. Similarly, while Thomi spoke of FISA's desire to develop lightweight rowing – and indeed the first FISA championships for lightweights[13] were staged, along with the fourth men's world championships, in Lucerne the following year – an absence of East European crews sometimes limited competition. The field for the inaugural lightweight men's eights event, for example, consisted of just four crews – an outcome described by Thomi as "a great disappointment". The FISA president's idea for annual veterans' meetings – characterised as "get-togethers of old friends during which some rowing is also done" – was an immediate success, though, with 600 participants attracted to the first such event in Berne.

In the absence for now of Coca-Cola-style football sponsorship, these ambitious expansion plans – along with the switch to annual world championships for both genders in non-Olympic years, replacing the old open European championships – were made at least potentially feasible by the much-increased flow of TV rights revenues, especially from the Munich 1972 Olympic regatta. But Thomi was also aware that a cash-flow issue for FISA was looming because of the absence of the sort of advance payments made by Munich on revenues that would eventually be generated by the Montreal 1976 Games.

When he used a meeting of the IOC tripartite commission to request that advance payment to international sports federations for Montreal be considered, he was told by Killanin that this would be "impossible". The US contract was, the IOC president added, subject to two conditions: that the Games took place and that the US team took part. The funds were consequently "frozen".[14] When, at the end of 1974, treasurer Charles Riolo came to tot up FISA's revenue for the year from TV rights, the total was a meagre SFr1,061.50.[15]

No sooner was the 1973 congress over than Thomi took yet another transatlantic flight to Montreal, donning his Swiss Timing hat as the aircraft entered Canadian airspace. A crucial negotiation with organising committee bosses resulted in the Swiss industry being awarded the timing contract for the 1976 Games. The restructuring which had led to Thomi adding the Swiss Timing string to his bow was, in large part, duly vindicated. With plans for the Olympic rowing course being revised, the FISA president paid two further visits to North America ahead of the GAIF meetings at which Jannette and Dassler's Adidas made its grand entrance in 1974. With those responsible for televising and keeping time at the Games also present at GAIF, Thomi commented that "very valuable coordination" had been ensured, resulting in "more fruitful work".[16]

The tripartite commission meeting a couple of days later in the IOC city of Lausanne was the last such occasion attended by Sir Stanley Rous prior to his replacement by Havelange a week later. Sir Stanley's departure paved the way for Charles Palmer, the colourful, Japanese-speaking president of the International Judo Federation and an increasingly important ally of Thomi's, to take up one of the international sports federation slots on the commission. A future chairman of the British Olympic Association, Palmer shared Thomi's enjoyment of cooking and piloted his own Piper Cherokee plane. Nally describes him as "a good support act to Thomi".[17]

Late August and early September saw Thomi back in Lucerne for a welcome two-week interlude of rowing, which included the inaugural women's world championships on the Rotsee and an epic men's eights race, won by the United States, in which the first five crews home were separated by just three seconds. Thomi also took the opportunity to host a slightly premature fiftieth-birthday celebration aboard a vintage steam-boat on Lake Lucerne. Unsurprisingly for guests who knew him personally, the evening ended with a firework fusillade.

International sport, as we have seen, was finding it ever more difficult to avoid becoming a pawn in the polarised politics of the era. And in October, in the once-occupied city of Vienna, came an IOC session which under different circumstances could have degenerated into a proxy for the Cold War. This was because Moscow and Los Angeles were competing there for the right to stage the 1980 Olympic Games. In fact, the Californian city waged a low-key campaign as if content with leaving themselves in a good position to win the subsequent race for the 1984 Games.[18] This was certainly the interpretation of Killanin, who wrote some years afterwards that the 1980 LA bid was "paving the way for their city to be selected four years later". Though the IOC president took pains to ensure that the voting figures were never issued, he later described the verdict, in favour of Moscow, as "almost unanimous". He went on: "Most of the West voted for Moscow. Had it become a political vote the IOC, which is basically conservative, might have voted differently. But this was the height of the East–West *détente* and, in any case, the voting was purely on sporting grounds."[19]

Typically, Thomi had been in Moscow, inspecting the regatta course, just a couple of weeks before the contest's low-octane dénouement in the Austrian capital. Like Jannette, Nally and other leading sports industry figures, he would return frequently over the balance of the decade. First, though, there was more work to be done in Canada.

CHAPTER 14

Sitting Pretty

It is a little before 10am on 17 July 1976 in Montreal's Bonaventure hotel and, after the ironing-out of a glitch in the simultaneous translation system, a buoyant Thomi regales the FISA congress with a "quite astonishing" fact. "At these Games", he tells delegates, "rowing has progressed to a position of the sport to which the greatest number of medals are awarded".[1]

When I first read this, I thought he had made a mistake: granted, Montreal 1976 would feature the first women's rowing events in Olympic history, but surely more medals would still be awarded in the likes of athletics and swimming. So I did the maths. And – what do you know? – he was right. By a score of 162 medals to 147 (athletics) and 114 (swimming), rowing – with twenty-seven medals awarded in its biggest events – was top dog by this particular yardstick. The statistic somehow puts the seal on a two- or three-year purple patch in Thomi's career as a sports administrator when he really did seem to carry all before him.

Contrast this with the troubles besetting the Olympic Movement. That same day, it was becoming clear that scores of athletes, including 1500-metre world record-holder Filbert Bayi of Tanzania, would experience the same disappointment as the FISA president had in 1956. This was because of a boycott of the Games by some twenty-five African countries in protest at New Zealand's sporting links with apartheid South Africa. When the IOC did not ban New Zealand from the Games over a rugby tour, the African nations walked out. A damaging new era of political boycotts of the Olympics was under way.

The Movement was already facing a reputational hit over the scale of cost overruns afflicting the problem-plagued Montreal project. These were assessed in 2016 at an eye-watering 720% in real terms in a research paper by Oxford University's Saïd Business School.[2] No wonder IOC president Lord Killanin summed up his "Montreal years" as "agonising" both for the Movement and himself. "My wife believes the coronary I suffered in 1977 was due in part to the increasing burden of problems I had to face during 1975 and 1976," he explained. "The abiding memory of Montreal must be the escalating costs… The story tarnished the reputation of the Olympic Movement and undoubtedly frightened potential hosts, who believed that it was no longer possible to stage the Games at reasonable cost, and free from politics."[3]

From a rowing perspective, Thomi was sitting pretty. Thanks in part to his diligent preparatory labours, the regatta course – for which the 1975 men's junior championships would act as a sort of test event – was the first of the new Montreal Olympic sites to be completed.[4] But, of course, he had other responsibilities. And when, in May 1975, as a result of strikes and other issues, concerns really began to mount that Mayor Jean Drapeau's majority French-Canadian city was not going to be ready in time, he made strenuous efforts to help. In a friendly but firm letter to Killanin written four days before that month's tripartite commission meeting in Lausanne, he states bluntly that while the Olympics are the IOC's property, "the IFs are contributing essentially towards their organisation and running". Were the Games to be cancelled, "we have to rearrange the schedule of our next year's competitions". So "we would... like to know what the IOC's plans are in case constructions cannot be finished in time".[5] He persisted with this line at the Lausanne meeting, stating that the federations were "very concerned" and arguing for the IOC to "investigate the possibility of alternative plans". On a characteristically practical note, he suggested that construction expert Karl Mertz – "responsible for the sites in Munich" – should go to Montreal to make a survey. While Killanin felt that October would be "the point of no return", the meeting was "of the unanimous opinion" that the IOC should nominate a commission to "study the possibilities of moving the Games either partially or totally from Montreal in the case of non-completion of sites".[6] The IOC president later acknowledged that "by the middle of 1975 I was worried" and "decided that we should make some contingency plans for an alternative to the Games". His plan was to hold "as many events, if not all the twenty-one sports of the programme, at venues in northern Germany".[7] The extent of his concern is underlined by a terse letter to organising committee head Roger Rousseau in which he asserts it is "essential that there should be some contingency plans made by Montreal".[8]

During his next Canadian visit in late June, Thomi saw both Rousseau and Drapeau, reporting to Killanin that the mayor "asked me to trust his word and that of his workers". For Drapeau, Thomi concluded, "the local reporters are obviously the black sheep. He feels that they are after him and would welcome any possible sign of distrust e.g. by the IOC. They would attack him personally and spread the news around the world, thus achieving exactly the opposite result of what we wanted."[9]

The situation was looking bleak. And yet, as tends to be the way with Olympic projects, as the clock ticked down inexorably towards the appointed day when the eyes of the world would fall upon the host city, the unthinkability of failure appeared to concentrate minds and the prospect that Montreal might not be ready began to recede. Killanin, writing in retrospect, had a clear view of who was responsible for this welcome change. "It was," he said, "early in October that I heard the Quebec Government were moving in to take over the construction board, appointing Dr Victor Goldbloom, the provincial minister of the environment and municipal affairs. I think at first I believed that here was just another man to join in the squabble... I was wrong, and in the year after the Montreal Games when one could reflect on the tangle and put a sharper perspective to all events, I feel that without Goldbloom the Games would not have taken place."[10]

Thomi, his authority undiminished, was able to avert his gaze to more agreeable matters. The world championships at the new artificial course in Nottingham went off well, proving a triumph for Norwegian double scullers the Hansen brothers. Early March 1976 saw him on the other side of the world in New Zealand, where the 1978 world championships were to be staged. Later the same month, a well-populated fiftieth edition of the Head of the River race in London, featuring 380 eights of all abilities and ages, nourished his ambitious vision for recreational rowing. This was also the year when he was made a Steward of his beloved Henley Royal Regatta.

Speaking on the eve of the Games, however, he left his FISA audience in no doubt about either the narrowness of the escape the Movement had just had or the shadow which Montreal's problems would continue to cast. "It seems to me certain that these Games will have a decisive influence on the future of the Olympic Movement," he said. "The IOC must establish clear goals and definite concepts to tackle these problems if it is to retain its credibility. This will only be possible if a hitherto passive attitude gives way to definite and dynamic progress."[11]

Two days later, on 19 July, the first Olympic oarswomen began their competitions at the Île Notre Dame course, with the coxed fours first away at around 10am. Among the winners on that historic Monday were Svetla Otzetova, a Bulgarian doctor's daughter and architecture student, and Zdravka Yordanova, her double sculling partner.

One characteristic of the Montreal venue was that there was not a great deal of space; Thomi had tried to have an additional training centre provided on the Île de Charron, but this was abandoned for financial reasons.[12] Otzetova remembers being advised to warm up by running up and down the course. On finals day – 24 July – there was a false start, whereupon the Bulgarian pair rowed up to 200 metres out along the 1000-metre course "to warm up properly". Otzetova says that Thomi – who typically spent most of his time at the regatta either around the start area or in a car following races[13] – began to shout that he would disqualify them because they kept on rowing. The ruse nevertheless worked. "We started again, got a very good start and won the race," Otzetova recalls.[14] It was one of just five gold medals not collected by the awesomely powerful East German rowers.[15]

An hour or so later, the single-sculls event came to a less satisfying conclusion for Ingrid Munneke, the Dutch oarswoman whose appearance in front of the IOC in Munich had helped to get women's rowing onto the Montreal programme in the first place. "In 1972 I had said to myself I would go to the first Olympics," she told me. "But I was ill on finals day with a temperature of forty degrees. It was really frustrating."[16] Munneke trailed home in fifth place, thirteen seconds down on Christine Scheiblich, the gold medallist from East Germany.

In the men's finals the following day, Finnish single sculler Pertti Karppinen stole the show, coming from eight seconds down at halfway to overhaul Peter-Michael Kolbe of West Germany. The Hansen brothers were victorious again in double sculls, holding off Chris Baillieu and Michael Hart of Great Britain.

When not following rowing races, Thomi spent many contented hours, alongside other sporting heavy hitters, in a comfortably appointed townhouse on a hill in a well-heeled part of the city, which the increasingly influential marketing man Patrick Nally had arranged to rent to help further the interests of his growing list of clients. Catering – at all hours – was handled by a popular English chef. There was a cellar full of pina colada mix, in aid of promoting the 1979 Pan American Games in San Juan, Puerto Rico. A stash of tickets for Olympic events was kept, for want of a better place, in the freezer-box of the refrigerator. Here Thomi – the head of the umbrella group of international sports federations *and* of Swiss Timing *and* of rowing – could rub shoulders in a discreet and relaxing environment with everyone from Adidas's Horst Dassler to IOC members such as Juan Antonio Samaranch and fellow IF leaders such as Adriaan Paulen, new president of the IAAF.[17]

With Moscow next on the Olympic horizon, eyes were already starting to turn east. First, though, Thomi had his mind on beginning a new phase in development of GAIF – and on recruiting a deputy to help with the management of FISA's much-expanded activities.

CHAPTER 15

The Picturesque Principality

You would hardly describe it as a landmark moment of the Montreal Games. Nevertheless, the B final of the men's quadruple sculls at the Île Notre Dame course does warrant a footnote in Olympic history. This was twenty-nine-year-old Neuchâtel lawyer Denis Oswald's ninth and last Olympic rowing race.[1] It was, however, far from his last involvement with either the sport or the Olympic Movement.

For some time, Thomi had been keeping tabs on his talented compatriot, who often took part in the rowers' meetings Thomi would call to canvass opinion. After more than a decade and a half in command, the FISA president's thoughts were starting to turn, in rare idle moments, to securing his succession. Furthermore, the workload associated with the federation's activities was getting heavier. Throw in his other responsibilities and the likelihood that his faithful colleague Charles Riolo would sooner or later want to step down, and Thomi recognised it was high time to recruit a reliable deputy.

It was in late 1975, at a winter regatta in Zurich, that he made his move. "He came to see me and asked, 'How long are you still going to row competitively?'" Oswald recalls. "I said, 'I hope to qualify for Montreal; that will be the end.'"[2]

"Have you thought of joining FISA?" Thomi went on, revealing his cards.

"What do you mean?"

"We have a tradition in rowing. We want the athletes to become leaders. I was an athlete. We have several other council members who were athletes. I have been following your career, what you have been doing, your personality. I think you are the right man to succeed me. But as an athlete, you have no idea what these officials in their blue blazers are doing. I think you could join FISA as secretary-general to learn the job and then become my successor. I have other names as well, so think it over and we can talk about it in a few months."

It might have seemed a flattering and thought-provoking offer, but Oswald says he put it to the back of his mind. "I knew FISA was a federation without money," he explains. "And I knew the position would be a voluntary one but would take up a lot of time. I was young, I didn't have a wealthy family, I had to earn my living. I didn't know whether this could be combined."

A couple of months before the Games, Thomi was back.

"Have you made up your mind?"

"About what?"

"Joining FISA."

"Oh no, you never mentioned it again and you said you had several names."

"No, no, no!" the FISA president exclaimed. "I have only one name. It's you. Are you ready?"

As he remembers these conversations, Oswald occasionally mimics something of the imperious tone people often associate with Thomi. "Yes, he knew what he wanted; he was the boss," he acknowledges when I ask if this was how Thomi spoke. "Physically he was a tall guy. Strong voice. Really imposing personality. You didn't want to contradict him."

We return to the substance of their 1976 exchange, with Oswald saying he told Thomi: "First, you will have to explain to me what it means, the conditions and so on."

"OK, go to Montreal, do your best, then after your race, come and join me. I want to introduce you to the council."

And so, in late July 1976, this is exactly what Thomi did. "At the time, he was deciding everything at the federation," Oswald says. "He just told colleagues, 'I am introducing him. You probably know him. You have seen him racing. He will join FISA.'... He asked me if there was someone in my firm who would do the administration work and support me. I was not yet a partner, but I discussed this with the boss and he said OK. FISA was giving some small compensation for a secretary. For the rest, my expenses would be paid, but no more."

In fact, 1976 was a bumper financial year for the federation, with Olympic TV rights yielding a "handsome" SFr189,958.50, after deduction of various expenses. This, in turn, led to a "spectacular" increase in year-end assets to not far short of SFr300,000.[3]

Even so, Thomi told his prospective new secretary-general that he was expected to "give your time". He explained: "You have benefited from all the work done on a voluntary basis by a lot of people. Now you have to return to sport what sport has given to you. If you want the next generation to get the opportunity to have the same experience as you, you have to pay back and you have to take responsibility. If those who benefited from the system don't ensure it continues, it won't work."

He added: "You were critical of FISA sometimes. So help us to improve. Show us what we did wrong and do it better. You have your experience as an athlete and my time was long ago. Certainly you can be very useful for your sport."

Around fifteen months later, at an extraordinary congress in the Mediterranean resort of Monte Carlo, Riolo stepped down and Oswald was duly elected secretary-general.[4] "He just said, 'OK, I propose a new secretary-general,'" Oswald says.[5] "He told everybody then, 'He should become my successor'. It was very clear for everybody and there was no other candidate because the position was never announced or whatever. Nobody would have dared to propose something different. I was elected. I started in 1977, officially at the start of 1978. But I was already pretty much involved from right after Montreal."

It was no idle whim that Monaco had been chosen to host this important FISA gathering. The picturesque principality had been playing an increasingly prominent part in Thomi's professional life since just after Montreal. This was for reasons beyond rowing. As sports marketing pioneer Patrick Nally explains, the Monaco government, whose territory had long hosted the glitziest Formula One Grand Prix, were "keen to promote Monaco as a sports centre. [The Adidas boss] Horst Dassler asked me to act as liaison with Monaco and to try and help bring international sports federations into the principality. I spent quite a lot of time with Horst trying to persuade IOC president Lord Killanin and director Monique Berlioux to move the IOC to Monaco."[6] Dassler and Nally also founded a local company, the Société Monégasque de Promotion Internationale (SMPI), to sell rights on behalf of sports federation clients. These included marketing rights for the 1978 FIFA World Cup in Argentina.[7]

While Nally and Dassler's efforts to persuade the IOC to leave Switzerland were destined to be frustrated, they had more success with Thomi. GAIF – over which he still presided – had by now, a decade into its existence, become a fixture in the sporting landscape. The new revenue-generating opportunities opening up for its members had reinforced its usefulness as a forum where expertise could be pooled and strategies coordinated. But they had also underlined its shortcomings: the umbrella body had no real headquarters and no secretariat.

In October 1976 GAIF met in Barcelona as part of a week of Olympic- and sports-related meetings in the hometown of Juan Antonio Samaranch, the coming man of the IOC.[8] It was there that it took the momentous decision to draft statutes to replace its rules of procedure – and to move its offices to Monte Carlo. Both of these steps would serve to solidify its existence and emphasise its independence from the Olympic Movement, developments that would not have escaped the attention of their host for the week. For now Samaranch contented himself with delivering a welcoming speech proclaiming Olympism as sport's "spiritual summit", while warning that the IOC was losing its "quality of political and international independence".[9] Thomi, meanwhile, observed that the "highly concentrated" programme imposed "a considerable strain" on those taking part. Happily, he and Riolo were looked after in "exemplary manner" by friends in Spanish rowing.[10]

In April 1977, after Thomi's return from Puerto Rico, where he scouted by helicopter for the right location for the 1979 Pan American Games regatta course, FISA officials were able to meet at the new GAIF base, located – appropriately – on Boulevard de Suisse and named Villa Henri. Deftly attaching another string to the organisation's bow, Thomi emphasised that "those federations who have no professional and full-time office can avail themselves of these facilities". FISA, of course, was one such federation – and this was "one of the reasons" why the 1977 extraordinary congress, at which Oswald's appointment was formalised, was held in Monte Carlo."[11]

Thomi also saw the umbrella body's strengthening as a bulwark against the sort of political interference in sport which he was committed to combating yet which – as Samaranch's words in Barcelona also indicated – was posing a growing threat. He made no bones about pronouncing that "sports political activities have been added to purely sporting ones", adding: "One of our most important tasks is to protect the independence of non-governmental sports organisations against the growing influence of governmental organisations."[12]

In October 1977, just before Oswald's confirmation at FISA, GAIF's strengthened status was sealed with a subtle but revealing change of name (and acronym). From then on, the body would be known as the General Association of International Sports Federations (or GAISF).

Prior to this, Thomi had the pleasant duty of presiding over the official opening of the new premises, in formalities attended by His Serene Highness Prince Rainier. Thomi's bonhomie at the inauguration and subsequently while sampling buffet food on the villa's terrace with its spectacular view over the harbour far below, would, I am sure, have been only mildly affected by the crutches he was using at the time.[13] While the metaphorical sky was far from cloudless, he was more firmly ensconced than ever on the sun-kissed uplands of sports administration, and his new surroundings seemed to symbolise this. "In this period," says Nally, "the essential political go-between was Keller, not Killanin. Keller had the ear of all the international sports federations."

CHAPTER 16

Power, Vodka and Large Siberian Dogs

While Monaco was becoming an important second base for Thomi, the sporting world's centre of gravity for the remainder of the decade had shifted 1500 miles north-east – to Communist Moscow, prospective host of the 1980 Olympic Games.

The FISA president had, of course, been a regular visitor to Moscow since the build-up to the European rowing championships in the city in 1973. But not even Thomi was a match for Christian Jannette when it came to the number of Soviet stamps in his much-used passport. The Adidas man made no fewer than sixty-two visits to the Olympic city over the six-year Games preparation period.[1] While there, Jannette was able to dine frequently at the residence of the Spanish ambassador[2] – a post filled from 1977 by none other than Juan Antonio Samaranch of the IOC. With the Games earmarked for Moscow, the 1980 IOC session would also take place in the Soviet capital. The post accordingly left Samaranch, in the words of his Olympic biographer David Miller, "perfectly placed to conduct a camouflaged campaign for election as IOC president".[3]

Jannette's Moscow engagements came so thick and fast that it was sometimes not worth him returning to France between meetings. Instead, he would head off on excursions with the assistance of

Sergei Pavlov, the Soviet sports minister for whom he had facilitated a clandestine trip to Niagara Falls during the Montreal Games.

One such excursion, to Novosibirsk, far to the east on the Ob river, helped engender a vogue for large Siberian dogs among international sports leaders. Jannette was given one of these dogs there for whom he eventually found a mate called Chaika, or Seagull. After they had produced a litter, he gave Chaika to Thomi for a friend. Jannette says that IOC director Monique Berlioux also came to own a Siberian dog called Sokol, or Falcon. Thomi himself was presented with two Siberian dogs over the years, one of which – Wassili, a rather fierce grey-brown male with four white socks, a part-white muzzle and a white-tipped tail that curved back to brush the base of its spine – he was utterly devoted to in later years. Almost everyone who encountered Thomi in the mid- to late 1980s retains a vivid recollection of Wassili. Beatrice Rothenbach-Seiler, his personal assistant, remembers walking up Zurich's Üetliberg mountain with Thomi and Wassili at a rapid enough pace to leave her short of breath. The only food-related item Thomi always kept in his Zurich office, she told me, was a can-opener to open tins of dog food for Wassili. The sports marketing specialist Patrick Nally used to joke that, given his provenance, Wassili was probably bugged.[4]

Nally and his business partner Horst Dassler of Adidas had decided that just because the Olympics were heading behind the Iron Curtain, there was no reason why sport's burgeoning new role as a marketing vehicle for large corporations should be curtailed or interrupted. "Moscow was going to be the turning-point of Olympic marketing," he told me. The young Englishman was hence frequently in the Soviet capital himself. As early as 1976, he presented a paper to the Olympic Games organising committee on how best to approach multinational companies such as Exxon, Coca-Cola and Procter & Gamble with a view to recruiting them as sponsors. Such companies were, he argued, "very concerned over their image with the general public", while "we must presume" that most of them – "certainly those based in the USA" – have "a particular interest in Russia". Nally emphasised, however, that it was essential to offer potential sponsors exclusivity in their particular product categories and in as many of the territories that interested them as possible. He also advised how best to approach NOCs in these territories so that the desired coverage could be achieved most efficiently.[5] This blueprint remains the basic model for blue-chip sports sponsorship today.

Of course, the Soviet invasion of Afghanistan and the subsequent United States-led boycott threw a spanner in the works. Nonetheless, a January 1980 US intelligence assessment of the state of preparations for the Games provides an intriguing insight into just how extensive involvement by US and other western companies might have been. "To date, Soviet planners have placed orders with Western firms for an estimated $500 million worth of equipment and services," the document stated. It went on: "The figure would be higher but for the successful Soviet solicitation of free equipment and services in exchange for 'Official Supplier' status... Numerous American as well as other Western firms have purchased 'Official Supplier' status to the 1980 Olympics either for the title's advertising value or to help the firm break into the Soviet market... Most cash donations have been in the $100,000 to $250,000 range, but Coca-Cola paid $6 million in cash and is providing $4 million in beverage concentrate and a new bottling plant for the exclusive right to supply soft drinks at the Olympics... Levi Strauss is donating 23,000 sets of blue jeans and jackets for officials and workers attached to the Games."[6]

The boycott did not prevent West Nally from concluding twenty-one sub-licensing contracts in various countries on Adidas's behalf. As well as official-supplier status, the sporting goods company had

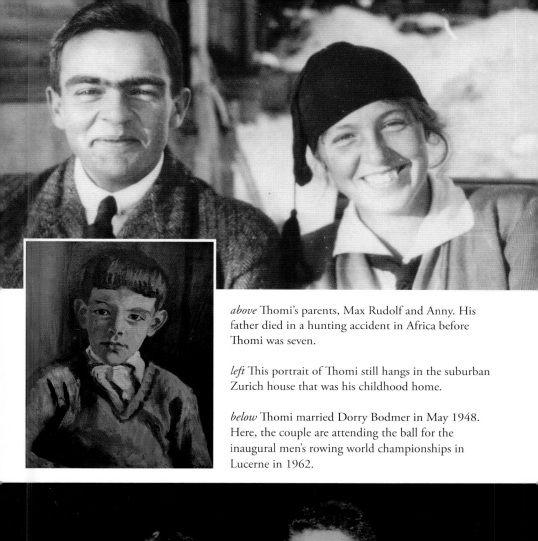

above Thomi's parents, Max Rudolf and Anny. His father died in a hunting accident in Africa before Thomi was seven.

left This portrait of Thomi still hangs in the suburban Zurich house that was his childhood home.

below Thomi married Dorry Bodmer in May 1948. Here, the couple are attending the ball for the inaugural men's rowing world championships in Lucerne in 1962.

left Thomi, pictured with his son Dominik and rowing partner Hans Frohofer, won both single and double scull events at the Swiss national championships in 1956, Olympic year.

below The Grasshopper Club on Lake Zurich was a regular haunt of Thomi's for almost half a century.

© NICOLINE SCHAUB, ZUERICH

above During military service, Thomi was in a motorcycle unit. Here, he rides the lead bike in an escort for the visiting Winston Churchill in 1946 in Berne.

left Henley here we come! Thomi made an arresting sight when driving with his shell from Zurich to the famous regatta course on the Thames in 1955.

below Once there, he and Hansruedi Vollmer lost narrowly after a scintillating duel with a Soviet crew. Newsreel commentary said the midsummer weather was "warm enough to melt the Cold War".

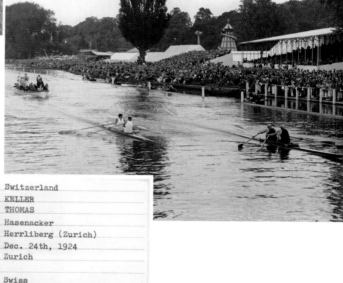

below Thomi's identity card for the 1956 Melbourne Olympics. To his bitter disappointment, it was never used.

COUNTRY/PAYS	Switzerland
SURNAME/NOM DE FAMILLE	KELLER
GIVEN NAMES/PRENONS	THOMAS
ADDRESS STREET/RUE	Hasenacker
ADRESSE TOWN/LIEU	Herrliberg (Zurich)
DATE OF BIRTH/NE(e) LE	Dec. 24th, 1924
PLACE OF BIRTH/NE(e) A	Zurich
PROFESSION	
NATIONALITY/NATIONALITE	Swiss

THE NATIONAL OLYMPIC COMMITTEE OF

(Name of Country)

certifies that the information contained herein is true and that the photograph is a true likeness of the owner of this identity card who is travelling to Melbourne, Australia, as a non-immigrant temporary visitor to attend the Games of the XVI Olympiad in the capacity stated herein.

POSITION QUALITE Participant (rowing)

ORGANISING COMMITTEE FOR THE XVIth OLYMPIAD MELBOURNE, 1956

Chairman   Chief Executive Officer

right This presentation in June 1958 may be the last meeting between Thomi and his predecessor as FISA president, Gaston Müllegg (on right, in suit). Six weeks later, Müllegg died in a plane crash.

above A tense-looking Thomi makes a brief acceptance speech after being chosen as FISA president in Vienna in 1958. It was a month before his thirty-fourth birthday.

right After this, his last victory in an international regatta, with Stuart MacKenzie (left), in 1959, Thomi had to rush off and don presidential attire to present another trophy.

left Playing football (in Adidas boots) with FIFA president João Havelange, whose election in 1974 showed that sport's Anglo-Saxon/ North European elite would no longer get everything their own way.

right Presenting Soviet sculler Vietcheslav Ivanov with his winner's medal at the 1959 European Championships in Macon. Thomi always maintained great affinity with athletes.

left A new FISA logo, comprising the blades of five oars in the colours of the Olympic rings, was introduced early in Thomi's presidency.

below The Palace of Culture and Sports at Varna in Bulgaria, where Thomi emerged in 1973 as "a big man with a big future".

© ALEXANDER RYABOV/GETTY IMAGES

above The conference chamber in Varna where Thomi delivered his landmark speech on international sport and its problems.

above Thomi was thrilled to be made a steward at his beloved Henley in 1976.

left With future FIFA president Sepp Blatter and others at Innsbruck in 1976. Thomi provided Blatter with his entrée to the football body.

right Thomi, pictured with Claus Hess and Walter Wülfing, could make wonderfully happy and appropriate speeches when the occasion demanded.

above With Avery Brundage, the IOC president who asked Thomi in 1969 if he would be interested in becoming an IOC member.

right With Lord Killanin, who was IOC president while Thomi was at the peak of his influence in the 1970s.

© JOHN SHORE

above Greeting West German president Karl Carstens at the 1981 Olympic Congress where IOC head Juan Antonio Samaranch (back to camera) made his mark. Also in shot is IOC director Monique Berlioux.

right In his element: Thomi doing one of the things in life he most enjoyed – umpiring at Henley.

below Thomi gazing down on his final world championships in 1989 at one of his favourite venues, Bled.

© TINA FISHER CUNNINGHAM

acquired the exclusive right to use the official Moscow 1980 emblem on bags, T-shirts and certain other items.[7]

In a way, Moscow's designation as Olympic host tended to reduce the amount of attention international sports federations such as FISA needed to devote to the Games over the preceding four-year period compared with previous editions. This was because, while the diplomatic landscape was always going to be treacherous to navigate, the sporting facilities for a prestige project intended in part to underline the excellence of the Communist model were just as sure to be top-notch. Given the number of balls Thomi was now juggling, this was probably just as well.

On the rowing front, the federation had made the adventurous choice of New Zealand to host the 1978 world championships. While this was easily justifiable for a sport striving to boost its international appeal, it involved, as Thomi acknowledged, "considerable risks"[8] and an extra administrative and logistical workload. In fact, through "skill and luck", the event could scarcely have gone better. Organisation and facilities were exemplary, the weather over Lake Karapiro behaved, and the crowds flocked in: 35,000 on men's finals day alone. For Thomi, that finals day, which culminated with a bronze medal for New Zealand in the men's eights and a row-past by two Maori canoes each with a crew of sixty, "will remain a unique experience in the history of rowing for all who were present". It was a further sign of the FISA president's clout at this time that the IOC agreed to award the Olympic Cup to the organising committee. He also presented prime minister Robert Muldoon, under whom New Zealand would later join the boycott of Moscow 1980, with FISA's medal of honour.[9]

The introduction from the 1960s onwards of new high-tech materials, replacing wood, persuaded FISA at this time also to set up a new boat-construction commission. According to

Klaus Filter – the East German recruited by Thomi as one of the new body's members – "a kind of armaments race in respect of rowing material had started" which the FISA president was worried might undermine fairness by favouring nations with the most money to spend.[10] With characteristic bluntness, Thomi duly proposed that he head the commission in its first year "in order to decide which of the members was the most suitable to take over responsibility".[11]

Meeting for the first time in early 1979 at Werder in the then German Democratic Republic, the body drafted a list of subjects for study, noting that "essential" tasks included "examining whether a [minimum] weight limit for elite-level boats is feasible, so as to prevent a rise in the cost of construction materials". The dryness of this language masks elements of the commission's modus operandi. Says Filter, this foundation meeting turned into a "hard day" because the GDR federation had stocked the refrigerator in Thomi's room generously with bottles of Stolichnaya vodka. Each decision had to be toasted in order to be confirmed and by evening Thomi's fridge was "at least half-empty". Realising the way things were heading, Filter says he mostly sipped at his shots rather than downing them in the time-honoured manner. When Thomi finally retorted by saying Filter would be "perfect" for the job in hand if only he could learn to drink, the German replied that as the only master boat-builder and naval architect present, he needed to stay sober to make sure they reached the right decisions. Like many others, though, Filter also remarks that, after an evening's drinking, Thomi would always be the first back at work the next morning, while disparaging latecomers. "I only remember," he concludes, "that my colleague Bjørn Hasløv from Denmark, whom we chose as the first chairman of the commission, was still not sober the next day when I took him to his train home".

With the IOC on the defensive over costs post-Montreal, and political pressures seemingly posing an ever greater threat to sport's independence, Thomi exploited his position as an IOC outsider who, nonetheless, sat on many top bodies and had the ear of everyone who was anyone in the sector to keep asking tough questions, usually with little regard for diplomatic niceties. For example, at a tripartite commission meeting in Prague in June 1977, he bluntly asked if "any candidates had been received" to host the 1984 Olympic Games. A seemingly discomfited Lord Killanin replied that the closing date for candidatures was not until 31 October. "It appeared from the press that Tehran was no longer considering making a bid, although it had not withdrawn its letter of invitation," the IOC president continued. "It was probable that an American city would make a bid, although the United States Olympic Committee would not decide until just before the closing date which city out of a possible four it is to propose. No official requests for the Winter Games had so far been received."[12] Los Angeles subsequently emerged as the sole Summer Games bidder, giving it the whip hand in negotiations and leading to many tense moments. The saga, however, had a relatively happy ending, with the California metropolis helping the IOC to obliterate the Montreal effect by demonstrating that the Olympics was not a sure-fire loss-maker and could in fact generate a large profit.

The delicate political situation facing sport resulted in a series of often turgid discussions and, eventually, a four-page tripartite commission statement seeking to delineate which organisations, governmental or non-governmental, ought to be responsible for what. The document produced a measure of mainstream press coverage, with the *New York Times* proclaiming it "the first shots in the battle to determine who will control international sports". Yet it counted for little two years later when Soviet troops crossed into Afghanistan.[13]

Thomi was unable altogether to sidestep these discussions, at one point paying a visit to Amadou-Mahtar M'Bow, director-general of UNESCO. In early 1978, indeed, he expressed concern that the boycott phenomenon could be poised to spread beyond the Olympics, warning IOC director Monique Berlioux that "there is a possibility that the socialist countries will boycott different world championships for political reasons". Suggesting that rowing once looked to be at risk but was now under control, he stated that "the socialist countries intend to boycott the 1978 shooting world championships which will be staged in Seoul, South Korea". Moreover, "in some other sports rumours are popping up as well, e.g. gymnastics".[14] The shooting event was to prove an important staging-post on the Korean capital's path to the 1988 Olympic Games, as well as the rise to prominence of Un Yong Kim, a key figure of the IOC's Samaranch years, who in 1986 succeeded Thomi as president of GAISF.

Following its installation in Monaco, the late-1970s brought further enhancement of GAISF's authority and efficiency. The boost to its authority came when, in 1978, the IAAF, global body for the bedrock Olympic sport of athletics, decided at long last to join the organisation. Efficiency began to get better from late-1979, when director Luc Niggli arrived to take over headquarters management.[15] Another sign of GAISF's strength was the impressive list of corporate backers – including Coca-Cola, Polaroid, Philips, ABC, NBC and (perhaps unsurprisingly) both Adidas and Swiss Timing – which it had collected by the end of the decade. A perception that Montreal's problems might make the IOC more reluctant to countenance the addition of new sports to the Olympic Games programme was, meanwhile, adding momentum to another sports federation project. This was the World Games, intended primarily to be a platform for non-Olympic sports whose governing bodies were GAISF members. Back in those days, such sports included the likes of taekwondo and badminton, which have since been welcomed into the Olympic fold.

On a less positive note, the build-up of members' non-Olympic TV revenues appears to have been going frustratingly slowly. A resolution labelling television "a vast and complex problem" was proposed to the annual meeting. Examples of less than satisfactory deals are set out, such as a rowing world championship sold to Japan for $5000 but incurring technical costs of $17,500.[16] Another setback was the December 1979 defeat of Charles Palmer, one of Thomi's closest allies, in the International Judo Federation's presidential election. Palmer, who went on to become chairman of the British Olympic Association, lost to Japan's Shigeyoshi Matsumae by a clear-cut sixty-seven votes to twenty-six, ending a fourteen-year stint as president.[17]

Another of the balls Thomi was juggling as the decade drew towards its end was his growing preoccupation with rowing's need to embark on a meaningful geographic expansion. While he had boasted in comments reflecting on his twenty years as president that FISA had become "a genuine worldwide federation",[18] he plainly felt that the job was only half done. He had found time to attend the 1978 World Cup in Argentina as FIFA's guest, and it was on Latin America in particular that he initially focused. While attending the Pan American Games regatta in Puerto Rico the following year, he was told that regional federations received little support, with the result that the sport in Central and South America was "generally in retreat". He concluded that it was "absolutely necessary" to establish closer contact between these federations and FISA. "If we are to fulfil our responsibilities as an international federation," he told colleagues in Bled soon after his return, "we must help in this situation".[19]

A potential new source of funding for the sport in underdeveloped countries had emerged in the shape of Olympic Solidarity for which money was being earmarked from the IOC's growing TV revenues. Tensions between the international federations and the NOCs had developed, however, over the federations' repeated requests for representation on the Solidarity Commission. Now, though, a new man was on the scene, with Mexico's Mario Vázquez Raña elected president of the Association of National Olympic Committees in Puerto Rico while Thomi was making his way there via California. The FISA president clearly recognised the potential significance of this new connection, since Vázquez Raña was invited to address the forthcoming GAISF annual meeting in Monte Carlo. He may even have hoped for a meeting of compatible minds, as the Mexican, like Thomi, was a wealthy businessman.[20] Yet it quickly emerged that in the alliance game, the new man was minded to throw in his lot with Samaranch, Spain's ambassador in the Olympic host city.

Before the full consequences of this could play out, politics cast its long shadow over the Olympic Movement and the Games to an extent that made Melbourne and Montreal look like the most trivial of warm-up acts.

CHAPTER 17

Ignoring Margaret Thatcher

On Thomi's fifty-fifth birthday, on Christmas Eve 1979, Soviet troops crossed into Afghanistan. The chain reaction which resulted some seven months later in a large-scale boycott of the 1980 Olympic Games in Moscow is well-known and has been widely chronicled. What concerns us here is how Thomi responded to these momentous events. And the verdict has to be that – after a commanding and decisive start when he stood up impressively to attempts by the Carter administration in Washington to bully others into line – the head of GAISF overplayed his hand. Whether from ambition or frustration, he seriously underestimated the recuperative powers of the Olympic Movement. This miscalculation in turn hastened his demise as one of international sport's very heaviest hitters.

The United States was an Olympic host too in 1980 – in February at the Adirondack town of Lake Placid in upstate New York, where the Winter Games were held. Swiss Timing had again won the Olympic timing contract, against competition from Seiko of Japan and Finland's Nokia.[1] By the time Thomi popped up to present a chronograph from the 1932 Los Angeles Olympics to organising committee president Bernard Fell on 18 February,[2] lines had been drawn for what IOC president Lord Killanin called "the biggest battle in Olympic history".[3] This was due largely to a strongly worded speech at the opening of the IOC session in Lake Placid by Cyrus Vance. The US secretary of state used what was by convention a ceremonial occasion to call for the transfer, postponement or cancellation of the Summer Olympics while underlining that Washington would oppose participation of a US team in Moscow. According to Killanin, the speech was greeted by "absolute silence".

There was also talk at around this time of putting on an alternative Games for athletes unable or unwilling to go to Moscow. Such an event would plainly have required the cooperation of international sports federations and, after Lake Placid, Thomi was received at the White House for discussions with Carter administration advisers. The idea had enough momentum for representatives of twelve countries to gather to discuss it in mid-March in Geneva. At this point, Brisbane and Nairobi were mentioned as potential sites of any alternative Games.[4] Within a few days, though, Thomi had undermined the venture's credibility by emphasising that international sport was "under the control and direction of the international sports federations" and revealing that nineteen of the twenty-one sports on the Olympic programme had "told me that they support their commitment to the Games in Moscow". As journalist John Rodda commented: "If there had been any lingering doubt in this week of sporting farce among the politicians that the pursuit of alternative Games was the most hopeless cause, Thomas Keller... killed it with one powerful lunge of the authority he carries."[5] Thomi's subsequent summary was dispassionate yet devastating. "It was made clear... that it is not for governments to organise international sporting competitions," he wrote. "With the exception of the Olympic Games, this falls exclusively within the competence of the international sporting federations and their affiliated national federations. Our point of view was eventually accepted."[6]

So far so good for the FISA president, and in April his standing as a man to be reckoned with was further reinforced at meetings in Lausanne, where he marshalled an impressively unified show of support for the IOC from the assembled international sports federation leaders. A statement published by the federations on 22 April protested "energetically" against pressure being put on NOCs by a number of governments to boycott the Moscow Games. Such measures could, the federations claimed, have "disastrous consequences for the future of world sport". In an assertion redolent of Thomi's pent-up frustration at being deprived nearly twenty-four years earlier of his one shot at an Olympic medal, they also asserted that "a boycott of a sporting event is an improper method to use in trying to obtain a political end". The statement ended by saying that all Summer Olympic federations would be present at Moscow.[7]

This backing was appreciated by Killanin, who was also pleasantly surprised by the participation of Prince Philip, husband of Queen Elizabeth II, who was then president of the International Equestrian Federation. "He did not always come to these gatherings," Killanin wrote, "so I was, frankly, astounded to hear that he had arrived in view of the attitude of the British Government over the Games". Thomi, who must have realised that the Prince's presence would catch the eye of news editors, displayed his cunning side by calling a press conference and telling reporters that the statement's "finishing touches were even made by Prince Philip". Killanin, a former journalist, recorded that: "At that moment, I could feel a movement among the pressmen and realised that it was the British reporters moving swiftly to the telephones".[8]

The deadline for acceptance of invitations to compete in Moscow was 24 May and, as the key date drew closer, attention began to focus on how many countries would stay away. Killanin later wrote that the more he looked back on 1980, the more he realised that, but for the support of western European countries as well as Australia and New Zealand, "the Olympic Games would now be something of the past".[9] It came as a heavy blow, therefore – and not just to the calibre of the Olympic rowing competition – when West Germany voted on 15 May not to attend. Norway also joined the boycott but, in the end, other leading west European nations did not. The Spanish NOC, for example, voted by twenty to thirteen against accepting its government's advice not to go to Moscow. With the benefit of hindsight, this result was of truly momentous significance for the IOC's future, since, had it gone the other way, the leadership ambitions of Killanin's eventual successor, Juan Antonio Samaranch, might well have been confounded. According to David Miller, Samaranch's Olympic biographer, had the government's advice been accepted, "Samaranch knew that his ambition would have dissolved and that he might even have had to resign from the IOC itself".[10] In the event, the boycott may actually have speeded the Spaniard's accession to the top job. This was because Killanin had been minded, as he subsequently acknowledged, to stay on for two further years until 1982, only to decide ultimately that the prospect of a leadership election in Moscow ought to ensure that the attendance level among IOC members was high.[11]

In the end, just eighty teams participated in Moscow, the fewest since Melbourne 1956. Sixty-six did not. It was in assessing the likely consequences of this that Thomi made his big mistake. He appears to have concluded – rightly – that the Olympic Games were in dire trouble and – wrongly – that they might well have outlived their usefulness.

Commentators have alighted before upon a letter that he wrote on 1 July, eighteen days before the Moscow opening ceremony. It concerns the programme for the 1981 Olympic congress, which was to be held in West Germany. Thomi suggests to fellow members of the IOC's tripartite commission that the programme be rearranged "in view of the recent developments" and proposes somewhat provocatively that the theme for the third day – the future of the Olympic Games – be handled by the international sports federations. More importantly, though, the very fact of circulating the letter could be interpreted as a gesture of insubordination. The normally placid Killanin, in his final month in office, took it seriously enough to fire back a reply from Moscow nine days later. "I must protest strongly against this action," the IOC president retorted. "The normal matter of circulating information, not merely as a matter of courtesy, is to approach the president of the commission with suggestions, which can then be discussed, and, if agreed, distributed to the other members. I must remind you that:– 1. The tripartite commission is an IOC commission, presided over by me. 2. The congress is an IOC congress, called by the IOC."[12]

In mitigation, the manner in which the commission was then operating makes Thomi's breach of procedure at least somewhat understandable. As Killanin later acknowledged, "unfortunately, after the Soviet Union entered Afghanistan, I had not been able to devote the amount of time I would have really wished to the planning of Baden Baden".[13] Much of the legwork, accordingly, was being done by a sub-committee consisting of IOC director Monique Berlioux, IOC vice-president Vitaly Smirnov of the USSR, Lieutenant-Colonel Raoul Mollet, president of the Belgian NOC,[14] and Thomi. The FISA president may, to a degree, have regarded his letter as a natural consequence of this operational structure. His boldness may equally be a symptom of his apparent conclusion that the boycott had exposed the Olympic Games as a busted flush. Comments in his annual report to the FISA congress in Moscow on 19 July 1980 – probably penned, like the letter, in early July – leave little room for doubt as to the extent of his disillusionment. "The Soviet presence in Afghanistan,[15] the decision of the American president to boycott the Games and the inability of the IOC to carry out its duties under present circumstances, have brought the

Olympic Games into a very serious situation," he argued. "This event which in the past has rendered a major contribution to the development of sport has now become counterproductive. It is damaging competitive sport and takes away much of its credibility."[16]

Killanin described Moscow 1980 as "joyless"[17] – a characterisation with which two Britons who attended the Games would doubtless concur. Chris Baillieu, who finished fourth in the double sculls with partner James Clark, recalls staying in the Soviet capital only for a short period: Great Britain was one of a number of participants whose athletes took no part in the opening ceremony. He remembers the female interpreter assigned to the team remarking how brave they had been to "defy your prime minister". To this he retorted, "Aren't we lucky to have the choice?"[18] Mike Sweeney, the team manager, evokes the uncomfortable atmosphere in the dining-hall which was stocked with a huge array of Eastern Bloc delicacies. The athletes would frequently overestimate their appetites, whereupon staff, for whom this must have seemed unimaginable extravagance, were obliged to dump the copious leftovers into bags. He remembers passengers on his flight back to England cheering when the plane took off.[19]

Sweeney also says that Moscow 1980 was the only occasion on which he fell out with Thomi. The issue was cox-boxes, small gadgets used for a range of functions such as counting stroke-rates.[20] The Englishman, who is no shrinking violet, actually told Thomi that his ruling was "unfair" – a charge Sweeney now accepts was inappropriate. What has stuck in his mind is how deeply the accusation affected Thomi. "It really cut him," he says. The recollection chimes well with the reaction of another (Swiss) interlocutor, who, when asked what the FISA president most disliked, immediately answered "unfairness". The two men patched things up quickly enough, however. Over a drink soon afterwards Thomi conveyed his gratitude to the team for not joining the boycott with the phrase, "Thank you, Great Britain, for ignoring Margaret Thatcher".

With West Germany and the USA absent, there is no doubt that the boycott affected the quality of the Moscow regatta. Most women's events were able to muster only six or seven crews. The same four Eastern Bloc countries – East Germany, the USSR, Bulgaria and Romania – occupied the first four places, in various permutations, in five of the six women's disciplines.

In theory, events with six entrants could have been settled by straight finals, with no need for qualifying heats or repechages. However, technical delegate Børge Kaas-Andersen remembers that Thomi had the idea of using the risk of side winds as a pretext for reducing the number of lanes in use in certain races and hence maintaining the regatta at its pre-planned length. Three of the six women's disciplines had five-boat finals. "There was no wind," Kaas-Andersen says.[21]

In the men's races, only Pertti Karppinen's victory in the single sculls prevented an East German clean sweep, although Great Britain managed two bronze medals and a welcome silver in the eights.

Much the most significant victory in Moscow for the future both of Thomi and the entire Olympic Movement, however, was Samaranch's comfortable win in the race to succeed Killanin. Assisted by Mexico's Mario Vázquez Raña, who coordinated his campaign, the Spaniard triumphed in the first round of voting against three opponents. These included Marc Hodler, one of the Swiss IOC members, who was also the long-serving president of the International Ski Federation.

Whether he realised it or not, Thomi was now a marked man.

CHAPTER 18

A New Shadow

It was during the countdown to Moscow, with sport stranded uneasily on the front line of the Cold War, that a new shadow fell over rowing. On 14 June in Lucerne it was revealed that two Soviet rowers had tested positive for anabolic steroids. The pair – Valentina Semenova and Sergei Posdeev – were banned for eighteen months. This was the first time competitors had been disqualified from rowing competitions for doping infractions.

The extent to which this was responsible for the host nation's meagre haul of just one 1980 Olympic rowing gold medal is hard to say.[1] It undoubtedly posed a stiff public-relations test for Thomi and FISA. It had been nearly twenty years since the growing phenomenon of athletes using potentially harmful substances to boost performance had been acknowledged in Article 9 of the new *Code des Courses*, which pronounced – with magnificent but undefined clarity – that "doping is strictly forbidden". Over this period, drug cheats had brought unwelcome publicity for some sports; seven athletes had tested positive at the Munich Olympics in 1972 and eleven at Montreal four years later. But rowing had managed to stay out of the firing-line, even though enhanced strength might be thought a distinct asset for the sport's practitioners.

Tests for anabolic steroids had been conducted for the first time at the 1975 world championships in Nottingham. They actually gave rise to one "doubtful case". However, as explained by the head of the then sub-commission six on medical questions, Hans Howald,[2] in his congressional report, "as a positive result was not provided by at least two tests, no action was taken against the oarsman in question". The episode evidently caused enough misgivings for the Swiss doctor to accept that FISA would have to "consider further the question of anabolic steroids". It had already been decided to introduce testing for the drugs at international regattas other than the world championships and Olympic Games.[3]

All drugs tests on rowers at Montreal were negative. Nonetheless, the tone of Howald's report is extremely wary. The results showed that "the athletes who underwent the control had not taken any anabolic steroids during the last weeks before their arrival in Montreal," he said. "But this does not necessarily mean that rowers have not tried to accelerate muscle growth and augment strength by taking anabolics." Moreover, in Montreal, it became "evident that today's lists of forbidden substances and respective controls are no solution for the existing doping problem. The new, hard-to-detect manipulations such as blood doping and 'performance stabilising' vitamin injections must," Howald said, be "openly discussed."[4]

In a development that was later to assume relevance for women's rowing, the medical commission had also been asked for advice on "an eventual reduction in competition distance to 1000 metres". Howald and his colleagues pulled no punches. "In our opinion," they said, "it is an illusion to think that the intensity of training would be reduced. Training would quite simply focus on strength and interval training instead of endurance, as has happened in other sporting disciplines. Even more than at 2000 metres, very big, muscular rowers would have an advantage and it is more than likely that the problem of anabolic steroids would resurface with a vengeance." They concluded: "By tradition, rowing is an endurance sport, which is why it has very positive health benefits. From a doctor's viewpoint therefore a reduction in distance must be rejected categorically."

At Lake Karapiro in 1978, no testing for steroids was done, as regional laboratories were not able to perform the necessary analysis. Rowing officials were starting to take pride in the sport's anti-doping record, though there was renewed talk of extending tests to more regattas. Testing was far from intensive at this early stage in the sport's anti-doping history: for example, the number of urine samples taken for other drug tests at those 1978 world championships was forty. By way of comparison, over 5000 tests were conducted under the London 2012 Olympic doping control programme.

It was at the Mannheim international regatta in West Germany in late April 1980 that the samples which were to result in the two Soviet positives were taken. It was reported that twelve competitors had undergone tests in all. The Russian rowing federation had been given the results ten days before the June announcement.[5] FISA deeply regretted that its doping regulations had been "abused for the first time in the history of rowing". It promised to make "all efforts" to ensure there was no repeat, while introducing "more intense" doping tests and demanded "strong steps" against the responsible officials.

Thomi was on hand in Lucerne to supervise the announcement. However, the most eye-catching aspect of rowing's response to this confirmation that it was not exempt from a phenomenon fast becoming one of elite sport's chief scourges did not emerge until a month later on the eve of the Olympics. At a media event on the same day as Lord Killanin's last press conference as IOC president, Thomi revealed his intention to set up a "flying squad" to test rowers around the world during winter training.[6] This was a first.

Indeed, it is an ideal which anti-doping authorities across sport still struggle to accomplish with any degree of comprehensiveness today. Not surprisingly, it was greeted with immediate scepticism. "This, I think, is not practicable," wrote *The Times*'s man at the press conference, Jim Railton. "Can you imagine, for example, applying for a visa to test the Russian team in training during April in the Caucasian mountains?" Can you imagine, indeed. But few, I think, would have doubted the sincerity of Thomi's intentions and most would have accepted that if anyone in sport had the clout to make an initiative like this work, it was the FISA president. And because of this, the comment put rowing back on the front foot in the public-relations game.

The following season produced another failed test: a young Bulgarian was found to be positive for anabolic steroids at an early-season regatta at Vichy.[7] But Thomi again spoke bullishly of tabling proposals for out-of-season testing for these drugs at the 1981 Olympic congress which was then just three weeks away. Howald's analysis, once again, was distinctly downbeat. "These positive analyses confirmed our fear of seeing anabolics used systematically in rowing with the aim of increasing the volume of training to a degree the human body cannot bear without a contribution from artificial hormones," the medical commission head observed. "The FISA council can in no way tolerate this harmful development and intends to become even stricter in anti-doping controls in future." He said that "several countries" were disposed to permit Thomi's idea for out-of-season testing.

In 1982 reality bit, with Howald admitting that "tests which had been planned for the training season had, unfortunately, not taken place". Thomi referred to "unexpected difficulties" which had prevented implementation of FISA's plans. "It has become apparent," he elaborated, "that the realisation of our intentions is only possible if all interested parties, which include the relevant governmental and intergovernmental authorities, agree to undertake joint action. To my mind there is no more suitable field for this kind of cooperation between governmental and non-governmental authorities than the fight against doping with all its side-effects." In the meantime, a fifth positive test had come to light, this time at the 1981 world championships in Munich.[8]

A breakthrough of sorts was achieved that winter, with twenty-five federations agreeing to take part in an "experiment" which saw out-of-season testing conducted on a voluntary basis. Even if the number of samples analysed was "not very great", FISA claimed to have done "pioneer work" and demonstrated that these tests could be carried out "without too much difficulty". It appealed to all federations to join in the experiment in 1983–84. Labelling anabolic steroids "the greatest doping menace in rowing", Howald acknowledged that the problem of their abuse was "far from being solved by this first action". Nevertheless, FISA had proved that international random spot-testing was possible "if national federations are willing to cooperate".[9] The number of cooperating federations in the second winter of voluntary out-of-competition tests rose ultimately to thirty-four, including every country which took part in the regatta at the boycott-marred Los Angeles 1984 Olympics. Even so, two federations not represented in LA were said to have rejected participation.[10]

Speaking in 1989, almost a year after the Ben Johnson bomb-shell in Seoul had put doping in sport at the top of almost every global news bulletin, it was clear that Thomi remained proud of his "flying squad" initiative. "We are certainly the first international federation that started already with anabolic tests in the training period on a voluntary basis," he said. "Now we have been able to get all the federations to cooperate and now they are on a mandatory basis... We can go in winter and check whether the national team use anabolics or not. We are absolutely the leading federation in the world and nobody else did it. We are the first one which put it into their statutes and we will start this programme. It costs us a lot of money – about SFr70,000 this year."[11]

From today's vantage point, it seems probable that rowing's efforts to stamp out doping in the 1970s and 1980s were little more effective than anyone else's. Equally, the sport has never been among those whose reputations have been most besmirched by the phenomenon; far from it. True, rowing was among the disciplines in which the now-notorious East German sports machine excelled. But as Howald told Christopher Dodd for his 1992 book *The Story of World Rowing*, "It is too easy to say that their success was due to doping. They were good at all aspects."[12]

The timing of that first 1980 case cannot have been easy for Thomi, with the Soviet Union building up to its great Olympic moment, even if it was already clear that many nations would not be attending. By resisting any temptation to be lenient, or even to brush the results under the carpet, the FISA president can be said to have got his sport off on the right foot in this most difficult and dreary of battles. For that he deserves credit.

CHAPTER 19

Post-Moscow Blues

A fraught, tetchy atmosphere enveloped the Olympic Movement in the wake of the Moscow Games. This was hardly surprising. The susceptibility of many Olympic bodies to political pressure had been demonstrated beyond question. The autonomy of the entire Movement appeared to have been jeopardised as a result. Thomi was far from alone in considering that the Games themselves were in trouble. The IOC was under new leadership. There seemed scant reason to have confidence in the ability of the new man – soft-spoken and little-known outside the sports politics domain – to steer them to a better place. The only heartening trend for the future was the willingness of broadcasters and multinational corporations to lob ever bigger wads of cash at the most compelling and attractive sporting properties. Even this came at a price, dependent on the nature and extent of the influence sport's new paymasters expected in return for their investment.

The niggling tension comes across very clearly in the record of the tripartite commission meeting held in Monte Carlo at the end of September, less than two months after the Games. The NOCs were plainly irritated that this supposedly vital body had not convened once throughout the duration of the crisis. Thomi's ally Charles Palmer was thirsty for blood, wanting to know – wholly unrealistically – "if the IOC should not consider the possible exclusion for one or two Olympiads of those NOCs who had boycotted the Games". Raoul Mollet, the influential president of the Belgian Olympic Committee, whose athletes had competed in Moscow, said in more measured terms that he favoured warning NOCs of "the possible sanctions political decisions would oblige the IOC to take". This all came after new IOC president Juan Antonio Samaranch had pleaded for unity in a welcoming speech, while admitting that the Movement was "vulnerable".[1]

Samaranch later told author and journalist David Miller that he had regarded Thomi as "a problem way back".[2] For the time being, though, there was little outward indication that GAISF president's number as one of the most powerful figures in sport was nearly up. After listening to the Spaniard's speech, Thomi had the chutzpah himself to welcome commission members to Monaco, "the headquarters of the GAISF". And at the conclusion of proceedings he contrived to underline Samaranch's novice status, congratulating him on "a most fruitful meeting, which was also the first occasion upon which he had presided over a meeting of the IOC".

Thomi was able to preside as king in his own castle just a couple of weeks later when GAISF held its general assembly, with Samaranch in attendance, again in the principality. The FISA president was also still very much in the inner circle of those preparing the next Olympic congress, scheduled for September 1981 in the West German spa town of Baden-Baden.

His personal travel schedule was ever more demanding, however. For one thing, the geographic expansion of rowing was becoming an increasingly urgent priority. This was partly to try and counter the way that, as Thomi had lamented many times, the sport had slipped down the pecking order over the decades in favour of cheaper or more spectacular alternatives. It was also partly because income from television was starting to provide FISA, for the first time, with the sort of funding necessary to underpin a worthwhile development effort. Even with the boycott, the broadcasting-rights money generated by Moscow for the Olympic Movement would be well over double the corresponding figure from Montreal, at $88 million.

Thomi had felt obliged too to undertake a number of visits to California. While those last two Summer Olympics had certainly had their problems, the location and specification of the respective rowing venues had, by and large, not been among them. Los Angeles 1984 was proving more akin to earlier Olympics during Thomi's FISA presidency in this respect. Under an early proposal, a new venue would have been built in the San Fernando Valley. According to Peter Ueberroth, president of the Los Angeles Olympic organising committee, Mayor Tom Bradley and the city's recreation and parks department "pursued a plan that tied a rowing channel to a San Fernando Valley water reclamation project".[3] There was strong local opposition to this, however, and the project was eventually killed.

In the meantime, in Ueberroth's evocative phrase, Thomi and organising committee official Dick Sargent "toured every body of water between Seattle and San Diego". Organisers of what was to be a privately financed event were plainly keen to locate a natural site to keep costs down, even though, as Ueberroth acknowledged, the FISA president had initially been promised an artificial course.

In June 1979, Thomi embarked on a two-hour helicopter flight as part of this venue quest. He reported back to FISA on "opposition from ecologists" to an artificial installation, while alluding to a proposal to stage the event in San Diego Bay. This solution offered "a number of advantages". Organisers, who had arranged a luncheon in Thomi's honour while he was in LA, were to put forward "definite proposals" before the Moscow Games.[4]

In December, Thomi was still expecting a "definite decision" on the course to be taken when he returned to the city in April 1980.[5] In the event, this did not prove possible. The Afghanistan crisis, of course, was in full swing and an inspection of the proposed Mission Bay site in San Diego revealed that it could "not really be considered because of the tide and the narrowing of the course near the finish". Other possibilities – including Lake Buena Vista in the neighbourhood of Bakersfield – were being considered. A decision was not now expected until the following year.[6]

A further visit ensued in December 1980, but it was only in late June 1981 that the Olympic venue was confirmed as Lake Casitas about eighty miles north-west of LA. On 24 July, Thomi visited the site with Denis Oswald, reporting that he had been "immediately won over" because of its resemblance to Lake Karapiro, setting for the 1978 world championships in New Zealand. "The air there is certainly cleaner than in Los Angeles," Thomi went on, adding that competitors would be lodged at the "magnificently situated and equipped" university campus in Santa Barbara, almost a forty-minute bus ride away.[7]

Los Angeles had been awarded the Games on a provisional basis in May 1978 while Thomi's influence was close to its apogee. Though it was the only bidder, the IOC's disenchantment with the terms on which the city wanted to act as host meant there was much uncertainty when the Olympic world gathered in Athens as to whether the city would get the green light. Thomi and Adidas's Horst Dassler had been asked to help. As sports-marketing specialist Patrick Nally recalls: "Thomi at that stage was still the kingpin. LA was seen as being a major commercial opportunity for us and everyone else. Even then, the projected profit for the Games was estimated at $250 million."[8]

This put Thomi in a situation where, if Los Angeles did get over the line with his assistance, he could reasonably expect some sort of *quid pro quo*. A story in the *Los Angeles City Historical Society Newsletter* gives an idea of what he had in mind, as well as highlighting that his methods could be unorthodox. The story involves Rene Henry, a public-relations man working on behalf of the LA bid, who had been an associate of Nally on different projects since the middle of the decade. According to the article, Henry met Thomi and Charles Palmer in a disco at the Athens Hilton, whereupon the trio made their way to the middle of the dancefloor where the music was blaring and there was no chance they might be overheard. The publication reports Henry's account of the message delivered by Thomi in this singular setting in the following terms: "You want the Games; I want a guarantee that Swiss Timing will be the Olympic official timer."[9]

Nally confirms that Thomi would "often ask for meetings to be held on the dancefloor". While some may be struck by the insight into how deals might sometimes be put together in this era, for many of us it is hard to get beyond the spectacle of that distinguished triumvirate establishing the basis of an understanding against a backdrop of strobe lighting, serenaded by the Bee Gees' "Night Fever" or "Love is in the Air" by John Paul Young.

By 1980, a "gentlemen's agreement" had set an upper age-limit of sixty-five for FISA council members.[10] According to Denis Oswald, Thomi had been minded initially to advocate that the ceiling be set at sixty, but had encountered resistance from FISA colleagues who felt this would be too young. Still only in his mid-fifties, the FISA president had decided that he was not yet ready to hand over the reins, while Oswald, for his part, was agreeable to the idea of serving another term as secretary-general. At the FISA congress in 1981, both men were duly re-elected by acclamation for four years.[11]

Thomi had been enduring the stresses and strains of office for well over two decades, though, and it is tempting to interpret a small misunderstanding at the GAISF meeting in October 1980 as a sign that this sustained pressure was starting to tell. Thomi had arranged for his old pal IOC director Monique Berlioux to come to Monaco to update Olympic sports federation presidents on TV rights post-Moscow. She was to do this between 11am and 12.45pm on Thursday 16 October. On showing up at the designated place and time, however, Berlioux was surprised – and clearly displeased – when Thomi allowed proceedings of the meeting to go on without allowing her any time to make her presentation. At 12.50pm, she took her leave. She heard nothing further from the GAISF president over the subsequent two days, except when she was told he had informed colleagues she had not responded to his request for information. She was sufficiently cross that she spelt all this out to federation presidents the following week in a letter.[12]

As it turned out, Berlioux's days as the most powerful woman in sport were numbered too. However, this was an inopportune moment – with Samaranch getting ready to strike – to inject tension so carelessly into a relationship with a key ally, particularly someone with whom Thomi had previously been on such warm terms. Meanwhile, more of the individuals who would go on to assume prominence as sports officials in the Samaranch years were starting to become established.

Immediately after his first trip to Lake Casitas, Thomi headed for the town of Santa Clara – known nowadays as the base of chipmaker Intel – for the opening of the inaugural World Games. This multi-sports event was conceived as an alternative platform for non-Olympic sports who saw little immediate prospect of making it onto the Olympic programme. It was, however, proving an additional point of friction among administrators, not least because certain Olympic sports looked set to participate. In the months leading up to the Games, they provoked terse exchanges involving Thomi at meetings of the IOC's tripartite commission. With the

Cold War raging, disenchantment with the event was even a rare point of consensus between the United States and the USSR. Soviet IOC vice-president Vitaly Smirnov was "of the firm opinion that the concept of the World Games was in opposition to the Olympic Movement", even if their staging could not be prevented. Former United States Olympic Committee (USOC) president Philip Krumm emphasised that, although the Games were being held on US soil, "the USOC was not in favour of them".[13]

Samaranch adopted the position that he was not against the event "as long as sports and events on the Olympic programme were not included". In the end none were, although boxing's withdrawal came too late to prevent its inclusion in some Games promotional material. In what turned out to be a precursor of the boycott of the 1984 Olympics by several Eastern Bloc nations, meanwhile, Soviet athletes did not take part.

Whether or not out of respect for Thomi, a Swiss team competed in the Games' opening event – a tug-of-war match against Wales.[14] A dearth of spectators meant that the Games were not a financial success. They were, however, another feather in the cap of Un Yong Kim, the South Korean head of the World Taekwondo Federation, who was president of the event's council and of the non-Olympic sports federations. Kim's fast-developing front-line nation was, moreover, about to be thrust under the international sports spotlight as its capital, Seoul, surprisingly defeated Nagoya for the right to stage the 1988 Summer Olympics.

Then in the final weeks before the Baden-Baden congress, a new man replaced Adriaan Paulen at the head of the IAAF, the athletics body. At the IAAF congress in Rome, Primo Nebiolo – a guileful and publicity-hungry Italian, born ironically in the same city as FISA,[15] who had headed the international university sports federation for many years – pulled off a noteworthy coup. As explained by Steven Downes and Duncan Mackay in their excellent book on the sport,

Running Scared, Nebiolo managed to convince Paulen "that he had himself collected sufficient promises of votes that if it came to a contested election… the incumbent would suffer a humiliating defeat. Paulen, Nebiolo suggested, should retire gracefully and maintain his dignity". In the authors' judgement, this amounted to a "masterful sleight of hand" and a "classic bluff". If a vote had taken place, they maintain, the "upstart Italian challenger would probably have been trounced".[16]

In any event, Thomi would soon have cause to regret the change.

CHAPTER 20

Divide and Rule

If the 1973 Olympic congress was where Thomi made his mark as a figure of real substance in international sport, its 1981 counterpart, held in Baden-Baden, enabled Juan Antonio Samaranch to accomplish a similar feat.

The IOC's new president had kept a remarkably low profile in his first year in office, biding his time and showing great circumspection like an opening batsman in a cricket Test match playing himself in at Lord's or Sabina Park. In Olympic historian David Miller's phrase, everything about that first year was "marked by caution and exploration". The Spaniard's sole big decision of note – a crucial one – was to disregard the examples of his two immediate predecessors and base himself in the IOC's home city of Lausanne. If he was to assert the level of control he aspired to, he quickly recognised that being a largely absentee president was no longer an option. He later described this as "the best decision I ever took".[1]

It was in the leafy spa town in divided Germany that Samaranch broke cover. The shadow cast by Cold War politics was at its longest. Yet, with worldwide media exposure assured, the Spaniard pushed ahead with changes in areas such as eligibility and athlete involvement which suggested the crusty club over which he presided was starting to modernise. After eighty-seven years of existence, the IOC elected its first two women members.[2] As Romanian IOC member Alexandru Siperco put it: "He led the congress in Baden-Baden outstandingly, kept everything in hand, including Keller. Held the three arms of the Movement together. That was the moment when he established himself."[3]

While some might have paused to bask in the glow of this achievement, Samaranch now moved to press home his advantage. One of the ideas to surface at the congress was for reform of the tripartite commission, the joint IOC/international sports federation/ NOC body that had assured Thomi of the ear of Olympic leaders throughout the Killanin years. Samaranch now wanted it tripled in size, incorporating the entire IOC executive board, and rebranded as "something like the Commission of the Olympic Movement", as Thomi dismissively told sports federation colleagues.[4]

Not surprisingly, federation leaders were suspicious. Wrestling head Milan Ercegan warned that if the commission were expanded, "there would be a reduction and eventually a cessation" of the meetings of the federations with the IOC executive board "because there would no longer be any reason for them". His volleyball counterpart, Paul Libaud, pointed out that if the IOC "intended to nominate" NOC and sports federation representatives, "it would only ever be an IOC commission and not truly a tripartite commission".[5] The most damning verdict was delivered long after the reform's implementation by rowing man and shrewd sports politician Peter Coni while he was giving Thomi's eulogy in Zurich's St Peter's Church. "The Olympic tripartite commission was enlarged from nine to twenty-seven members," Coni stated matter-of-factly, "with the inevitable result that it became too large to be of any real use at all".[6]

What need concern us here are not the rights and wrongs of the expansion, but that the proposed changes provided the pretext for a showdown between Thomi and Samaranch after which it was

clear that their views would not be reconciled. As Un Yong Kim –
the South Korean who succeeded Thomi as president of GAISF in
1986, two years before the Seoul Olympics – explained: "[Thomi's]
philosophy was that international sports federations... should be in
charge of sports, while the IOC is in charge of the Olympics. IOC
president Samaranch's philosophy was that the IOC controls both
the Olympics and sports. They collided openly at the GAISF general
assembly in 1981 in Monte Carlo and [Thomi] and GAISF lost."[7]

This general assembly took place in mid-October around three
weeks after the congress. Samaranch attended and gave a substantial, business-like address. It was in a subsequent question-and-
answer session that the collision occurred. Official minutes are not
tabloid newspapers; it is their nature often to downplay emotions,
generalise specifics and to convey proceedings in measured, sometimes ponderous prose. Yet working through the five dense pages
which constitute the record of these exchanges, the impression is
of a saucepan simmering on the hob and ultimately boiling over.
Thomi and Samaranch are not the only participants, but little by
little what begins as some fairly gentle jousting over the timescale
for proposing the nine sports federation representatives to the new-
look tripartite commission appears to spin out of control.

By the fifth page, Thomi's stance has hardened into what, even
through the prism of the institutionalised prose, amounts to open
defiance. Agenda item 15:1:0–q is the key passage and is worth
quoting in full. It reads as follows:

> o) President Keller stated that discussion with his colleagues here
> had led him to believe that it would not be possible to arrive at
> nominations for the new commission until they knew more clearly
> what were its terms of reference and its spheres of competence.
> He did not believe that it would be possible to have this done by
> the forthcoming spring.

p) IOC president Samaranch repeated his hope that it would be possible to have these names at least by the IOC session in May in Rome and, in reply to a further question from president Keller, stated that he did not really believe it was necessary to nominate persons but rather that federations should be appointed to the commission and that the federations should decide who their representatives were on the tripartite commission. If it transpired that such a representative was already a member of the IOC, he did not believe that that posed any particular problems or would not exclude them from membership thereof.

q) President Keller pointed out that this was a completely new principle which had now been mentioned because, previously, all elections had been of persons and not federations, and he believed that this would have to be studied very carefully by the federations.

What is particularly telling is that the next, unrelated, question from Thomi – on referees' expenses – merits just a single-word response. The IOC president's patience, it seems, has snapped.[8]

One other excerpt from these minutes is illuminating in the way it pinpoints a difference in philosophical approach that, besides any innate rivalry, made it impossible for these two great sports leaders to see eye to eye. Since the name of the revamped commission would include the phrase "the Olympic Movement", Thomi asks, returning to an old bugbear, would it not be "desirable to have a clear definition" of what the Olympic Movement is? To this Samaranch artfully replies that he "wondered in fact whether it would be a good idea, since the Olympic Movement changed so much". There you have it: on the one hand, a competitor's desire for clear rules objectively applied; on the other, a politician's desire for the exact opposite, leaving him scope to reshape the landscape for his own convenience. No wonder they clashed. Gian

Franco Kasper, a leading Swiss sports official who knew both men well despite being twenty years their junior, remembers Samaranch commenting a trifle nervously, "This Thomi Keller, the number of strokes in rowing is more important to him than international politics".[9]

There is no doubt that Samaranch always intended to undermine Thomi, just as he later disposed of Monique Berlioux, the IOC director who had become such a powerful figure under Killanin. The Spaniard told David Miller that Thomi wanted "more influence" and was "emphatic that the IOC should only deal with the Olympic Games". He went on: "I told him that the IOC had some responsibility for the whole of sport. Face to face with me, he was very correct and friendly, and I knew well that for all his bluff he was not a particularly strong man, especially as he was not from one of the major federations. We had the means to destroy him, and did so."[10] Following those Monaco exchanges, the increasingly self-confident IOC president wasted no time in putting his plan into action.

While many would, of course, take issue with Samaranch's ungenerous characterisation of Thomi as not a particularly strong man, there was a key weakness in his, and GAISF's, position – and the Spaniard had identified it. It was quite simply that the bulk of the new income that had been coming the Olympic federations' way was derived from an event – the Olympic Games – which the IOC, not the federations, controlled. What is more, with GAISF open to non-Olympic as well as Olympic sports, and winter sports as well as their summer counterparts, its members' interests were far from identical on many issues. They could be expected to adopt different stances on different problems. This represented potentially fertile territory for implementation of the ancient strategy of divide and rule.

Samaranch told Miller that Thomi wanted Summer and Winter Games' finances amalgamated and then shared. Instead, the Spaniard moved to separate them once and for all. He had already taken a number of steps likely to find favour with the Winter Olympic sports federations. These included underlining that the Winter Olympics were "the Games of snow and ice", hence forestalling any push by summer federations to have disciplines included, and offering to increase the number of winter sport representatives on IOC commissions. The move to give federations a far stronger say over athletes deemed eligible for Olympic competition in their particular sport would also have gone down well in winter sports circles, particularly skiing, which had had such problems with Avery Brundage's inflexible doctrine on Olympians' earnings. It is noticeable, indeed, that much the most positive response by a federation president to Samaranch's speech in Monte Carlo came from Marc Hodler of the International Ski Federation (FIS). Speaking – significantly – in the name of all six winter Olympic sports federations, Hodler thanked the IOC president for "the positive reaction with which the few requests expressed by the winter sports federations, especially with regard to the Winter Games, had been received".[11]

It was another innovation that would turn out to be the most important of all for accomplishing the IOC president's designs in the short term. A decision had been taken to hold the next meeting between the IOC executive board and the international sports federations in the 1984 Olympic host cities. This was sensible on grounds of enabling leading sports federation figures to familiarise themselves with venues and organising committee personnel. But it also meant, plainly, staging two separate meetings – one in Winter Games host Sarajevo in December, one in California in February. It was in the snowbound then-Yugoslavian city – ahead of site visits to Zetra and Trebević, the bobsled and luge centre destined years later to be turned into a warzone – that a key step in Samaranch's plan to undermine Thomi was taken.

On 2 December 1981 it was decided, as summarised in the IOC periodical *Olympic Review* that "an Assembly of International Winter Sports Federations would be considered by the [IOC] executive board". If this new body were "accepted", Hodler, an IOC member since 1963, would head it. The IOC president and his colleagues wasted little time: the body was "approved" the very next day.[12]

Whether or not they immediately realised it, this was a hammer blow for GAISF and for Thomi. As Samaranch explained: "Without the television money, the proportion for the Olympic federations coming from the Games, GAISF was finished... I realised the solution was to split the Olympic federations, summer and winter, into two associations... They had the right to deal with the IOC on television income. This left GAISF without power."[13]

While the ground was being cut from beneath his feet in wintry Yugoslavia, Thomi spent the last weeks of the year immersed in the pressing issue of sport's strained relationship with national governments. He attended first the fifth European sports conference in Warsaw and later a UNESCO gathering in Paris.[14]

It seems likely that he had realised the precariousness of his position as the most powerful international sports federation leader by January 1982, when he attended the opening ceremony of the alpine ski world championships in Schladming, Austria, and doubtless saw Hodler. The ski federation president was also involved in the formulation, starting that spring, of a number of proposed changes to GAISF's statutes. This exercise, which would have created a number of sub-groups within GAISF, may have been in part a rearguard action intended to limit the damage caused by the new Olympic winter sports body. However, the proposals were comfortably voted down and hence not implemented.[15]

While Thomi and Hodler were fellow countrymen and associates of long standing, one can readily comprehend the appeal of Samaranch's plan to winter sports leaders. There were only six of them – compared to more than twenty summer Olympic federations – and this would leave them to divide the IFs' share of Winter Olympic TV rights revenue between them. Amalgamating summer and winter payments would have produced a much bigger pool of money, but also far more rightful recipients. Winter federations would, moreover, have exercised much less control over how the spoils were divvied up. According to Samaranch, Hodler was "wholly co-operative" and "also wishing to protect winter sports".[16]

With the new Olympic winter sports body a fait accompli, and Thomi's authority palpably slipping, it was only a matter of time before pressure started to mount for formation of an Olympic summer sports equivalent. Meanwhile, confirmation came that the restructuring of the tripartite commission would indeed undermine its influence: the first meeting of the new-look commission for the Olympic Movement in Rome on 23 May 1982 turned out to be as underwhelming an occasion as Thomi's friend Coni would no doubt have predicted. "While the nine international sports federation members attended, only three NOC delegates were present with three replacements and the IOC representation was not complete either," Thomi reported back to GAISF colleagues frustratedly. "The whole meeting lasted only two hours," he went on, "and no decision was taken".[17]

By the 1982 GAISF general assembly in October, following rejection of the proposed statute changes, the die seemed cast. Wrestling's Ercegan spoke of a need to "do something to save the GAISF", and a working group to prepare draft rules for a grouping of summer Olympic federations was set up. Thomi retained enough respect to be re-elected by acclamation for another four-year term as GAISF president. However, concern was starting to grow about the potential consequences for federations if they took the rowing man's side unwaveringly in his feud with Samaranch.

Both secretary-general Charles Palmer and treasurer Charles Riolo were re-elected far from convincingly by twenty-five votes to twenty. "Keller clearly didn't like Samaranch and I think his attitude did a lot of harm to GAISF," Palmer, for years a loyal lieutenant, later opined.[18] Un Yong Kim told me that if he had not later changed GAISF policy to "collaboration with the IOC as its second, technical, pillar and junior partner, I do not know what would have happened to GAISF".[19]

It seems clear, though, that Samaranch – his hold on power growing stronger by the day – would only ever have been prepared to tolerate GAISF as a subservient body rather than a rival one. Thomi's insistence on speaking his mind and standing up for what he saw as the federations' – and sport's – best interests might have speeded this evolution. But it would have happened anyway.

On 20 July 1983, Primo Nebiolo, still less than two years into his reign as head of world athletics, was able to write to his key ally Samaranch, on newly printed headed notepaper, to inform him "officially" that the Association of Summer Olympic International Federations (ASOIF) had been – that word again – "officially constituted".[20] As perhaps betrayed by the repeated adverb, the Italian must have felt like all his birthdays had come at once. Not only had he secured the presidency of this new body much desired by the IOC president, but the inaugural World Athletics Championships would get under way in Helsinki in less than three weeks. Here – unlike at the Moscow or, as it turned out, Los Angeles Olympics – all the sport's stars from both sides of the Iron Curtain would be free to compete unaffected by political boycott. He had every reason to expect that IOC membership would swiftly follow.

Thomi took part in the first full ASOIF meeting on 31 May at Lausanne's Palace hotel. Indeed, Palmer even suggested that the new body, "given the option", would "probably" have elected him as president, though "he tended to be nervous about elections".[21]

This outcome cannot be ruled out, though it is hard to believe that an operator as canny as Samaranch would have permitted his grand design to be subverted in that way. As it was, Nebiolo's path to the post was smoothed by his emergence as chairman of the original working group. At the constitutive meeting on 30 May, after nine federations had proposed transforming this working group into the new council, the Italian was elected unanimously to the presidency.[22]

The minutes of the full meeting the following day make frankly fairly breathtaking reading. Having inflicted huge damage on GAISF, much of the talk is of unity and solidarity. A proposal that the TV money they stand to receive from the 1984 Olympics be divided equally among participating federations gains immediate traction, even though it demands a considerable sacrifice by Nebiolo's own sport of athletics which would normally have got 20% against the others' 4%. With a showman's instinct, Nebiolo requests a break in proceedings, "in order to consult the members of his federation", before agreeing, "considering the fantastic atmosphere which we have found". In a final twist, the other federations agree to chip in to ensure athletics receives no less than it did from the Moscow Olympics, when the overall cheque was considerably smaller.[23]

How should we interpret Nebiolo's generosity with his own sport's money? Perhaps it was a by-product of his sudden propulsion to the top rank of international sports power-brokers. On the whole, though, I see no reason to demur from Miller's characterisation of the gambit as the Italian's "covert move towards personal membership of the IOC".[24]

More than three decades on, ASOIF and its slightly older winter counterpart, the Association of International Olympic Winter Sports Federations (AIOWF), are still in place. It seems strange to think that they are a relic of a personal showdown between two of the great sports leaders of their time.

CHAPTER 21

For Whom the Bell Tolls

It had been a bruising twenty-odd months, but a presentation made to Thomi in Duisburg's Mercatorhalle on the morning of 23 August 1983 must have given him immense pleasure.

The year was his twenty-fifth as FISA president, and to mark the anniversary Christopher Davidge – the council member and former Oxford University stroke who as president of the Amateur Rowing Association had been in the front line of British sport's tussle with the Thatcher government over the Moscow Olympics – presented Thomi with a brass bell. The assembled congress then accorded him a long and heartfelt standing ovation.[1]

What I imagine touched Thomi the most was the amount of thought that had gone into the gift. The bell was not intended to help him chair that day's deliberations; it was not as if he needed that kind of assistance. It was a ship's bell for the steam launch he had recently had constructed which was to be one of the joys of his later years. A snapshot from his penultimate summer shows Thomi at the controls of the vessel on Lake Zurich, the bell stationed above his head. Beatrice Rothenbach-Seiler, his former personal assistant, describes the boat as "his biggest toy".[2]

Tronador – "Thunderer" in Spanish – was built at the Peter Freebody & Co. boatyard in the tranquil Thameside village of

Hurley, four miles downstream from Henley. Sitting a matter of feet from where the boat was crafted in the yard's atmospheric workshop and where he has worked on a freelance basis for nearly half a century, Richard Way tells me he made the patterns from which the parts for Tronador's engine were cast. "The engine we duplicated was a Bellis – very fine nineteenth-century steam engineering," he says, sporting a white beard and a navy-blue and white-spotted neckerchief. "Steam engines have to be very accurately machined if they are going to be silent." With Tronador, "when it was running, the only sound you could hear was the steam going through the regulator".[3]

The bell was by no means the last Tronador-related gift Thomi would receive. For his sixtieth birthday in December 1984, a chauffeur at the family firm who was a former pastry chef fashioned a magnificent chocolate model of the boat. The driver, Sepp, was the partner of Irmgard Meister who got to know Thomi's everyday habits as well as anyone during twenty-one years with the company. Among the small tasks she performed for him was to painstakingly remove half the elastic from new pairs of socks so they would not be too tight on his legs, constricting his troublesome circulation.[4]

Thomi was slow to accept that his role at the top table of international sports affairs outside rowing was set to dwindle as a consequence of the emasculation of GAISF. No sooner were the meetings that established the agent of GAISF's enfeeblement –ASOIF – over than the FISA president headed off to Magglingen for the general assembly of yet another contributor to the sector's indigestible alphabet soup of acronyms: the International Association of National Organisations of Sport (IANOS). There he was appointed IANOS president for the next four years.

IANOS does not seem to have left an indelible imprint on sporting history. Founded in Australia, it was merged into the

Association for International Sport for All in 2009.[5] One might be forgiven for surmising, accordingly, that Thomi's move to take up its reins was almost a neurotic response to being cut out of the loop elsewhere. This would though, I think, be to overlook the tense, fast-changing environment in which sports leaders were operating in the early 1980s. At least one sports federation president, wrestling's Milan Ercegan, seemed to be taking the new body very seriously in 1981, alluding to an "embryo organisation" created in Melbourne that "appeared to have pretensions to directing world sport".[6] Thomi, for his part, made it clear that IANOS would focus its activity on "mass sport".[7] In this sense, his involvement there chimed well with his growing preoccupation with grass-roots development and geographical expansion in his own sport of rowing.

Development of the sport had become a critical issue for rowing, as it strove to prevent at least a modicum of youngsters from being seduced by the commercialised, spectator-friendly alternatives being popularised by television. It was also all-pervasive. It embraced politics through the need to reach out to countries outside rowing's European heartland with no real grounding in the sport. It embraced equipment through the need for low-cost, standardised boats which would be affordable for hard-up communities. And it embraced competition formats, since the vast majority of rowers in the vast majority of targeted countries were lightweights. Because so much of the associated travel was inevitably outside Europe, it also added greatly to Thomi's already heavy flight schedule.

As noted previously, South America appealed to Thomi as a continent where early progress might be possible – so much so that, with characteristically high ambition, he would have liked to have seen the 1987 world championships staged there.[8] In early 1982, he took advantage of another Olympics-related trip to California to embark on a gruelling journey that took in Venezuela and

Chile, both future Pan American Games hosts, as well as Peru and Argentina. Not everything went altogether smoothly. Iván Dibós, the former Peruvian rowing champion and long-time IOC member, still remembers finding Thomi fuming in a hotel he did not like after he got in early from Caracas. "He had no baggage, only carry-on," Dibós told me. The Peruvian rescued the situation by putting the FISA president up in his beach house, complete with cook, butler and chauffeur. "So he enjoyed Lima," he concludes.[9] The city certainly has an affinity with the sport, including a rowing club founded in 1875.

By this time it was becoming clear that a more systematic approach was called for, which raised an immediate problem: where would the money to mount a sustained development push come from? Economic conditions were not easy, with the world-wide recession said to be having a negative influence on women's rowing.[10]

True, the sport's escalating TV money was a help, enabling sec-retary general Denis Oswald to propose, for example, a significant cut in subscription fees in 1982.[11] But there were many other calls on resources. In particular, it had been clear for some time that escalating workloads would demand that the central administrative function be placed, sooner or later, on a professional footing. In any case, the sums passing through FISA's books were still small enough at this time for the enforced replacement of a typewriter to be deemed worthy of mention.

It was vice-president Claus Hess who articulated the answer, in Duisburg, a few hours after Thomi had received his brass bell: Olympic Solidarity. It was, Hess said, "essential to enlarge the FISA family" and to "develop rowing in countries where it is too little known". He went on: "We must also reduce the gap between countries where rowing is developed and those where it is less so. To do this we must organise elementary courses on a regional or continental basis, making use of, *inter alia*, Olympic Solidarity, which can give appreciable financial support."[12]

Olympic Solidarity is the construct through which the IOC channels assistance to NOCs, particularly those in underdeveloped regions of the world. By utilising it to help fund its own development efforts, FISA would, in effect, just be ensuring that a bit more of the Olympic TV money from which it was already benefiting would go to help rowers and rowing. Another Baden-Baden era change had seen the fund restructured to embrace the international sports federations.[13] There was a potential problem, however: Thomi's feud with Olympic boss Juan Antonio Samaranch meant that he might not take kindly to the notion of going cap in hand to the IOC. Happily, while the FISA president did not relish doing this himself, he had no objection if others did.

Thor Nilsen, the Norwegian viewed as prime architect of FISA's development strategy, remembers that when he proposed going to talk to Olympic Solidarity officials, Thomi replied: "You can go. I don't want to have anything to do with it." Nilsen, who had coached in Spain, thereupon went to see Anselmo López, the Spanish basketball man, Olympic official and friend of Samaranch who had been brought in as Olympic Solidarity director in 1982. "I went to Anselmo and explained to him what we wanted to do," Nilsen told me. "Anselmo asked his secretary to come in and said: 'Pamela, give Thor $85,000 for the next four years. He will use it well.' I went back to Thomi. He said: 'You run it'. That's when we really got aggressive with the FISA development programme. We had nothing before that."[14]

Nilsen also offers an insight into the care with which Thomi monitored those ushered into FISA's inner circle. "He more or less selected the people around him personally," he recalls. "He picked people... If somebody was proposed from outside, he was always very exact to see if they could use them. When I was proposed in

1975 or '76, he came to Norway to interview me to see if he could accept me in the competitive rowing commission. He took things very seriously."

According to Christopher Dodd, by 1990 the booklets written by Nilsen and his team after the Olympic Solidarity money made it possible for FISA to launch its development programme in 1985 had been translated into eighteen languages. "We were forced to present things in a simple manner so that people without a scientific background in exercise physiology and without much rowing experience could learn something and use it in daily work," the Norwegian told him. Dodd describes them as the "building blocks for the seminars and courses conducted by the programme's coaches".[15] From fewer than sixty in the mid-1980s, FISA/World Rowing membership has risen to more than 150 national federations today.

On 8 May 1984, the announcement the Olympic world had been bracing itself for since 1980 finally came: the Soviet Union would not be taking part in the Los Angeles Games. Given the near-certainty that other Eastern Bloc nations including the East Germans would follow Moscow's lead, this was a big blow for rowing. Thomi calculated that, set against 1983 world championship fields, the sport risked losing around one-third of men's entries and no less than 43% of women's. "A substantially reduced number of entries may have a disastrous effect on the future of rowing as an Olympic sport," he warned, appealing for other countries to apply "lenient" selection criteria. At the FISA congress in Lucerne in June, he expressed sympathy – his mind no doubt flashing back to 1956 – for "those athletes who had prepared for the Los Angeles Olympic Games and whose National Olympic Committees had decided not to take part".[16] There had been a time when Thomi had been purring about the "excellent television coverage" the sport could expect owing to its planned early-morning starts.

"The Californians could watch it at breakfast, on the eastern sea-board of the United States it would be lunchtime and in Europe, the end of the afternoon and the beginning of the evening," he enthused.[17] That was all very well, but how many crews would they be watching?

In the event, Romania – a country under the thumb of the maverick dictator Nicolae Ceauşescu – decided not to join the boycott. It was rewarded with six rowing gold medals, including every women's event bar the eights. Overall, there was a 5% drop in men's entries compared to Moscow 1980, but a 20% rise in women's, even though both the coxless pairs and the eights were decided by a straight, six-lane final.

An exciting men's competition saw Finnish sculler Pertti Karppinen take his third consecutive Olympic title, catching West Germany's Peter-Michael Kolbe in the final stages, as at Montreal eight years before. Italy's Abbagnale brothers overwhelmed all rivals in the coxed pairs, while there was a home victory in the double sculls as Brad Lewis and Paul Enquist came from behind to deny Belgium. Their story became part of the subject matter for David Halberstam's bestselling book *The Amateurs*. The regatta also brought the start of perhaps the most remarkable Olympic rowing career of all, with Steve Redgrave part of the crew that won the coxed fours for Great Britain. This would be the first of five gold medals at five consecutive Olympics for Redgrave. His compatriot Davidge once jokingly claimed that he was the only Englishman to witness this first triumph. This was on grounds that he had fol-lowed the final from a launch while fog on the lake was too thick for spectators on the bank to see.[18]

Dominik Keller, Thomi's son, remembers this as the "happiest" regatta he ever attended, with bands playing and plenty of specta-tors. "Yes, there were occasionally morning mists," he recalls, "but one did see the races".[19]

Ironically, given his strong views on the dangers of excessive commercialisation of sport, Thomi suffered the indignity of a ticking-off for unauthorised advertising at the regatta. A terse letter bearing Samaranch's distinctively perpendicular signature alludes to reports that boats are marked with "conspicuous advertising", contrary to contracts signed with the European Broadcasting Union. "I should be grateful," the IOC president orders, "if you could take immediate steps to remove this advertising from the boats".[20] According to Dan Bakinowski – a future president of the United States Rowing Association and head of FISA's marketing operation – who was working as a technical official at Lake Casitas, he had found a sponsor for US Rowing earlier that year: Hunt-Wesson Foods. He says Thomi had told officials that whatever happened at Lake Casitas was "up to him". If a sponsor wanted to put a logo on a boat, "he had been given assurances it was his fiefdom". On the second racing day, however, Bakinowski got a call from Thomi on his walkie-talkie saying that rowing events would no longer be televised unless the logos were removed. "So here I am, going to the US team saying, 'Take the logos off' after I was responsible for putting them on in the first place," a bemused Bakinowski recalls.[21]

Contrary to expectation, Los Angeles 1984 turned out to be a landmark for the Olympic Movement, demonstrating that hosting the Games could be profitable, and in the process puncturing the sporting boycott's reputation as an effective and relatively painless instrument for governments pursuing political ends.

Thomi was quick to identify and rejoice in this aspect of Los Angeles's success, while flagging up another familiar danger. "During 1984, the Olympic Games were in a difficult situation which they have overcome in an astonishing way," he told FISA colleagues. "The comment that they came out of it stronger than before seems to be justified. I am confident that it will be realised that boycotts and non-participation at sports competitions are not efficient means for the realisation of political aims.

"I am afraid that the unrestrained commercialisation of competitive sports, the ever-growing importance which money plays in top-class competitive sport and the consequences which result therefrom, are in the long run a much bigger danger."[22]

Money was, though, undeniably important, particularly with rowing now pushing hard to expand its geographical footprint. Striking the correct balance between exploiting new income-generating opportunities and keeping the sport true to its traditional virtues would be one of the chief recurrent concerns of his remaining time at the FISA helm.

CHAPTER 22

Lightweights, Sandwich-Men
and the Beginning of the End

Thomi still had a foot in the sports-business camp via Swiss Timing, the watchmakers' alliance. This was to afford him a privileged insight – as both potential customer and potential beneficiary – into a new commercial plan that the IOC had formulated. This aimed to capture some of the private sponsorship interest which had been monetised to such good effect by Los Angeles and thereby to generate a new revenue stream to supplement its growing income from broadcasting rights.

Two weeks before the Los Angeles 1984 Olympic opening ceremony, Thomi received a letter addressed to him in his capacity as Swiss Timing president from a company called ISL Marketing. Based, a touch ironically, in the Swiss rowing town of Lucerne, this was a relatively new entity involving the familiar figure of Horst Dassler of Adidas fame. The restless Dassler had split from British sports-marketing pioneer Patrick Nally and teamed up instead with Dentsu, a Japanese advertising company with deeper pockets.[1]

Among ISL's new clients was the Seoul 1988 Olympic organising committee. It had also been taken on by the IOC to, as the letter explained, "develop a coordinated worldwide marketing program for the Olympic Movement".[2] This would involve bundling sponsorship rights of as many NOCs as possible, including the Summer and Winter Games hosts, to facilitate dealings with – and enhance the programme's appeal to – multinational companies.

It was hoped in this way to be able to offer global exclusivity for the use of Olympic trademarks in a range of product categories. One of the categories it was intended to market was Swiss Timing's speciality: timing. "As your company is a leading sponsor of the 1984 Olympics," the letter said, "we would welcome the opportunity of having a meeting in Los Angeles to discuss our concept and review possible areas of future involvement by your company in the Olympic Movement." It goes on to give telephone and telex numbers at the Sheraton Grande and the Biltmore, where ISL representatives would be stationed. It is evident that ISL were keen to get discussions under way. "We would like to suggest," the letter continues, "that we contact you upon our arrival in LA and we would therefore be grateful if you could by return telex... inform us of your hotel in Los Angeles."

One must presume that the meeting did not make much headway. The nub of the matter, after all, was that Swiss Timing would in future be expected to pay for the publicity value of its official time-keeper status rather than being paid for providing a vital service.

In comments published more than a year later, Klaus Hempel, ISL's managing director, says that Swiss Timing "lack the musical ear for our marketing proposals". The Swiss group, he acknowledges, has "a great technical advantage" for events such as the Olympics. "This is known not only to ourselves, but also in [1988 Olympic host cities] Seoul and Calgary. The organising committees of both these cities want to have Swiss Timing. We are not opposed to this. We are merely faced with the problem that Swiss Timing will be the official time recorder, but that they are refusing in Bienne to provide the necessary funds for the exclusive sponsorship contract."[3]

In the same article, Denis Oswald, in his capacity as Swiss Timing secretary-general, is quoted as saying that: "Timing is a technical matter and has precious little to do with sponsorship". This chimes well with the recollection of ISL's Olympic project manager Michael Payne, who remembered how Swiss Timing executive Manfred Laumann had "called my bluff" after Payne implied that Japan's Seiko was "ready to jump in". Laumann told the ISL man that he "misunderstood the dynamics of the whole operation. You pay us to time the Olympics, we do not pay you."[4]

As it turned out, Payne acknowledges, Laumann was right: "Swiss Timing was paid to time the Seoul Games." This state of affairs did not last indefinitely, however. Seiko did indeed "jump in" for the Barcelona Games in 1992, prompting the Swiss to return for Atlanta 1996 with the comment, as Payne (by then IOC marketing director) recalls: "You won – how much?"[5] The so-called TOP worldwide sponsorship programme became a noteworthy success and now generates more than one billion dollars in cash and value-in-kind goods and services per four-year Olympic cycle.

This push on sponsorship was one example of how IOC president Juan Antonio Samaranch was striving to make the most of the improved economic climate surrounding the Olympics. He also brought TV negotiations under direct IOC control.

In this, he enjoyed immediate and spectacular success: in January 1984 ABC agreed to pay $309m for the US broadcasting rights to the 1988 Winter Olympics in Calgary. This was more than three times the fee for the 1984 Winter Games that were about to get under way in Sarajevo, and the most money paid up to that point for a single event in TV history.[6]

The economic climate was not so favourable for a relatively un-commercial and not especially TV-friendly sport such as rowing, whose leader was known to be zealous about prioritising sporting matters. FISA did, nevertheless, manage to negotiate a three-year deal with Eurovision covering the 1985–87 world championships. Figures written into the budget suggest this was expected to yield SFr165,000 over the term of the contract.[7] This amounts to just over one-ninth of the sport's share of TV revenues from the 1984 Olympics.

There was also a certain amount of experimentation with new, predominantly shorter formats aimed at popularising the sport and producing a more exciting spectacle. At the 1986 international regatta in Lucerne, for example, it was decided that, while heats would be over the standard 2000 metres, some finals would take the form of 500-metre sprints. As Thomi admitted, this was not "an unqualified success".[8] Journalist and author Christopher Dodd concluded that "rowing's greatest regatta appears to have taken leave of its senses", with athletes giving the experiment "a resounding thumbs-down". Television, Dodd went on, "made a mess of it. They failed to place a camera alongside the rowers so that viewers could not interpret what was happening."[9]

The move in any case sent out mixed signals because FISA had recently lengthened the standard distance for senior women's racing to the men's distance of 2000 metres. This followed a successful demonstration at the 1984 lightweight championships in Montreal. Part of the motivation was a sense that endurance disciplines were less likely to encourage doping. The medical commission noted the change with evident satisfaction, saying it was "always in favour of bringing the racing distance to 2000 metres in women's rowing".[10]

The sport was badly in need of the sort of decisive leadership which Thomi had provided so consistently for most of his long career. Unfortunately, his falling-out with Samaranch – coinciding with the post-Los Angeles revival in the Olympic Movement's fortunes – was contributing to an erosion of the authority he had wielded irresistibly in years gone by. The IOC president's presence at FISA's extraordinary congress in Rome in January 1985 did nothing to help matters and ended up underlining Thomi's diminishing clout.

The matter at issue in the Italian capital was FISA's desire to add lightweight events to the Olympic programme. A connection with rowing's development push had been made, since the vast majority of athletes behind the new geographic frontiers the sport was hoping to conquer were lightweights. A Chinese delegate rammed home the point, arguing that his country had one thousand million inhabitants, "most of whom were in the lightweight category".[11] Thor Nilsen, who had coordinated a working party on the subject, maintained that the "very future of rowing" was at stake. But Samaranch, having been presented with the FISA medal of honour by Thomi, responded coolly, asserting that there were many Olympic disciplines in which athletes of small build had "few chances of achieving the best results". The IOC, he said, would make a decision in June.

In the end the sticking-point was, on the one hand, rowing's reluctance to sacrifice existing Olympic disciplines to make space for lightweights and, on the other, the IOC's reluctance to enlarge rowing's quota. Lightweight disciplines did not ultimately make it into the Olympics until 1996 – more than a decade later – and then the overall number of rowing events remained at fourteen. The contrast between this episode and Thomi's success in the 1970s in getting women's rowing into the Games would have been apparent to anyone with a memory long enough to make the comparison.

A month after the Rome congress, Samaranch sent a small package to Thomi's Zurich office on Talstrasse, accompanied by a formal covering letter. "*Monsieur le Président*," the Spaniard wrote, "having found a medallion depicting the sport you preside over in an antique shop, it gives me pleasure to offer it to you... I hope that this piece, dating from 1922, will please you".[12] It would be possible to interpret this as either a thoughtful gesture without wider significance, or a peace offering. But the lack of warmth or any sense of kinship in the missive means it is tempting to regard it rather as the product of an old diplomat's reflex to reciprocate: you bestowed a medal on me, so I must respond in kind.

From now on, dissent becomes more of a feature than for many years at FISA meetings. Thomi was forced repeatedly to defend his handling of the lightweight question, as well as cautioning national federations against the "ill-considered step" of contacting the IOC on the issue directly.[13]

The Soviet Union revived attempts to change FISA policy towards apartheid South Africa, using the new emphasis on global development of the sport as a pretext. The Communist state had raised the issue several times before at FISA meetings in the 1960s and 1970s. On those occasions, however, Thomi had controlled the situation with relatively little fuss. FISA's stance was still to allow the national federation to stay on as a member while banning South African rowers from FISA championships. In 1986, though, after the international federation had changed its statutes specifically to outlaw all political, religious or racial discrimination, the matter was pushed to a vote, obliging Thomi to make an uncompromising speech supporting the status quo. While "convinced" that FISA was unanimous in wanting apartheid abolished, he warned that discrimination was widespread and that to "enter the field of political action" by excluding South Africa would create a precedent. FISA would then have to act in the same way towards "all the other federations whose countries, in one way or another, tolerated some form of discrimination". To do this, he concluded resonantly, "would really be suicide". The status quo held by sixty-nine votes to twenty-eight.[14]

At the same meeting in Nottingham, it became apparent that many national rowing leaders did not altogether agree with Thomi's cautious approach towards commercialisation. The previous year, the FISA council had decided to permit sponsors' logos to appear on rowers' clothing at some international regattas but not at world championships. When a succession of delegates spoke out in favour of allowing logos at all events, Thomi cut short the debate by declaring that the council had "no intention of turning the oarsmen into sandwich-men". He paid the penalty for this some months later after "fierce discussion"[15] on the banks of the Trent. The Danish and Australian federations, hosts respectively of the 1987 and 1990 world championships, had the temerity to appeal the council's original ruling, arguing that such championships were "almost the only televised event" in the sport's portfolio. Thomi duly spoke out against the change, suggesting that FISA would "lose much of our credibility". Despite this, the appeal was upheld, and while it mustered the very minimum number of votes needed to secure a majority, it was clear both that the federation was split and that Thomi's authority was no longer absolute.

The outcome of this vote must have jolted Thomi; it came, after all, less than a year after colleagues had reinstalled him as president by acclamation for another four-year term.[16] This is not quite the full story, however. Secretary-general Denis Oswald had tried to tell him about mounting frustration in the ranks as part of a frank response to Thomi's disclosure that he wanted to stay on. According to Oswald: "I said, 'Well, you know Thomi, FISA is growing. When you started, you had I think about forty national federations affiliated. You could do everything and you are still doing everything… We are lucky in our sport; we have well-educated people and these people I can tell you – they maybe don't tell you, but they tell me – they feel a bit frustrated.'" Oswald endeavoured to get Thomi's commitment to making the next four years, to 1989, his last in the hot seat. "I said, 'OK, let's now make a clear agreement,'" he told me. "'I am OK to continue for another four years, but with the condition now that you promise you won't ask for an additional term after that and that we can start reorganising ourselves in the direction I suggest. We need professional administration – not a big one at the beginning, but maybe a professional secretary-general and so on.'" Oswald indicates that Thomi readily consented to this, although the agreement was not written down. "To be honest," he concludes, "not really much changes".[17]

One thing that did change was the nature of Thomi's commitment to GAISF. After seventeen years as president, he announced in May 1986 that he would retire – and, five months later, he duly did.[18] By stepping aside, he must have realised that he was leaving the way open to re-establishment of more harmonious relations between the umbrella body and the IOC, which now held most of the aces.

This resignation, he told rowing colleagues, would "give me considerably more free time, which I shall use in full for FISA".[19] No doubt he did, perhaps partly in response to Oswald's cautionary words. By now though, after nearly three decades, it was becoming reasonable to postulate that the Keller era was entering its final phase.

CHAPTER 23

The State of Denmark

1986, the year of Chernobyl and Diego Maradona's hand of God, was Thomi's English year. Not only did the world championships return to Nottingham, but the FISA president paid no fewer than four visits to his beloved Henley between April and July. A new regatta headquarters building beside Henley Bridge had been opened in his presence by Queen Elizabeth II. The FISA council held its traditional spring meeting there at the start of May. He was back again in June for the opening of a boathouse, and in July to umpire at Henley Royal Regatta alongside his friend Peter Coni. For good measure, he spent a further week in the country in February 1987, visiting the Amateur Rowing Association and the "famous Eton College".[1]

Coni – a politically astute lawyer who was every bit as colourful a character as Thomi and who smoked hand-rolled Sobranie cigarettes in a tortoiseshell holder – was also chairman of the world championship organising committee.[2] So one can imagine the consternation, as well as the great personal sympathy, when he suffered a heart-attack just before the event. According to Christopher Dodd, Coni drove his Mini into a filling station and ordered an ambulance. "He appeared a few days later at the big dinner and the roof came off," Dodd recalls.[3] In spite of – or perhaps because of – the bloody-minded determination that this bespeaks, another heart-attack killed him, aged fifty-seven, in 1993.

Though strong winds had threatened to compound the event's problems, Thomi pronounced the championships "very well organised" and the quality of rowing "exceptional". The FISA president's only regret – though it was a significant one, given the sport's pressing need to drum up income to finance international development and the professionalisation of top management – was that more people did not turn up to watch.[4]

Correspondence in FISA's archive indicates that rowing's commercial push was a continual preoccupation through Thomi's remaining years in charge. Secretary-general Denis Oswald had overseen the build-up of a merchandising operation that was now a reliable income generator. Post-Los Angeles, the federation could afford an annual budget of SFr 480,000. That was a big jump from the SFr30,000 to SFr45,000 of annual income it could expect in the mid-1960s, but it was not enough to meet the sport's ambitions. Furthermore, it was derived for the most part from the Olympics, an event over which FISA had no control.

Thomi, who after all was a businessman, was certainly not impervious to calls for greater priority to be given to the quest for cash. The US rowing officials Dan Bakinowski and Paula Oyer were assigned as volunteers to beef up marketing and sponsorship efforts. FISA started to work with the US offshoot of ISL Marketing, the company piecing together the IOC's first worldwide sponsorship programme. ISL Marketing USA's president William Breen at one point comments on Thomi's "true American entrepreneurial spirit", adding: "Like Churchill, there must be some US bloodline".[5] For the FISA president, though, it was axiomatic that commercial matters must never take precedence over the athletes' interests or the sport's impeccable fair-play ethos. This could make him less flexible than some colleagues might have wished.

An episode involving speed tape offers a good illustration of the sort of money the sport might have been able to bring in and the compromises it was being asked to make in return. A letter from Oyer in Indianapolis announces: "Good news!" A company called 3M is interested in sponsoring FISA "as early as 1988".[6] This is a good call: 3M, a Minnesota-based conglomerate, plainly sees something in sport and will be a partner in the first two IOC worldwide sponsorship programmes. Specifically, the company is offering FISA between $50,000 and $75,000 in cash, as well as between $20,000 and $25,000 worth of 3M product. "Would you consider," Oyer asks, "allowing speed tape at the Olympic Games for one event, given that FISA could supply the tape at no cost to each country entered?"

The problem with this is that some months earlier, the FISA executive committee had decided to ban the product, Scotchcal plastic film, until 1989. "It is an expensive product and its effects are disputed [*contestés*]," Thomi alleged. He justified the ban on grounds of economy and fair competition.[7] Nonetheless, he plainly gave the matter some thought. He is said to have met a company representative on his way to visit his new granddaughter[8] and had a list drawn up of 3M products used in boat-building. There are seventeen in all, ranging from ear plugs to "Scotch-weld EPX, for joining deck and hull".[9] Yet when Bakinowski asks, nearly eleven months after Oyer's original letter: "Should FISA accept a donation of a product (such as 3M's speed tape)... if this will encourage 3M to sponsor rowing?" someone, presumably Thomi, has handwritten a one-word answer: "no".[10]

Almost thirty years after her pitch to 3M, and to Thomi, Oyer says she understood and accepted the FISA president's response. "I didn't have an issue with it. His resistance was over the risk of creating an unfair competitive advantage. Back then, lack of TV exposure was a much bigger challenge in securing sponsorship

than Thomi Keller was!" Oyer – now Paula Berezin – told me.[11]
"He wasn't an exception," she added. "When Dan and I introduced
sponsorship to the sport in the United States, there was a huge
resistance. It was a DNA/cultural thing. Audi was our first-ever
sponsor there for a $2 million contract. They were very smart. They
wanted to align and build an authentic relationship supporting the
rowing community. They knew that if they commercialised things,
it would have the opposite effect. The real value of affiliating with
rowing is the access to their very influential audience. Thomi wasn't
against sponsorship, but he was very protective about fair play."

In 1986, the Nottinghamshire crosswinds had preyed on the nerves
of world championship organisers. As it turned out, this was merely
a prelude to the problems that affected the event the following year.

The venue this time was Lake Bagsvaerd in the suburbs of
Copenhagen, with the finals split over two days on 29 and 30
August. For the first batch of finals, the course was assailed by
what future FISA council member Mike Sweeney described to me
as an "evil crosswind".[12] This made conditions terribly unfair.
Reporting for the *Guardian*, Christopher Dodd said the wind gave
"advantage to lanes six and five" while "rendering lanes two and
one almost useless".[13] Unfortunately, waiting for calm was not an
option because of stipulations in the TV contract. "We had to race,"
confirms Danish council member Børge Kaas-Andersen. "We could
not afford to lose the TV money."[14] It would have been little consolation that, in Britain at least, the event was assigned three choice
slots on the flagship *Grandstand* programme on BBC1, alongside
the world athletics championships and racing from Goodwood.

Faced with a no-win situation, FISA advanced the following
day's finals by an hour while giving the most favoured lanes to
the fastest qualifiers. Of course, Dodd records, the wind then
dropped, "so that the original timetable would have been fair for

most races". Unsurprisingly, the criticism was withering, with UK sports minister and Olympic rowing silver medallist Colin Moynihan saying: "The regatta could not have been organised worse for the competitors."[15]

The point about all this, as Sweeney explained, was that cross-winds "happen quite often in Copenhagen; it was not a surprise".[16] Failure to make a contingency plan thus further chipped away at confidence in Thomi and highlighted that the time had come for responsibility for managing the sport to be shared more widely. The days of the one-man band were over.

CHAPTER 24

When I'm Sixty-Five

On the eve of the Copenhagen regatta, Thomi announced to FISA colleagues that he planned once again to seek re-election as president in 1989. However, he added, he would retire at the end of 1990.[1] This would be a few days after his sixty-sixth birthday.

The reason he gave for wishing to stay on beyond the federation's nominal age-limit of sixty-five was that 1990 would be a particularly busy year. He listed three events to support this claim: the Asian Games; the Olympic congress (which did not take place); and the world rowing championships in Australia. There was no doubting which of these was closest to his heart.

Thomi had first visited the world championship venue at Lake Barrington in Tasmania in 1984. He described it as a "magnificent site" though "located in a remote place".[2] He still had fond memories of the 1978 world championships on New Zealand's Lake Karapiro, when FISA's faith in making an adventurous and demanding venue choice had been rewarded with a truly outstanding event. And, of course, returning to the region at the start of the new decade would dovetail well with the federation's development agenda. His enthusiasm had even survived hostility from a local resident in the form of a possum bite.[3] He later said that when he left office in 1990 "I would like a FISA flag signed by all participants in the Worlds in Tasmania – and no big speeches".[4]

The immediate reaction to Thomi's announcement is not recorded, but it must have stunned some delegates, most of whom had never known any other rowing leader. Secretary-general and heir-apparent Denis Oswald was surprised, since the move contradicted the agreement the two men had come to in 1985. He remembers, however, that Thomi had started dropping hints that he wanted to continue in office, saying, "I'm not so sure that I will go" and "the situation is changing, there are so many new elements".[5] Oswald was not about to make an issue out of one extra year, but he worried that if Thomi were simply re-elected for a standard four-year term in 1989, it was more than likely that he would find new reasons to stay on. FISA's centenary was coming in 1992 and unsurprisingly some national federations were comfortable with the status quo. Says Oswald: "I and other people on the FISA council were pretty convinced that he would not step down in 1990, and we felt that we could not wait any longer to modernise FISA management."

The issue became whether it was necessary to devise a mechanism to allow Thomi to be re-elected for just one more year. Since this could be interpreted as a question of trust, it is perhaps not surprising that relationships, notably between Thomi and his secretary-general, started to deteriorate. When taking over the chairmanship of the congress where the succession was finally resolved in September 1989, Claus Hess, a FISA vice-president close to Thomi, observed that the past few months had seen "one of the most serious problems" in FISA history.[6]

An attempt to agree a path ahead was made in early August 1988 in Milan, where council members held a number of meetings during the junior and lightweight world championships. According to Oswald, it was agreed that Thomi should stay until after the 1990 world championships, if he so wished, but no longer. Oswald was proposed as his successor.[7] Hess – who, in spite of his closeness to Thomi, believed that the FISA president ought to abide by the sixty-five age-limit that he had been instrumental in introducing and applying to others[8] – then asked Oswald to draft a letter to national federations setting out what had been determined.

If part of the purpose of this intervention was to calm things down and remove a damaging distraction from the other pressing matters confronting the sport, the plan backfired. As Oswald recalls, when he submitted his letter for Thomi's signature, he refused. "He said, 'I'm not prepared to sign it,'" Oswald told me. "I said, 'Thomi, it's what we agreed the day before yesterday.'" Thomi replied: "I don't care. I'm not going to sign it."

Oswald says he then called Hess who said he would sign the letter in his capacity as vice-president. The German also said he would call Thomi to try to convince him that he should go along with what had been decided.

Had Thomi heard something in the short interval while the letter was being prepared that caused him to have second thoughts about the specified course? Sports politics has long been endowed with a fantastically productive rumour-mill, but at this distance, it is impossible to know. What one can say is that it is rarely easy for sports leaders, who have spent their lives completely absorbed in their sport, to face up to the end of the road. Thomi, who had experienced no interval between the end of his sporting career and the start of his administrative one, would probably have found the prospect as hard to accept as any.

A month after Milan, the sports world assembled close to the Cold War's Asian front-line in Seoul, South Korea for the 1988 Olympic Games. The seven-year countdown to the event had been fraught with tension, much of it political, but some of it linked to concerns that what was essentially still a developing nation might find the ever-growing logistical demands of an Olympics beyond its capacity to cope.

Thomi had visited Seoul in both 1982 and 1983. Even so, the rowing venue did pose challenges, with the first two sites submitted having to be abandoned.[9] Once the eventual venue, near the river Han, had been identified, however, progress was smooth – aided no doubt by Thomi's relationship with Un Yong Kim, his successor as president of GAISF, who was vice-president of the Games organising committee. Thomi eventually proclaimed the entire nation's performance "stupendous" and the regatta "a complete success in every respect" – this in spite of weather conditions which forced a six-hour postponement of the semi-finals.[10] Oswald, though, complained at the "huge administrative workload" associated with arranging accommodation for delegates to the FISA congress which preceded the Games. The task, he said, "proved to be especially complicated and thankless... Some delegates did not understand that we do not have the flexibility of a professional travel agency."[11]

Thomi's last Olympics produced some special moments for him. At congress, he had the satisfaction of seeing the national federation of the Philippines, where he had lived and rowed as a young man in the 1950s, accepted as an extraordinary member of FISA. He also escorted Princess Anne and IOC president Juan Antonio Samaranch around the rowing venue, where he was reported to be "in good spirits".[12] Yet at other times he appears to have been at a low ebb. Wiwi Greve, wife of Børge Kaas-Andersen, the Danish FISA council member, describes observing Thomi during the Seoul regatta driving his car along the bank alone. He called her over and she got in. An emotional Thomi then started saying he felt everyone had left him. "He told me he felt alone in the world, that everybody in FISA was against him," Greve recalls. "I told him, 'You have a lot of acquaintances, but not close friends'."[13] There were other days when Thomi had plenty of passengers in his car, but it seems the events of August had taken a toll.

Notwithstanding Thomi's comments to Greve, he still had his supporters. The council's August letter seems also to have persuaded them to step up their efforts. Britain's Neil Thomas – the Amateur Rowing Association (ARA) president – had been an increasingly vocal presence at recent FISA meetings, and in January 1989 he called publicly for Thomi to "remain in his position until the centenary of FISA".[14] His view was echoed by the Belgian IOC vice-president and medical commission head Prince Alexandre de Mérode.

The UK also seemingly had some ambition to use the imminent appointment of a professional secretary-general, requiring extra office space, to entice FISA to set up its headquarters in Great Britain. Neil Thomas told FISA delegates that the British federation and the Sports Council, "recognising the importance of the international sporting federations, were very keen to see them established in Great Britain". They would, he added, "provide financial backing for up to 75% of the rent".[15] When I raised this with former ARA chief executive Ivan Pratt, however, he indicated he did not think this progressed beyond the informal discussion stage.[16]

FISA had been talking to the International Ski Federation (FIS) about taking space in the FIS's new headquarters building that was under construction in Oberhofen on Lake Thun. This ultimately was what happened. The first FISA council meeting in the new building was held in early May 1990.[17] By this time, the Australian John Boultbee, who got the secretary-general's job, had been in situ for the better part of a year, working from Oswald's law firm in Neuchâtel.

There is some evidence that Thomi, having shaken off the low spirits which overcame him at times in Korea, went along with those trying to keep him in place until 1992. A confidential memo from "PRCC" to "NRLT", "JAV" and "IWP" begins with the line, "I had a phone call from TK this morning." Given the content of the rest of the message, I think we can take it as read that of the many thousands of individuals with these initials who were knocking about in the late 1980s, the man on the end of the receiver was Thomi. Similarly, "PRCC" must be Peter Richard Carstairs Coni, Thomi's friend from Henley. As for the other three, they are surely Neil Thomas, John Veats and Ivan Pratt, who went as the three British representatives to the extraordinary FISA congress in Athens in late January 1989. The memo is undated, but a reference to this Athens meeting leads to the conclusion it was written either late in 1988 or, more likely, very early in 1989.

The most interesting passage confirms that Boultbee is the frontrunner for "professional Gen Sec", noting: "He speaks good German and is working on his French (I resisted pointing out that Australians can't speak English)". It then goes on: "TK has also identified a very possible swiss [sic] successor to himself as President in '92 – a guy called ?Shuter... who has managed[18] the main office of one of the big Swiss banks in the USA and for the last five years has been running a family industrial firm employing about 1000 in Switzerland with his brother. He travels a lot round the world to do with his job, and sounds very like another TK potentially. That is not something for formal raising at Athens, but at least it enables us to say in informal chats with other feds that we are satisfied that another swiss can be identified to succeed Thomi if need be – that is to say if we fear that some other Federations may see the whole of our proposals as a move by ARA to take over FISA!" Somebody has written at the bottom of the message by hand: "H.R. Schurter (a V-President of Lucerne Regatta)".[19]

When I asked Hans-Rudolf Schurter about this, he confirmed that he knew Thomi, and that the idea came up but that it put him in a difficult position because of the family business and because he also knew Oswald, so he did not agree. "I met him mostly during my time as sports director of the Lucerne regatta at the beginning of the 1980s," he told me. "We had long discussions in his office about how rowing should be developed. After a couple of years we started to have trust in each other. It was not an easy thing to have his trust." Schurter says his father had been secretary-general of the organising committee of the inaugural world championships in Lucerne in 1962. "He and Thomi got along pretty well." More than twenty years Thomi's junior, Hans-Rudolf wonders whether this family connection, along with his love of dogs, helped to overcome the generation gap that might otherwise have distanced them.[20]

Boultbee's recollection is that by the time he arrived properly on the scene in 1989, he found Thomi had decided that he wanted to stay on and was no longer confident Oswald was the right person to succeed him. When Boultbee visited Switzerland in February for what was, in effect, his job interview, it was "more or less well known that Thomi and Denis were not seeing eye-to-eye". The interview took place in the humdrum surroundings of the Thun railway-station cafeteria. Says Boultbee: "I knew of and felt the tension when the three of us were together in Thun, but both were committed to bringing on a professional secretary-general, so it was a cordial meeting, more or less."[21]

Seven months later, as the rowing world began to assemble once again in Bled, the atmosphere was distinctly worse. As Boultbee puts it, "the congress in Bled in 1989 was horrible".

CHAPTER 25

Checkmate

Bled Festival Hall is a largely glass-fronted building near the town's picturesque lake, which surrounds what today is the only island in Slovenia. It was originally built in 1961 for a chess tournament which helped to cement US teenager Bobby Fischer's reputation for brilliance. It was here on 2 September 1989 that Thomi's three-decade reign as the monarch of world rowing to all intents and purposes ended, even if his long spell as FISA president did not.

Thomi had been a frequent visitor in the months leading up to the congress. This was partly to nail down a TV deal for the world championships that would follow the FISA meeting and partly to monitor progress of an extensive renovation of the hall. Not surprisingly, given the political ructions starting to shake Eastern Europe at this time, this was said to have fallen behind schedule.[1]

Notwithstanding the leadership question and his advancing age, the FISA president was maintaining a heavy travel schedule during what were to prove his last months in office. Easter Saturday saw him once again on the Thames, where he witnessed his first Oxford versus Cambridge boat race – a contest won by two-and-a-half lengths by the Dark Blues. Other stop-offs during the year included Tel Aviv and Cuba. With Mike Sweeney, now a member of FISA's regattas' commission, he also inspected a string of future world championship candidates' facilities. Henley was celebrating its sesquicentenary and Thomi undertook his umpiring duties there with "particular pleasure". He "particularly enjoyed the fact that invitations had been issued to all the available former winners of the Diamond Sculls". Finals day was positively idyllic, being blessed with "the best of the weather, wind and stream," and producing a succession of course records.[2] The most dramatic achievement, according to management committee chairman Peter Coni, was "undoubtedly that of Nottinghamshire County R.A. who, after setting a new record time in the final of the Ladies' Challenge Plate and being required to re-row the race at 8pm, succeeded in winning that race in a still faster time to an enthusiasm from the banks which can rarely have been equalled at any previous regatta".[3] It is gratifying to think that Thomi's last experience of this place, which had brought him so much contentment over the years, was so rewarding.

He also had the opportunity to indulge in a final foray into international sports politics, playing a part in efforts in Barcelona in April to get Primo Nebiolo removed from the presidency of ASOIF. In the event, Nebiolo – the athletics leader who helped IOC president Juan Antonio Samaranch enfeeble Thomi's old fief, GAISF – clung on. Thomi's verdict, for all that, was unsparing. It was, he said, "the most perfect demonstration of how not to run a meeting".[4]

Proceedings in the remodelled conference hall in Bled on Saturday 2 September – the eve of the fiftieth anniversary of Britain's declaration of war on Nazi Germany – began at 9am. After a welcome from the head of the Yugoslavian Rowing Federation, Thomi set the ball rolling with a plea for "a spirit of friendship" when dealing with matters that were "somewhat sensitive".[5] What many in the hall probably did not realise, though Thomi's son and daughter-in-law did when they arrived in town that morning, was that the

FISA president was sick – more sick than Dominik Keller could ever remember seeing him.[6]

It is frequently the case with such formal proceedings that the ordering of the agenda bears little or no relation to the issues foremost on everyone's mind. So it was that delegates focused dutifully in turn on a whole range of subjects – the accounts, wind at the junior world championships in Szeged, rowing's second Universiade appearance, new full-time secretary-general John Boultbee's arrival, voting procedures for the world championship designations that were to be made when congress reconvened in six days' time, a recent positive doping test for ephedrine – before arriving at last at item 11: "Election of the Executive Committee".

It is also frequently the case that the most important votes are seemingly technical. So it was here.

Prior to handing over presidency of the session to vice-president Claus Hess, Thomi read out the council's proposal that delegates re-elect him president until the end of the 1990 world championships and then proceed immediately to elect his successor. It was, he said, necessary to vote on this proposal. If congress accepted, "then it would proceed today to the election of his successor"; if not, it would be "a different story". Until now, he emphasised, he had seen no reason to change his point of view regarding retirement from the statement he had made in Denmark two years earlier.

It was at this point that Great Britain's Neil Thomas, who had called in January for the FISA president to remain in situ until 1992, made an intervention that might have opened the door for Thomi to defy the council's wishes. The FISA statutes only permitted the election of a president for four years, the Englishman asserted cunningly. Congress was sovereign, but if it wished to proceed "in a different direction from that required by the statutes", a two-thirds majority was needed. He wanted to know, therefore, which majority would be applied to the forthcoming vote.

It is impossible, of course, to know what flashed through Thomi's mind at that instant. Was he resigned to the council getting its way or convinced that it wouldn't? Was he now willing to leave his fate in his colleagues' hands without trying to tilt the balance in his own favour? Was he too sick to care? What we do know is that Hess had once again underlined, after their arrival in Yugoslavia, that in his opinion it would look very bad if Thomi stayed on more than a year after his sixty-fifth birthday, having in the past insisted that others should not.[7]

Whatever Thomi may have been thinking, he did the honourable thing. "I am not a lawyer and you might possibly be right," he replied to Thomas. Even so, he thought it "the most correct procedure" for the decision to be taken by simple majority.

At this point, Hess took the chair, only for Thomas to come back with a second volley, asking if Thomi would accept a full term should that option be available, prior to answering his own question: he believed – like many others in the room, no doubt – that he would. Thomi seemingly made no further move to clarify the position, while Hess replied that delegates must accept "the fact that Thomas Keller is only available for one year, whereas we have to fill the position for four years".

With that, congress proceeded to the vote.

The result, when it came, must have produced gasps, as delegates processed its significance. Perhaps a resigned smile crept over Thomi's weary face; perhaps too there were gestures of frustration from the British contingent. In total, fifty-seven votes had been cast for the motion, and forty-four against. The council had thus won a clear majority, though not by a margin convincing enough to have satisfied the two-thirds criterion, had it applied. The rest was more or less routine.

Thomi was re-elected by acclamation until the conclusion of the 1990 world championships. He duly thanked his colleagues, observing with decorous understatement that what had been achieved in his thirty-one years as president was "not insignificant". Denis Oswald then won a convincing victory in the election to decide a successor for the balance of the term, beating Thomas by eighty votes to fifteen with six abstentions. The outgoing secretary-general made a brief plea, speaking partly in English, for unity to be re-established. He also revealed that Thomi had agreed to take charge of FISA's centenary celebrations in 1992. And that was that. It was left to Thomi, his thoughts no doubt racing, to resume the chair, to thank Hess for doing the honours during "this diffi-cult period", and to present retiring Soviet vice-president Evgeny Kabanov with a silver salver. After the election of vice-presidents and a few remaining items of limited consequence, he declared the session closed just before 2pm. And with that, Thomi retreated to his sick-bed in the Toplice hotel on the eastern shore of the lake.

He had a good view of the course from the balcony of his suite, but was reduced at times to watching from the bathroom window. Dominik and his wife were, of course, frequent visitors to Thomi's room – as was Helga Hess, partly out of concern, partly to relay messages to and from her husband, who had taken over some of Thomi's normal duties. Helga also made sure that Thomi's Siberian dog Wassili, who as usual was with him, got fed (though not with the sausage-rolls Thomi ordered). At one point she found Thomi lying on his bed – something she describes as "a unique case" which led her to conclude that he must have been feeling very bad.[8]

The stricken FISA president was also being attended to by the Australian team doctor. John Boultbee thinks he remembers mention of a relapse of malaria, contracted during Thomi's years in the Philippines.[9] This might have been a factor. On the whole, though, I am more inclined to see his sickness as a consequence primarily of a worsening of the longstanding circulation issues. These presumably in turn induced the heart failure that was soon to kill him. It was later suggested, indeed, that Thomi had suffered a mild heart-attack in Yugoslavia, brought on in part by the enormous stress he was under. Hans-Rudolf Schurter recalls thinking Thomi looked far from well at the Lucerne regatta in July, referring to a severely discoloured leg.[10] On 25 August, moreover, Thomi had telexed the Chinese rowing federation to cancel a proposed two-week visit due to have begun in late September. "Some health problems could not be attended to during our rowing season," he explained. "They have to be tackled immediately after the rowing world championships in Bled, early September."[11] By the time he gave a final extended interview to Tina Fisher Cunningham, he had been sick for three days. "Are you feeling better?" she asked. "More or less," Thomi replied unconvincingly. "I ask him [that] every day," another colleague who was with them observed, "and he always says, 'More or less.'"[12]

Thomi had recovered sufficiently by the end of the week to preside over the second session of the congress, as well as his last FISA closing ceremony in the glorious setting that was one of his favourite rowing venues. A feature of the championships had been the slim pickings scavenged by the once-mighty Soviet rowing machine: a solitary silver medal in the women's competition and one bronze in the men's. The world was about to change.

CHAPTER 26

Too Early

On Thursday 28 September 1989, Irmgard Meister made Thomi a light lunch of soup at his office at 65 Talstrasse, as she had done many times before, and said goodbye. She meant until the following week when he would be back from a short trip to Monaco. It turned out to be for good. The next morning, she took a telephone call from Luc Niggli, secretary-general of GAISF in Monte Carlo. Niggli had been trying without success to reach Thomi's wife and children at their respective workplaces. Now he wanted to know how to get in touch with other members of the FISA president's family. Though he did not explain why, Meister says she could tell from the tone of his voice that something had happened.[1]

What had happened was that Thomi had died during the night from heart failure. It was less than four weeks after the vote in Bled which confirmed he would cease to be FISA president the following year and just under three months before his sixty-fifth birthday.

Thomi had gone to Monaco to meet Niggli, his old colleague from GAISF days. Knowing his former boss was unfailingly punctual, Niggli became anxious when the appointed time came and went with no sign of him. After waiting half an hour, he contacted the manager of Thomi's hotel and went up to his room. No answer.

Gaining entry, they found Thomi lying on the bathroom floor. The story goes that he wore a peaceful expression.[2]

Peter Coni had had a long phone conversation with Thomi on 25 September. This was to make arrangements to meet in London at the end of October, when Thomi was planning a visit that would take in a couple of West End musicals. He had already had his assistant fax Christopher Dodd, who was about to start work on the all-encompassing rowing book Thomi had commissioned, to ask for a copy of *Time Out* so he could make his theatre selections. Thomi told Coni that he had had a "complete medical check-up" after getting back from Bled and been pronounced "completely fit". The two men were to have begun detailed planning for FISA centenary celebrations at Henley in 1992. Coni was already sure these would culminate with a "monstrous" firework display.[3]

Thor Nilsen, the Norwegian mastermind of FISA's development programme, had arranged to call Thomi early on 29 September. There was no reply. When he found out why – like so many others in the sport to which this charming, forceful, occasionally infuriating man had dedicated his life – Nilsen was knocked sideways or, as he puts it, "really out of order". It is, he muses, "unfair that some good people die too early".[4]

Mike Sweeney was due to have dinner with another of FISA's younger generation, Svetla Otzetova, the evening after he heard the bad news. The former Bulgarian oarswoman wanted to improve her English and so had come to Cambridge to study, he told me. "I had to tell her Thomi Keller was dead."[5]

Dominik says his father had had an appointment with an eye doctor after getting home from Yugoslavia, but had seemed well. He remembers him being unusually considerate and kind during this brief period. "He called me up after I did a small errand for him and thanked me profusely," he says. "Later I heard he had called a number of former employees of EDAK, the metal products company he managed in his professional life, to ask how they were." He wonders whether Thomi was subconsciously saying goodbye. "It is a painful affair with lots of formalities to move a body over an international border," Dominik continues. "Finally, his remains arrived in a lead coffin, tightly closed. All you could see of him was through a small window."[6]

Newspaper obituaries underlined the magnitude of Thomi's accomplishments, while emphasising the special relationship he always retained with his sport's athletes and his consequent determination to resist unreasonable commercial pressures. *The Times* pointed in its unsentimental way to "a vein of insecurity", while observing reductively but not inaccurately that he "sought to challenge the pervasive power of the IOC, but was outmanoeuvred".[7] It seems unlikely, though, that many, then or now, would disagree with the verdict of rower-turned-journalist Hugh Matheson, who described Thomi as quite simply "the outstanding figure in the history of international rowing".[8]

Coni condensed this epitaph further in the course of an eight-page eulogy, delivered to a congregation of more than 1000 gathered in St Peter's church in Zurich on 6 October. "Literally," he said, "he has been the sport of rowing". The English barrister's heartfelt text is worth quoting at length for the sense of stunned, almost wronged, incomprehension it conveys on behalf of those crammed into the pews. Yes, rowing had steeled itself for the loss of its colossus – had even hurried the process along – but a rupture so brusque, cruel and absolute had not been anticipated by anyone.

Coni dwelt on the human side of rowing's "indomitable character", noting that when you were with him, "life was always good fun". But he also heaped praise on the administrative qualities of a man who Coni's compatriots in the Amateur Rowing Association had, after all, wanted to keep in the FISA presidency until at least 1992. There are "many high sports administrators who appear to be carrying out little worlds for themselves," he said, doubtless with the air of someone who knows. He went on:

"Thomi was not at all interested in that. Lord Killanin, the immediate past president of the IOC, said of Thomi that of all the senior administrators he met during his term of office, Thomi was the one who was closest to his competitors; and all of us in rowing know how very true that was. He had the ability to appear on stage on formal occasions, and to give wonderfully happy and appropriate speeches when that was required; but what mattered to him far more was to have contact with the competitors and coaches. It was something you could always see at medals ceremonies at championships: the number of competitors he knew by their christian names and whose medal meant even more to them because they felt they were being given it by a friend.

"I do not believe that anyone could argue when I say that no other sport has enjoyed such wisdom and such personal involvement from its president. In all that he did as president, he showed common sense, honesty and integrity. He saw very clearly how some sports were rapidly ceasing to be about honest amateur competition, and he was determined to protect rowing at least from becoming a commercially-run circus... His energy and the workload he set himself as president was massive. He was always willing to make himself available for another trip or another meeting; always anxious to speak with rowers and hear their views; and it was these attitudes which ensured that when we speak of the FISA family, that is exactly what the sport has been, under his guidance as head of that family."[9]

Speaking solely in English, after apologising to his audience for feeling "wholly unable to address you in German", Coni continued by remarking on how fortunate rowing had been that Thomi's position with his family company "enabled him to devote so much of his time every year to sport". He was "sure that none of us has a full picture of just what an important personal sponsorship of FISA he actually provided in that way. His concern that sport should not become a media spectacle rather than being based on fair competition did not mean that he was blind to change; but he aimed, and for rowing at least he succeeded, in ensuring that the sport kept control of its destiny."

Coni concluded with the lines of "Success", a poem that is much-used at funerals but might almost have been written with Thomi in mind. Yes, the long-time FISA president had "laughed often" and "filled his place". Yes, he had "looked for the best in others". And, yes, most definitely he had given "the best he had".

Afterwards, mourners regrouped at the Limmatquai headquarters of Thomi's Saffron Guild for a meal of tomato-and-basil soup and veal with mushroom sauce. The absence of the man who used to dominate any room he entered must have been overpowering.

The following day – 7 October 1989 – forty-two-year-old Denis Oswald was named FISA president with immediate effect.[10] The Keller era in rowing was over, even if its legacy persists to the present day.

When they sorted through his things, Thomi's family realised that, while he had some wealth, he had few personal belongings. Besides his boat Tronador and Wassili, they found perhaps twenty navy blazers, twenty pairs of grey trousers, a gold watch given to him by his mother-in-law at the time of his wedding, and that was about it. "He left no will," says Dominik, "but I am somehow certain that he did not really plan for retirement – even though he maintained that he would go out on the lake in Tronador and read history books. His life in sports was what really mattered to him."[11]

Some time between the end of the 1989 world championships and his departure for his last trip to Monte Carlo three weeks later, Thomi had also found time to compose a 600-word assessment of his final FISA event. This was published in the federation's newsletter two weeks after his death.[12] It is an entirely characteristic appraisal, combining generous praise of the Yugoslav hosts' efforts, radiant pride at this sport's capacity to stage world championships with "157 different competitive sections, without one single act of unfairness occurring",[13] and gruff censure of the "large number of crews" who "do not keep to the essential simple traffic regulations during the races". It is tempting to imagine rowers all over the world hearing what Christopher Dodd described as Thomi's "rasping voice from the bank"[14] in their heads as they read this in the weeks after his death. The piece also contains a last echo of Thomi's unease at the direction in which the unavoidable quest for cash was taking rowing and sport in general. "FISA has granted the TV rights for the championships 1989–1991 and 1993 to a private agency," he announces. "It will be interesting to see how the situation develops and whether FISA has set off down the right path..."[15]

And with that, the voice which guided rowing through three turbulent decades is finally stilled. Goodness knows what he would make of the fees being paid by broadcasters for some sporting properties today.

Afterword

"Enjoy life," Thomi used to say in his later years, "because in the end, no one will thank you for what you did".[1]

As a philosophy, it is cynical, reflecting his disillusionment with the direction sport was taking[2] and his dwindling personal influence in the international sporting circles he once dominated. But was he right? In the wider world of sport, yes, perhaps. Nowadays nobody much thanks Thomas Keller for his role in harnessing the power of the international sports federations and creating a force that the IOC had no choice but to respect. There is a simple explanation for this: it did not last. Sport's commercial revolution enriched the IOC far more than most other sporting bodies, and the astute leadership of Juan Antonio Samaranch made sure that increased wealth generated increased power. History, as the cliché has it, is written by the winners. Though wielding enormous power for close to a decade, Thomi was not ultimately a winner in this world. So his contribution has been widely forgotten.

It is a different story, though, if one narrows the focus to rowing. As I have discovered over the past eighteen months, this sport – which perhaps more than any other continues to embody the values Thomi stood for – is jam-packed with individuals who are profoundly thankful for what their former international federation president did.

There is no clearer manifestation of Thomi's undimmed aura than the reverence attached to the gold medal that bears his name.

First awarded in 1990, the year after his death and the year in which he would have stepped down, the medal recognises truly outstanding international rowing careers. The 2017 winner was Britain's Dame Katherine Grainger, five times an Olympic medallist – and I can vouch for how moved this tough competitor was after the presentation ceremony in Lucerne.[3]

This was Thomi's milieu. I have no doubt he would have accepted other posts, up to and including IOC president, had his fellow international sports leaders decided to bestow them upon him. He had a generously proportioned ego and, while a good listener, did not readily accept that he might be wrong. His natural charm, intelligence and business acumen, allied to a complete absence of snobbery and suspicion of careerist politicians, made him a talented Cold War-era negotiator. But, while he was prepared to wheel and deal for the good of rowing, the backroom bargains, dubious alliances and tense back-of-envelope arithmetic of international power politics left him cold. His long-time ally Charles Palmer interpreted this as nervousness.[4] I wonder whether boredom was not a bigger factor – plus a sense that such politicking was self-defeating, since promises made to attain or retain power might later hem you in, restricting your room for manoeuvre on issues that really mattered. Thomi's attitude to obtaining – or more often extending – a mandate was more like: "Here I am, warts and all; you have seen what I have done; take me or leave me."

Though he became one of the most powerful – and popular – sports administrators of the twentieth century, there was a side of Thomi which remained as uncomprehending and innocent as that pink-jumpered boy we met staring out of the portrait at the beginning of this story. Like a child, he took things personally. That's why the end came so hard.

Thomi Keller's Speech to the Tenth Olympic Congress in Varna 1973

Mr Thomas Keller
President of the Fédération Internationale des Sociétés d'Aviron

THE OLYMPIC MOVEMENT AND ITS FUTURE

In order to avoid any misunderstanding I would like to stress that the speeches of the three delegates from the International Federations reflect above all their personal opinions, which have come into being from the discussions held within the International Federations over the years.

THE DEVELOPMENT OF MODERN SPORT

Sport, formerly the hobby of a privileged minority, has today become a necessity of life for a great part of humanity. When the Olympic Games were reintroduced by Baron de Coubertin the organisation of sport was limited to local and regional events and most competitions were also on this level. There were therefore no unified rules for competitive events. With the progressive development of modern techniques the tempo of life has changed more and more and during the course of the last century the whole framework of sport has grown in stature. National Federations were given clearly defined terms of reference and in many branches of sport they joined together to form International Federations. In some countries the various Sports Federations formed national governing bodies which function sometimes independently and sometimes as government organisations. With a few exceptions these governing bodies are, together with their affiliated Federations, today responsible for sports in their countries.

THE DEVELOPMENT OF THE MODERN OLYMPIC GAMES

The Olympic Games have grown from a modest sporting event into a gigantic undertaking and this has led to a fundamental change in their character. The principles of the original Olympic rules were that the object of the reintroduction of the Games was not primarily to give competitors the opportunity to win medals, nor to break records. The Games were not principally to entertain the public nor were they to provide athletes with a means of furthering their professional careers, nor were they to provide an opportunity to prove the superiority of one political system over another. These basic principles have long been overtaken by events. The changed role of sport in modern industrial society and the success of the Olympic Games have made them pointless.

It is a fact that what counts above all in the Olympic Games is winning medals. In general, an Olympic win enjoys greater prestige than a world championship title, although both demand the same level of performance. In many cases Olympic medals act as a springboard for a career as a professional sportsman and they often lead to professional advancement. Successes are more or less openly rewarded by material compensations. The International Olympic Committee cannot prevent medal tables being drawn up and political conclusions being drawn from them. For the spectators in the stadium and for those watching the events on television the Games have become a vast spectacle.

These successes have given magical sound to the word "Olympic". We speak of the "Olympic spirit" meaning the spirit of fair play in general and not limiting ourselves to Olympic competitions. We talk of "Olympic sites", even if Olympic competitions have never been held on them, meaning sites which comply with the requirements of the various international governing bodies. Financial sources are available to ensure participation – in the Olympic Games which are denied to other sporting events. The Olympic Games are selected for political and ideological demonstrations as they afford greater publicity than other events. The interest of the mass media and the number of television viewers is very great indeed. I believe it can be stated that there is no other function that is regularly held which enjoys such popularity. If a city is entrusted with the organisation of the Games, its town planning programme is speeded up. In spite of all the efforts of the International Olympic Committee the word "Olympic" and the symbol of the Olympic rings have become a much sought after means of commercial advertising. The number of these examples could be multiplied almost at will.

In spite of, or rather because of, the unbelievable success of the Olympic Games it seems to be appropriate to make some critical observations.

QUALIFICATIONS FOR TAKING PART IN THE GAMES

Rule 26 lays down qualifications for taking part in the Games. Thirty (in special cases sixty) days of full time training are allowed in the year. Only a dwindling minority of the athletes who competed in the Munich and Sapporo Games complied with this requirement. The same applies to the conditions regarding material compensation. Yet, the Presidents of the National Olympic Committees, the national governing bodies of the various sports and the athletes all certified that Rule 26 was complied with. Everyone interested in sport knows that entries for the Olympic Games have largely become an open exhibition of lying which is quite incompatible with the ethics of sport and the spirit of Baron de Coubertin. These anomalies cause the proposals which we put forward for the benefit of sport to lack credibility and mean that they are regarded by many as unsound. All this is happening at a time when we are desperately seeking all possible means to instil into our youth a feeling of respect for society.

The International Olympic Committee attempts to support the fiction of amateur games with the help of Rule 26, although it is fully aware that most National Olympic Committees and Sports Federations are primarily concerned to ensure that these conditions are circumvented as discreetly as possible, in order to be able to nominate their best athletes for the Games.

These facts do not mean that the present day state of top level sport is altogether bad. What is bad is only that we lack the courage to face the true consequence in the case of the Olympic Games.

The fear of possible consequences of non-observance of Rule 26 has led, among other things, to the concealment of certain very urgent social problems. Some sports demand of future top level athletes a very onerous training programme, even in extreme youth. This leads to serious problems, not only as regards health, but also as regards education and professional training. The reintegration of former top athletes into ordinary life is also often attended with serious difficulties. In both these cases co-operation on an international level is urgently necessary. It is high time that the International Olympic Committee recognises that the changes which have come about since 1896 are irreversible and that it should act accordingly.

The majority of International Federations hold the view that conditions in the various branches of sport are so varied that it is no longer possible to find a solution to the amateur problem which would be suitable for all of them. Political, economic and public factors and the consequences flowing from them can no longer be divorced from modern competitive sport.

The International Olympic Committee should confine itself to a few basic criteria for the right to take part in the Games. It is the task of the International Federations to draw up rules governing amateur status which take reasonable account of the situation in their respective sports and to see that they are adapted to changing conditions with the passing of time. It is not for the International Olympic Committee, nor for National Olympic Committees, to ensure the observance of these rules. This is the task of the National Federations. On the basis of these rules and of a few additional criteria which I shall be mentioning, the International Olympic Committee should decide which sports should be admitted into the programme of the Games.

THE PROGRAMME OF THE GAMES

Hitherto the recognition of a sport by the International Olympic Committee has been meaningless in practice, but the acceptance of a sport into the programme of the Games is of great importance to its development. The work of the Csanadi Commission was a step in the right direction, but the Commission's work must be completed. Above all, we lack a definition of what physical and mental performance is required in a sport in order that it may be recognised by the International Olympic Committee. If we have such a definition, then only the question of amateur status and how it applies to the sport in question, as well as the extent to which it is practised throughout the world, should be taken into consideration in deciding the eligibility of that sport for admission into the programme of the Games. This latter criterion was incompletely laid down in the report of the Csanadi Commission since it is not enough to establish where a sport is practised; the way in which it is practised is equally important. In this regard information as to the number of persons registered as practising the sport, the holding of national and international competitions and other similar data would be useful.

The members of the International Olympic Committee cannot possess the necessary technical knowledge to decide which events should be included in the various sports making up the programme of the Games. They can say that there are too many events in a particular sport or that the number of competitors is too great and indicate suitable limitations to the relevant federation. It should be left to the latter to decide in detail how to effect any necessary reductions.

If the Olympic Games are to retain their place as the most important international sporting event, the number of sports included in the programme should not be limited. On the contrary any sport complying with the conditions set out above should automatically be qualified to take part. Any necessary measures to control the growth of the Games should be limited to establishing quotas in the number of events and for the number of competitors in each branch of a sport.

CEREMONIAL

Because of the nature of the original Games which were both religious and sporting festivals, Baron de Coubertin laid great stress on the ceremonial aspect. The Games open in accordance with clearly laid down rules of ceremony; the Olympic hymn, national anthems, parade of the athletes, speeches, firing of guns, flights of doves, ceremonies with the flame and with flags and the Olympic oath. In this way they are clearly distinguished from the world championships and other similar events, Recently, the organisers have attempted to add local touches as, for example, Alpine horns, dancing groups and children's dances in Munich. The National Olympic Committees, not wishing to be outdone, have turned the parade of the athletes into nothing less than a fashion show. Television allows millions of people to share in this spectacle and it very readily gives prominence to eminent guests. Free propaganda for politicians and the gratification of human vanity have become an appreciable part of the Games. No attention is paid to the fact that in the next few days the athletes will achieve the highest level of performance. In the past, the opening ceremonies have fortunately been generally favoured by the weather. A single wet day should suffice to demonstrate quite clearly the doubtful value of this spectacle.

It is difficult for an outsider to understand the importance still given to ceremonial and protocol by the International Olympic Committee and to find in it any connection with competitive sport.

I repeat what I have said before that sport is no longer the hobby of a privileged minority but a popular movement. This is a fact which should be borne in mind by officials of governing bodies.

TARGETS AND ALLOCATION OF TASKS

The importance of sport in modern society requires co-operation from all organisations dealing with these problems. If this is to come about it will be necessary first of all to have a clear definition of our objectives and to ensure an appropriate distribution of our necessary tasks. In my view, the general framework within which we should act is well summed up in Juvenal's often quoted words

"Orandum est ut sit mens sana in corpore sano" (the goal should be a sound mind in a sound body). Under present conditions the following basic principles seem to be applicable:

1. The development of mental and physical health in the young by means of competitive sport.
2. The maintenance of this state of mental and physical health through sport as a leisure activity.

Within this framework the following is the responsibility of the International Federations:

- The establishment of rules for competitive events.
- The establishment of requirements for equipment and sites.
- The division of competitors into categories (such as sex, age, weight, performance level).
- The definition of amateur status and the periodical adaptation of this definition to actual circumstances.
- The establishment of medical requirements for the protection of athletes.
- The organisation of world and continental championships and similar events.
- The supervision of international competitions.
- The fostering of the development of sport among the people.
- The co-ordination of the work of member federations.
- The co-operation of organisations having similar goals.

These clear definitions do not exist in the Olympic movement; consequently, the members of the International Olympic Committee have themselves widely differing views regarding its functions. Baron de Coubertin created the modern Olympic Games and the Olympic movement with the object of developing the character and physique of the young. This laudable goal has been submerged in the euphoria of the Games.

Today the Olympic movement is limited in practice to the Olympic Games themselves and to the more or less important events and functions held in conjunction with them.

The work of the National Olympic Committees varies between the following extremes:

1. Organisations which control sport in their countries.
2. Organisations which in practice only concern themselves once every fourth year with their country's participation in the Olympic Games.

These basic differences make it difficult to set up a common target for National Olympic Committees.

LEADERS OF SPORT

The most modern methods of science and research are used to foster the progress of athletes, but the government of sport is carried out by methods which in some ways are completely out of date. In industry, the success of leading personalities can be measured in figures. This is a yardstick which is lacking when estimating the work of a leader in the field of sport. A football coach whose team wins no matches is dismissed, but this does not hold good in the higher ranks in the hierarchy of sport.

An administrative career in sport is often misused to satisfy personal vanity. To my mind it should above all be the fulfilment of an obligation to youth.

Everyone holding a leading position in sport should have a thorough knowledge of it. [This means spending] time and close contact with the athletes themselves. It is not enough to have been a former competitor oneself, since conditions have changed in the meantime. The past should not intrude on the present as modern competitive sport is in a constant state of change. It is not enough to watch competitive events from the stand; there must be personal contact with the athletes on the training field.

COMPARISON BETWEEN INTERNATIONAL CHAMPIONSHIPS AND THE OLYMPIC GAMES

Today all International Sports Federations organise their own championships, but this was an exception in de Coubertin's time. These events are held in places which possess the necessary equipment and where an experienced team of organisers is available. The number of competitors is generally kept within limits which allow a smooth running of the event.

Generally speaking, these competitions can be well organised with relatively modest means. They are often allocated by the federations to small towns which identify themselves with the event and thus an excellent atmosphere is established. All competitors can be housed in the same place and personal contacts are developed among them as well as with the officials and the population. Championships of this kind become in a sense family events of the International Federations in which the spectators also take part.

The sports federations make use of these events to ensure their own cohesion and benefit by the fact that the mass media give them worldwide publicity.

In direct contrast is the uncontrolled "gigantism" of the modern Olympic Games and the requirement that all competitions must be held in the same place. For this reason costs have increased vastly in recent years and it seems to me that this trend is no longer acceptable and it is harmful for the image of competitive sport. Naturally, the holding of all Olympic competitions in the same town during the same two weeks is attractive to the public. This, however, requires very large and expensive sites and installations for which it is difficult to find any reasonable use in the future. This lack of planning has often been a heavy burden on the whole structure of the Games and has led the towns concerned into financial difficulties.

THE FUTURE OF THE OLYMPIC GAMES AND THE OLYMPIC MOVEMENT

All that has been said should provide a guideline for future Games – but this guideline must be determined in common by all concerned if it is to achieve unity. Above all the International Olympic Committee must establish clear goals. To my mind, there are two possible alternatives:

1. Either the International Olympic Committee must ally itself with modern competitive sport and be ready to face the full consequences, or
2. the International Olympic Committee must decide to limit the Games to genuine amateurs as Coubertin had originally intended and to make the necessary adaptations.

This second possibility may sound absurd at first sight but nevertheless it deserves to be examined. Top athletes, having increasingly less connection with the true amateur, will compete against each other in international championships. This would reduce the prestige now associated with the Olympic Games. The problem of the so-called "gigantism" of the Games would be non-existent. Under these conditions it would be possible to draw a dividing line between the amateur and the non-amateur.

If the International Olympic Committee does not decide firmly in favour of one of these two alternatives, it has a third possibility, the worst: to carry on as before without any clear goals and resorting to compromises and anomalies. The present unsatisfactory situation would get worse and, in my opinion, would sooner or later lead to the collapse of the Games and the Olympic movement.

All over the world people are tired of the insincerity, the excessive cost and the ceremony which accompany the Games. Their huge success in this century is no guarantee for the future.

We await with interest the developments during the course of this congress and the decisions which will be taken during the following session. If the International Olympic Committee comes to a decision regarding the future of the Olympic Games and the Olympic movement, it must be clear that co-operation with the International Federations is more than ever necessary. The federations are, as always, ready to co-operate but expect that this co-operation will be in a spirit of genuine partnership.

We must all agree that the stature of the Games and the Olympic movement in their present form is of diminishing importance.

In society the role of sport will be ever more important, either with Olympism or without, and therefore the role of the International Federations will not cease gaining importance. We are ready to take on the resulting responsibilities and hope that the IOC will do everything necessary.

T.K.

Acknowledgements

I have many people to thank. Top of the list is Dominik Keller, Thomi's son. Dominik funded the project and provided many insights into both family life and rowing events in Thomi's era. While naturally keenly interested in the product of my labours, he left me at perfect liberty to reach my own conclusions. Matt Smith set the wheels in motion with an email asking if I had "any ideas on who a suitable author might be" for a Thomi Keller biography. Since then, he has helped with contacts, introductions and other suggestions, and by putting the contents of the World Rowing archive at my disposal. Author and journalist Christopher Dodd was extraordinarily generous with his time, knowledge and contacts. Recognition is also due for his foresight in retrieving items of correspondence and other documents in the wake of Thomi's death which would otherwise have been lost.

Among interviewees, Denis Oswald, Patrick Nally and Beatrice Rothenbach-Seiler showed particular forbearance in the face of attempts to dredge up what must often have seemed like absurdly small details relating to events from three or four decades ago. This portrait of Thomi has benefited greatly from their contributions. The same could be said of Ingrid Dieterle who, in addition, translated and relayed questions on my behalf to Claus and Helga Hess. *Herzliche Grüße*, Ingrid! Mike Sweeney and Thor Nilsen offered insights nobody else could have provided. Chelsea Eves at the River & Rowing Museum in Henley could not have been more helpful; nor could Lucy Trochet, Elisabeth Waroux and Prateek Gumbar at World Rowing. I would also like to record my gratitude to Maria Bogner and her wonderful team at the excellent Olympic Studies Centre in Lausanne, especially Stéphanie Moreno and Sabine Christe.

I was delighted that Charlotte Atyeo was able to bring her valued editing and project management skills to the table. And, of course, thanks also for support on the home front, and exemption from stable duties, to Edi Smockum and Molly Smockum Owen.

I would finally like to thank the following for additional contributions of one sort or another: Chris Baillieu, Dan Bakinowski, Patrick Baumann, Paula Berezin, Sepp Blatter, John Boultbee, John Boulter, Sarah Bowron, Melchior Bürgin, Tina Cunningham, Michel Filliau, Klaus Filter, Melanie Freebody, Dessyslava Georgieva, Wiwi Greve, Philippe Gueisbuhler, Rene Henry, Christian Jannette, Børge Kaas-Andersen, Gian Franco Kasper, Un Yong Kim, Duncan Mackay, Denis Masseglia, Hugh Matheson, Irmgard Meister, Ingrid Munneke, Svetla Otzetova, Michael Payne, Presiyan Panayotov, Ivan Pratt, Marco Richon, Jean-Christophe Rolland, Andrew Ryan, Magdalena Šarbochová, Hans-Rudolf Schurter, Linda Stahnke Stepp, Lonny Stöckli, Charlotte van den Booren, David Wallechinsky and Dick Way.

Any mistakes are, of course, my responsibility. It has been a privilege retracing the steps of one of the best sports leaders of the twentieth century.

Notes to the Text

FOREWORD

1   Minutes of a meeting of the IOC tripartite commission for the preparation of the congress on 25 June 1973. Note that, as of 20 June, the organising committee had received 130 press accreditations.

2   "New voice in an old movement" by John Hennessy, *The Times*, 5 October 1973; "End to deception over genuine amateurs" by John Hennessy, *The Times*, 9 October 1973.

3   "Chien fou sans collier..." *Sport Belgique*, 3 October 1973.

4   Vizer resigned as SportAccord president some six weeks later on 31 May 2015, after a growing list of international sports federations and other bodies took steps making plain their disapproval of his action. SportAccord was renamed the Global Association of International Sports Federations in 2017.

5   "A tale of Marius, Juan Antonio and two Thomas-es, or did history repeat itself on the shores of the Black Sea?" by David Owen, insidethegames.biz, 17 May 2015, www.insidethegames.biz/articles/1027376.

1. PORTRAIT OF THE CHEMIST AS A YOUNG MAN

1   Face-to-face interview with Dominik Keller.

2   Details of Max Rudolf Keller's fatal accident, *ibid.*, plus Keller family archive.

3   "Such a good character", transcript of interview with Thomi Keller by Tina Fisher Cunningham, Fisher Forde Media, in Bled, Yugoslavia, 1989. This transcript is part of a collection of research materials given by author Christopher Dodd to the River & Rowing Museum at Henley-on-Thames.

4   "Hopeless banana", *ibid.*

5   Notes taken by journalist and author Christopher Dodd from an interview with Hans Frohofer, a one-time sculling partner of Thomi's who became a friend; Dominik Keller interview.

6 Tina Fisher Cunningham interview transcript.
7 *The Story of World Rowing*, Christopher Dodd, Stanley Paul, 1992, p.379.
8 Tina Fisher Cunningham interview transcript.
9 Details of Thomi's early rowing exploits taken mainly from a CV handwritten (in French) on notepaper headed with the emblem of the seventy-first IOC session held in Luxembourg 11–18 September 1971.
10 Tina Fisher Cunningham interview transcript.
11 Notes taken by Christopher Dodd from an interview with Frohofer.
12 Interview with Dominik Keller.
13 *The FISA Centenary Book*, Jean-Louis Meuret, FISA, 1992, p.101.
14 Tina Fisher Cunningham interview transcript.
15 *Manila Rows: The story of the Manila Boat Club*, Alan L. May, Vera-Reyes, 1979, pp.iv–v.
16 Letter written by Ian Purslow after hearing about Thomi's death. Part of the collection of research materials given by Christopher Dodd to the River & Rowing Museum. Dodd visited the club in 2015 and wrote about it for the Hear the Boat Sing rowing website. He describes a "homely place", with hens occupying the yard, the club pooch guarding the boatshed door and an oil depot on the opposite bank. His article may be read here: https://heartheboatsing.com/2015/02/21/thriller-in-manila/.
17 At a meeting on 28 April 1949 in Rome, the IOC selected Melbourne ahead of Buenos Aires by just one vote from a field of no fewer than ten candidates, including six US cities.

2. TWO MEN IN A BOAT

1 Thomi's foreword to *Manila Rows: The story of the Manila Boat Club*, Alan L. May, Vera-Reyes, 1979.
2 Face-to-face interview with Dominik Keller.
3 Newsreel footage of the 1955 Henley Royal Regatta may be found on the British Pathé website at http://www.britishpathe.com/video/henley-regatta-8/query/royal+regatta.
4 Face-to-face interview with Mike Sweeney.
5 Email exchanges and face-to-face interview with Beatrice Rothenbach (née Seiler). Dominik Keller remembers the family finding about ten pairs of these socks among Thomi's affairs.
6 Cited in *The Games: A global history of the Olympics*, David Goldblatt, Macmillan, 2016, p.41.
7 Dominik Keller interview; also email exchange with local bookseller Richard Way.

8   Eulogy delivered by Peter Coni at St Peter's church in Zurich, 6 October 1989.

9   Notes taken by journalist and author Christopher Dodd from an interview with Hans Frohofer.

10 Documents accessed at IOC historical archive in Lausanne.

11 A detailed account of the Olympic rowing competition and prior preparations can be found in the *Official Report of the Organizing Committee for the Games of the XVI Olympiad Melbourne 1956*, pp.532–557.

12 Details of various boycott discussions in the days running up to the Melbourne opening ceremony, compiled with the help of contemporary newspaper articles and telegram records held in the IOC historical archive.

13 Transcript of interview with Thomi Keller by Tina Fisher Cunningham, Fisher Forde Media, in Bled, Yugoslavia, 1989. Melchior Bürgin, a well-known Swiss rower of the 1960s who Thomi coached for a time, told me it was his father who first informed Thomi of the Swiss boycott when he jogged by on a forest run.

14 Email exchange with Dominik Keller.

3. THE YOUNG ONE

1   *The Times*, 8 August 1958. Details also drawn from other newspaper articles and tribute in IOC Bulletin no.64.

2   "He wanted me to become his successor...", transcript of interview with Thomi Keller by Tina Fisher Cunningham, Fisher Forde Media, in Bled, Yugoslavia, 1989.

3   Face-to-face interview with Dominik Keller.

4   Minutes of the FISA congress at Poznan, 27 August 1958; also *The FISA Centenary Book*, Jean-Louis Meuret, FISA, 1992, p.117.

5   "The other gentlemen...", Tina Fisher Cunningham interview transcript.

6   *The Story of World Rowing*, Christopher Dodd, Stanley Paul, 1992, p.381.

7   Minutes of the FISA congress at Vienna, 22 November 1958; also *The FISA Centenary Book*, p.119.

8   "The first time...", Tina Fisher Cunningham interview transcript.

9   *The FISA Centenary Book*, p.119.

10 The FISA presidency did not quite put an end to Thomi's competitive rowing career. In spring 1959, he partnered the well-known Australian-born oarsman Stuart MacKenzie to victory in the double at an international regatta in Lecco, near Milan. The event did, however, underline one potential hazard in endeavouring to combine roles as both administrator and athlete. No sooner was the ceremony for the double over than Thomi had to rush off

and don presidential attire in order to present a trophy to the winning crew in the eights.

11 Minutes of the FISA congress at Mâcon, 18 August 1959.

12 Times have changed: the share of revenues from the London 2012 Games allotted to Summer Olympic international sports federations amounted to well over half a billion dollars.

13 *The Official History of the Olympic Games and the IOC*, David Miller, Mainstream, 2012, p.147.

14 *Official Report of the Organising Committee of the Games of the XVII Olympiad Rome 1960*, p.355.

15 Miller, p.158.

16 *Official Report Rome 1960*, p.398.

17 Miller, p.147.

4. THOROUGHLY MODERN THOMI

1 "We had to remodernize...", transcript of interview with Thomi Keller by Tina Fisher Cunningham, Fisher Forde Media, in Bled, Yugoslavia, 1989.

2 "You see I competed...", Tina Fisher Cunningham interview transcript.

3 *The FISA Centenary Book*, Jean-Louis Meuret, FISA, 1992, p.122.

4 *Official Report of the Organizing Committee of the Games of the XVI Olympiad Melbourne 1956*, p.535.

5 *FISA Centenary Book* and *Official Report of the Organizing Committee of the Games of the XVII Olympiad Rome 1960*, vol.1, p.83.

6 *The Olympics: A history of the modern Games*, Allen Guttmann, University of Illinois Press, 2002, p.104.

7 Minutes of FISA congress, Prague, 22 August 1961.

8 The coxed pair and coxed four were included, as well as the eights. In 1993, FISA voted to remove the coxed pair and four as well as the women's four from the Olympic programme in favour of the lightweight men's four and double as well as the lightweight women's double. There was a further change in 2017 when FISA voted to remove the lightweight men's four in favour of returning the women's four to make rowing's Olympic programme gender-equal.

9 *The Story of World Rowing*, Christopher Dodd, Stanley Paul, 1992, pp.155–56.

10 Minutes of FISA congress, Lucerne, 4 September 1962.

11 As Thomi told Tina Fisher Cunningham in 1989, "the old FISA medal was a lady with big tits and an oar with an anchor".

12 Bled, in modern-day Slovenia, secured twenty votes in the one-round contest, versus eighteen for Vichy and ten each for Essen and Duisburg. At the time, ordinary FISA members were entitled to three votes each and extraordinary

members one vote. To qualify as an ordinary member, a national federation must have belonged to FISA for at least three years and have staged a men's continental championship, an Olympic regatta or a world championship.

13 *The Story of World Rowing*, Christopher Dodd, Stanley Paul, 1992, p.90.

14 *The FISA Centenary Book*, Jean-Louis Meuret, FISA, 1992, p.129.

15 "SFr" is used to denote Swiss francs (here and throughout the text). As a Swiss-based organisation, it is only natural that FISA should have used this as its reporting currency.

16 From his earliest days as president, Thomi was acutely aware that there was a downside for sport to throwing in its lot with broadcasters. In reply to a 1960 proposal to replace some European championships with a European or Eurovision Cup with more youth appeal, he retorted that he could not agree to sacrifice these championships for something dependent on a commercial organisation which would "coldly drop us" as soon as its interests changed. Minutes of FISA congress, Rome, 24 August 1960.

17 More than $500,000 at 1964 exchange rates.

18 Minutes of FISA congress, Duisburg, 24 August 1965.

19 *ibid.*

20 *The Times*, 16 October 1964.

21 *The Story of World Rowing*, Christopher Dodd, Stanley Paul, 1992, pp.383–84.

5 · FLAGS OF INCONVENIENCE

1 *The Times*, 14 August 1961.

2 Details on the Justicz affair taken mainly from *The Story of World Rowing*, Christopher Dodd, Stanley Paul, 1992, p.382, and *The Times,* 12 August 1961.

3 The vote was thirty-five against and seven in favour.

4 Minutes of FISA congress, Prague, 22 August 1961.

5 *The FISA Centenary Book*, Jean-Louis Meuret, FISA, 1992, p.110.

6 Minutes of FISA congress, Prague, 22 August 1961.

7 Email exchange with the author. Filter, who was born in 1933 and spent the post-war years in East Germany, vividly remembers Thomi's first words to him while he was toiling away in the Prague boathouse. "The bow balls on your boat are too small," the FISA president shouted out from behind. "Check for yourself," Filter replied, passing a measuring device over his shoulder without troubling to check who the owner of the voice was. A few minutes later, Thomi presented himself and apologised, saying, "Yours are the right size, all the others are too big." Says Filter: "I think that was the moment when we started to respect each other."

8 *The Story of World Rowing*, p.382.

9 Minutes of FISA congress, Lucerne, 4 September 1962.

10 West German crews had won every category in the row-offs in 1962 to determine who represented Germany at the inaugural 1962 world championships. *The FISA Centenary Book*, p.128.

11 Minutes of FISA congress, Copenhagen, 13 August 1963.

12 Minutes of FISA congress, Amsterdam, 14 August 1964.

13 Minutes of FISA congress, Duisburg, 24 August 1965.

14 Minutes of sixty-third IOC session, Madrid, 7–9 October 1965.

15 Klaus Filter says he came to understand during meetings with Thomi and the two federation heads Wülfing and Neumann that the FISA president favoured two independent organisations. This, once again, was for practical, not political, reasons: it would enable more top athletes to compete at international championships.

16 Minutes of Extraordinary FISA congress, Vienna, 13 November 1965.

6. A KIND OF ASSOCIATION

1 In a 1981 interview with Olympic specialist and author Allen Guttmann, an IOC member from the United States called Doug Roby said of Brundage: "We'd have meetings with the NOCs or the international sports federations and he'd say, 'We'll take it under advisement'. It was a brush-off... He just wouldn't listen... Let them talk, and then forget it".

2 *The Official History of the Olympic Games and the IOC*, David Miller, Mainstream, 2012, p.184.

3 This was the forerunner of today's Association of National Olympic Committees (ANOC), which dates from 1979.

4 The forerunner of SportAccord, which was again renamed the Global Association of International Sports Federations in 2017.

5 Minutes of the sixty-fourth IOC session in Rome, 25–28 April 1966.

6 Minutes of FISA congress in Bled, 6 September 1966.

7 A letter from D.T.P. Pain, secretary treasurer of the IAAF, to International Amateur Boxing Association president Rudyard Russell, dated 11 January 1967, alludes to Pain's "surprise that a meeting is being suggested in April". Pain makes clear that the IAAF sees "no reason" for this gathering to take place this year and "quite definitely" will not be represented.

8 Minutes of the meeting note that the acronym "IF" for international sports federations was used because "ISF" was the abbreviation for the International Ski Federation ("FIS" in French).

9 Minutes of the meeting of the international sports federations in Lausanne, 21–23 April 1967.

10 Minutes of the sixty-fifth IOC session in Tehran, 6–8 May 1967.

11 *ibid.*

12 Letter from Avery Brundage to William Berge Phillips, 22 May 1967.

13 Minutes of FISA congress in Vichy, 5 September 1967.

14 *ibid.*

15 Face-to-face interview with Dominik Keller and email exchanges with Beatrice Rothenbach-Seiler.

16 "You forget, we are older than they are", he reminded Tina Fisher Cunningham at one point during their interview in Bled in 1989.

17 Minutes of FISA congress in Vichy, 5 September 1967.

7. A LONG SPRINT

1 According to Christopher Dodd, the Munich 1972 rowing course was at one point "planned to end within the municipal boundaries of Dachau", but was moved a few hundred metres. *The Story of World Rowing*, Christopher Dodd, Stanley Paul, 1992, pp.390–91.

2 "The first rowing course specifically built for an Olympic Games", *ibid.*, p.295.

3 Minutes of FISA congress in Klagenfurt, 5–9 September 1969.

4 Minutes of FISA meeting in Tokyo, 7 October 1964.

5 Minutes of FISA congress in Duisburg, 24 August 1965.

6 Minutes of FISA extraordinary congress in Vienna, 13 November 1965.

7 As equestrian events for the Melbourne 1956 Games were staged in Sweden.

8 Minutes of FISA congress in Bled, 6 September 1966.

9 Letter to IOC president Avery Brundage from GAIF dated 26 April 1967.

10 Minutes of FISA congress in Vichy, 5 September 1967.

11 Details on Oswald's early years in rowing and his Mexico final taken mainly from a face-to-face interview with the author in Lausanne in 2016.

8. AN OPPORTUNITY DENIED

1 Minutes of FISA congress in Mexico City, 10 October 1968.

2 The other Swiss IOC member at this time was Marc Hodler, president of the international ski federation.

3 *The Games Must Go On: Avery Brundage and the Olympic Movement*, Allen Guttmann Columbia University Press, 1984, p.197.

4 *ibid.* p.180.

5 Minutes of the sixty-seventh session of the IOC in Mexico City, 7–11 October 1968.

6 *ibid.* Also letters from Avery Brundage to R. William Jones, president, International Amateur Basketball Federation, 24 August 1968, and to Lord Killanin, 13 and 19 January 1970.

7 Letter from Brundage to the IOC's executive board, 4 March 1969.

8 Allen Guttmann alludes to a comment made by Brundage to Willi Daume, the West German IOC member: "We need a leader, and Michael [Killanin] isn't a leader." *The Games Must Go On*, p.247. Daume is said to have recalled the remark in an interview with the author.

9 He told Tina Fisher Cunningham in Bled in 1989: "I am one of the few individuals who refused to become a member of the IOC. They are relatively rare. I refused personally to become a member of the IOC because I said I prefer rowing to the IOC."

10 *My Olympic Years*, Lord Killanin, Secker & Warburg, 1983, p.58.

11 Minutes of the IOC executive board meeting on 22 and 23 March 1969 state regarding members' expenses: "The reimbursement of expenses will be made as follows: 1) members of the executive board are reimbursed for travel, tourist class, but are responsible for their own accommodation expenses; 2) the members of commissions are reimbursed for their accommodation on the day before the meeting of the commission and on the day after – but are not exonerated from their travelling expenses."

12 Minutes of IOC executive board meetings, 5–9 June 1969, in Warsaw.

13 IOC executive board meetings in this period were generally recorded. However, on inquiring with the IOC's excellent archive service, I was told that recordings from these Warsaw proceedings do not appear to be in the collection. In any case, it is IOC policy that audio files of the executive board are for internal use only and not accessible for research purposes.

14 Telephone interview with the author, May 2015.

15 Minutes of IOC executive board meetings, 5–9 June 1969, in Warsaw.

16 *Olympic Revolution: The Olympic Biography of Juan Antonio Samaranch*, David Miller, Pavilion Books, 1992, p.246.

17 *The Games Must Go On*, p.185.

18 Thomi suggested to Brundage that the situation be reviewed in "say, two years' time".

9. A GIANT LEAP

1 Phillips, Australian president of the international swimming federation, was again unable to attend the meeting at which he was succeeded by Thomi, "because of his wife's illness".

2   Minutes of a meeting of the sub-committee of the international sports federations in Lausanne, 27 April 1968.
3   Minutes of a meeting of the General Assembly of International Sports Federations in Lausanne, 31 May–2 June 1969.
4   Noel-Baker won a silver medal in the 1500 metres at the 1920 Olympics in Antwerp and was awarded the Nobel Peace Prize in 1959. An advocate of multilateral nuclear disarmament, he had been the minister responsible for organising the 1948 Olympics, the so-called Austerity Games, in London.
5   Minutes of IOC executive board meeting in Dubrovnik, 23–27 October 1969. These minutes though also cite senior IOC member Comte Jean de Beaumont as "arguing for the IOC not to fight the permanent general assembly of NOCs".
6   Florence, Los Angeles, Montreal and Moscow (Summer); Denver, Sion, Tampere and Vancouver (Winter).
7   Minutes of GAIF general assembly in Munich, 20–22 March 1970.
8   *ibid.*
9   Minutes of IOC executive board meeting in Dubrovnik, 23–27 October 1969. Also letters from Brundage to Killanin dated 13 and 19 January 1970.
10   Letter from Brundage to Stoytchev, 12 June 1970.
11   Minutes of IOC executive board meeting in Lausanne, 21–23 February 1970.
12   In the referendum on 2 November 1969, Zürcher voted No to a bid by the convincing margin of 145,347 to 40,912. Commentators suggested that the city was doing so well at the time that it had no real need for the Games.
13   Minutes of FISA congress in Klagenfurt, 5–9 September 1969.
14   *The FISA Centenary Book*, Jean-Louis Meuret, FISA, 1992, p.149. According to minutes of the 1969 congress, FISA's governance structure comprised a five-member administrative council or board, a three-member technical commission and a three-member umpires' commission. By the following year, the umpires' commission was four-strong, while the technical commission had grown to seven, including Nely Gambon-de Vos. It was after a later reorganisation in 1978 that Gambon-de Vos became the first female member of the FISA council.
15   Minutes of FISA congress in Klagenfurt, 5–9 September 1969.
16   *The FISA Centenary Book*, pp.153–5.
17   Face-to-face interview with the author, September 2016.
18   Email exchange with Dominik Keller.
19   Record of meeting at Château de Vidy, Lausanne, 2 October 1970.

10. PERSUASION

1   Minutes of FISA congress in Copenhagen, 13 August 1963.
2   Minutes of FISA meeting in Tokyo, 7 October 1964.
3   *The Times*, 23 August 1954.
4   Minutes of FISA meeting in Tokyo, 7 October 1964.
5   Minutes of FISA congress in Mexico City, 10 October 1968. Hess beat Kabanov by forty-three votes to twenty-one. This is spite of the presence on the ballot of another western candidate, France's Jean Rodenfuser, who secured nine votes. There were also two abstentions.
6   Minutes of FISA congress in Klagenfurt, 5–9 September 1969; minutes of IOC executive board meetings in Warsaw, 5–9 June 1969.
7   Minutes of FISA congress in Klagenfurt, 5–9 September 1969.
8   Email exchanges between Ingrid Dieterle and the author.
9   Šarbochová described to me how being presented one of these medals with her sculling partner personally by Thomi was an "unforgettable experience".
10 Letter from Thomi to Avery Brundage and IOC colleagues sent to Château de Vidy, Lausanne, 18 March 1970.
11 Minutes of meeting of IOC executive board in Lausanne, 21–23 February 1970.
12 Minutes of FISA congress in St Catharines, 1 September 1970.
13 Minutes of the seventy-first IOC session in Luxembourg, 15–17 September 1971.
14 Minutes of FISA congress in Copenhagen, 17 August 1971.
15 Telephone interview with the author.
16 Minutes of the seventy-third IOC session in Munich, 21–24 August 1972.

11. GOOD TIMING

1   *Official Report of the Organizing Committee for the Games of the X Olympiad Los Angeles 1932*, p.94.
2   Face-to-face interview with the author.
3   Minutes of IOC executive board meeting, 22 and 23 March 1969.
4   According to former Longines man (and future FIFA president) Sepp Blatter, Thomi insisted at the General Assembly of International Sports Federations in Munich in 1970 that Junghans could not provide timing for the Games alone. He therefore brought Longines in. "This situation gave me personally the opportunity to be responsible for the timekeeping in this Munich Olympics," Blatter told me.
5   Blatter told me that he proposed Thomi as Swiss Timing chairman. In this account of the formation of Swiss Timing, I have also drawn on extracts

from the book *Omega Saga* kindly sent to me by Marco Richon, president of Chronométrophilia, and contemporary newspaper articles.

6 Conversation in Zurich with Beatrice Rothenbach-Seiler and her former colleagues Lonny Stöckli and Irmgard Meister.

7 Sourced from email exchanges with Beatrice Rothenbach-Seiler, who started working for Thomi in April 1986.

8 Minutes of a meeting of the IOC tripartite commission for the preparation of the Olympic congress in Munich, 28 August 1972.

9 Minutes of tripartite commission meetings on 29 May and 28 August 1972.

10 Minutes of tripartite commission meeting in Munich, 9 September 1971.

11 Letter from Thomi to Lord Killanin, IOC president, 26 October 1972.

12 Report by Thomi of a meeting with the All-China Sports Federation in Beijing, 14 April 1973.

13 Minutes of FISA congress in the Palace hotel Lucerne, 25–28 October 1973.

14 Programme of seventh annual meeting of GAIF in Oklahoma City, 21–26 May 1973, and president's annual report on GAIF activities since May 1972.

15 Letter from IOC director Monique Berlioux to Thomi, 29 August 1973.

16 *Le Figaro*, 27 September 1973.

12. BIG MAN WITH A BIG FUTURE

1 Sources include: a letter from Bulgarian IOC member General Stoytchev to Lord Killanin dated 13 April 1972; minutes of a meeting of the IOC tripartite commission for the preparation of the congress, in Lausanne, 25 June 1973; and "Undercurrents as the bikinis parade" by John Hennessy, *The Times*, 1 October 1973.

2 Minutes of meeting of IOC tripartite commission for preparation of congress in Varna, 30 September 1973.

3 Independent views: problems of international sport in competition by Thomas Keller, *Olympic Review*, November/December 1972, pp.431–36.

4 The full text of Thomi's speech is included in the Appendix.

5 "Honest opening to conference" by John Rodda, *Guardian*, 2 October 1973.

6 "New voice in an old movement" and "End to deception over genuine amateurs" by John Hennessy, *The Times*, 5 and 9 October 1973.

7 *The Olympic Games: 80 years of people, events and records* by Lord Killanin and John Rodda (ed.), Book Club Associates, 1976, p.153; *My Olympic Years* by Lord Killanin, Secker & Warburg, 1983, p.82.

8 Letter from IOC president Lord Killanin to Thomi dated 5 November 1974.

13. NEW FRIENDS

1 *Pitch Invasion: Adidas, Puma and the Making of Modern Sport*, Barbara Smit, Penguin Books, 2007, p.58.

2 Telephone interview with the author.

3 *ibid*.

4 Details from *Pitch Invasion* and from telephone interview with Jannette.

5 *The Sports Business*, Neil Wilson, Piatkus, 1988, pp.176–78.

6 Like Horst Dassler, Davidge attended the 1956 Olympic Games which Thomi missed, rowing in the Great Britain eight.

7 Interview with the author.

8 Havelange too had been at the 1956 Olympic Games, serving as *chef de mission* for the Brazil delegation.

9 *Pitch Invasion*, p.157.

10 Email exchange with the author.

11 Telephone interview with Jannette and *Pitch Invasion*, p.182.

12 Minutes of FISA congress in Lucerne, 25–28 October 1973.

13 The average weight of a crew, excluding coxswain, was limited to 70kg, as was the weight of single scullers. No other individual oarsman could weigh more than 72.5kg.

14 Minutes of meeting of IOC tripartite commission, Lausanne, 4 June 1974. According to author Allen Guttmann, the network ABC had secured the US rights with an offer of $25 million. The Games generated $34.9 million in broadcasting revenue in all, approximately double the Munich 1972 total.

15 Minutes of FISA congress in Nottingham, 25 August 1975.

16 Minutes of FISA congress in Lucerne, 3 September 1974.

17 *Daily Telegraph* obituary of Palmer, published 20 August 2001, and interview with Patrick Nally.

18 It is also worth noting that another US bidder, Lake Placid, was competing for the 1980 Winter Olympics, to be awarded on the same day. Lake Placid duly got the better of Vancouver–Garibaldi, its Canadian rival, and walked off with this consolation prize for the United States. Another US city, Denver, was originally awarded the 1976 Winter Games, but subsequently withdrew.

19 *My Olympic Years*, Lord Killanin, Secker & Warburg, 1983, pp.5 and 168.

14. SITTING PRETTY

1 Minutes of FISA congress in Montreal, 17 July 1976.

2 *The Oxford Olympics Study 2016: Cost and Cost Overrun at the Games* by Bent Flyvbjerg, Allison Stewart and Alexander Budzier. The 720% figure is for sports-related cost overruns.

3 *My Olympic Years*, Lord Killanin, Secker & Warburg, 1983, pp.120 and 137.

4 Minutes of FISA congress in Nottingham, 25 August 1975.

5 Letter from Thomi to Lord Killanin, IOC president, dated 20 May 1975.

6 Minutes of tripartite commission meeting in Lausanne, 24 May 1975.

7 *My Olympic Years*, pp.123–24.

8 Letter from Lord Killanin to His Excellency Ambassador C.O.R. Rousseau, president and commissioner general of the Montreal 1976 organising committee, dated 29 May 1975.

9 Letter from Thomi to Lord Killanin, dated 3 July 1975.

10 *My Olympic Years*, pp.124–25.

11 Minutes of FISA congress in Montreal, 17 July 1976.

12 *ibid.*

13 According to Dominik Keller, when Queen Elizabeth II came to watch the rowing finals, she mentioned to the FISA president that it would be fun to follow a race. This would be easy, Thomi replied. The vehicle he used for this purpose was ready near the grandstand. And so off they went, to the consternation of those responsible for security and protocol.

14 Face-to-face interview with the author.

15 Another medallist at these Games was future IOC member Anita DeFrantz, who was part of the US eight that placed third behind the German Democratic Republic and the Soviet Union.

16 Telephone interview with the author.

17 Interview with Patrick Nally and *Pitch Invasion: Adidas, Puma and the Making of Modern Sport*, Barbara Smit, Penguin Books, 2007, p.179.

15. THE PICTURESQUE PRINCIPALITY

1 The Swiss boat including Oswald finished second, behind France.

2 Interview with the author.

3 Minutes of FISA congress in Amsterdam, 23 August 1977.

4 *The FISA Centenary Book*, Jean-Louis Meuret, FISA, 1992, p.190.

5 Interview with the author.

6 Interview with the author.

7 *Pitch Invasion: Adidas, Puma and the Making of Modern Sport*, Barbara Smit, Penguin Books, 2007, p.160. Tellingly, Dassler controlled 55% of SMPI shares and West Nally 45%.

8 "For a week, Barcelona will be a hive of intense Olympic activity," Samaranch boasted in an article bearing his distinctive signature in the September/October 1976 edition of *Olympic Review*.

9 Speech by Juan Antonio Samaranch, IOC member, welcoming GAIF members to Barcelona in October 1976.

10 FISA president's annual report included in minutes of FISA congress in Amsterdam, 23 August 1977.

11 *ibid.*

12 FISA president's annual report included in minutes of FISA congress in Hamilton, New Zealand, 30 and 31 October 1978.

13 A crutch is visible in a snapshot of the occasion supplied by Patrick Nally, who was also there. This may be a consequence of a bad knee or of circulation problems starting to become more manifest. Dominik Keller remembers him suffering from two embolisms in the heart region. "Once he said it was like death creeping up from the bottom of the body," Dominik told me. On that occasion, the sensation stopped when it reached chest level.

16. POWER, VODKA AND LARGE SIBERIAN DOGS

1 *Pitch Invasion: Adidas, Puma and the Making of Modern Sport*, Barbara Smit, Penguin Books, 2007, p.180.

2 Telephone interview with the author.

3 *Olympic Revolution: The Olympic Biography of Juan Antonio Samaranch*, David Miller, Pavilion Books, 1994, p.4. Spain had reopened diplomatic relations with the USSR in 1977 for the first time in sixty years.

4 Details on Siberian dogs from *Pitch Invasion*, telephone interview with Christian Jannette, email exchanges with Beatrice Rothenbach-Seiler, and interview with Patrick Nally.

5 Part of Nally's proposal to Moscow 1980 may be read here: http://westnally.com/past-projects/olympic-developments-including-moscow-1980/

6 The US intelligence assessment may be found here: https://archive.org/stream/OlympicBoycottCIA/Olympic%20Boycott%20CIA_djvu.txt

7 *Official Report of the Games of the XXII Olympiad*, p.501.

8 Minutes of FISA congress in Bled, 4 September 1979.

9 Details on 1978 world championships from 1979 FISA congress minutes and *The FISA Centenary Book*, Jean-Louis Meuret, FISA, 1992, pp.192–94.

10 Klaus Filter comments taken from email exchanges with the author.

11 Minutes of FISA congress in Hamilton, 30 and 31 October 1978.

12 Minutes of IOC tripartite commission meeting in Prague, 12 June 1977.

13 Statement from the tripartite commission of the IOC, 20 March 1978; "IOC Rebukes UNESCO On Olympics Interference", *New York Times*, 21 March 1978.

14 Letter from Thomi to IOC director Monique Berlioux dated 13 January 1978.

15 Minutes of FISA congress in Moscow, 19 July 1980.

16 Minutes of GAISF annual meeting in Monte Carlo, 18–20 October 1979.

17 Minutes of 1979 International Judo Federation congress.

18 Minutes of FISA congress in Hamilton, 30 and 31 October 1978.

19 Minutes of FISA congress in Bled, 4 September 1979.

20 Los Angeles 1984's Peter Ueberroth recalls attending a wedding party for Vázquez Raña's daughter on his estate in Mexico City in his book, *Made in America*. "While showing us the sumptuous grounds," Ueberroth writes, "he'd led us past his own private soccer field and tennis courts toward a large, caged area. Inside, we were shocked to see a huge bear. 'A gift from the Moscow organising committee,' Vázquez had explained."

17. IGNORING MARGARET THATCHER

1 Final report of the XIII Olympic Winter Games Lake Placid 1980, p.68.

2 This presentation is mentioned in the book *Omega Saga*, relevant extracts of which were sent to me by Marco Richon, president of Chronométrophilia in Bienne. Los Angeles 1932 marked the start of Omega's long relationship with the Olympic Games.

3 *My Olympic Years*, Lord Killanin, Secker & Warburg, 1983, p.181.

4 "Nations play the Olympic power and glory game" by Gareth Parry, *Guardian*, 18 March 1980.

5 "Keller puts it straight" by John Rodda, *Guardian*, 22 March 1980.

6 FISA president's annual report included in minutes of FISA congress in Moscow, 19 July 1980.

7 "Duke joins Olympic protest on boycotts", *The Times*, 23 April 1980.

8 *My Olympic Years*, pp.195–96.

9 *My Olympic Years*, p.220. Four New Zealand athletes competed as independents.

10 *Olympic Revolution: The Olympic biography of Juan Antonio Samaranch*, David Miller, Pavilion Books, 1994, p.12.

11 *My Olympic Years*, pp.198–99.

12 Letter from Thomi to IOC tripartite commission members, 1 July 1980; letter to Thomi from IOC president Lord Killanin, 10 July 1980.

13 *My Olympic Years*, p.229.

14 Mollet was a former modern pentathlete who suffered a bad fall at the London Olympics in 1948. His *Daily Telegraph* obituary on 19 August 2002 described him as "the most notable Belgian sporting figure of the last century".

15 Thomi had initially used the phrase "Soviet intervention in Afghanistan", but had agreed to modify it.

16 FISA president's annual report included in minutes of FISA congress in Moscow, 19 July 1980.

17 *My Olympic Years*, p.217.

18 Telephone interview with the author.

19 Interview with the author.

20 The issue was whether the gadgets should be included in the minimum weight.

21 Interview with the author.

18. A NEW SHADOW

1 Soviet rowers also won nine of the fourteen silver medals.

2 Howald, head of the scientific research laboratory at the Swiss federal sports school at Magglingen, was elected to replace Ludwig Prokop on the FISA technical commission in 1974.

3 Minutes of FISA congress in Montreal, 17 July 1976.

4 Minutes of FISA congress in Amsterdam, 23 August 1977.

5 "Two Russian athletes in drugs ban" by Jim Railton, *The Times*, 16 June 1980; "Russians shipwrecked", *Guardian*, 16 June 1980.

6 "War declared on drugs in rowing", by Jim Railton, *The Times*, 19 July 1980. Thomi also disclosed, rather embarrassingly, that a third rower, a Swede, had failed a test taken at Lucerne, this time for ephedrine. However, he had "turned up with a nasal spray he was using when picked out for a random test". His disqualification period was set at six months. He was said to be present in Moscow as a boatman. Thomi said, with his characteristic empathy for athletes, that he would like to "have a drink and talk to this young oarsman".

7 Minutes of FISA congress in Garching, 31 August and 1 September 1981.

8 Minutes of FISA congress in Lucerne, 21 August 1982.

9 Minutes of FISA congress in Duisburg, 27 August 1983.

10 Minutes of FISA congress in Lucerne, 15 June 1984.

11 "We are certainly the first...", transcript of interview with Thomi Keller by Tina Fisher Cunningham, Fisher Forde Media, in Bled, Yugoslavia, 1989. According to one former volunteer, those dispatched to collect samples

would travel in pairs, one male and one female, one from the Eastern Bloc and one from the West.

12 *The Story of World Rowing*, Christopher Dodd, Stanley Paul, 1992, p.138.

19. POST-MOSCOW BLUES

1 Minutes of IOC tripartite commission meeting in Monte Carlo, 29 and 30 September 1980.

2 *Olympic Revolution: The Olympic biography of Juan Antonio Samaranch*, David Miller, Pavilion Books, 1994, p.27.

3 *Made in America*, Peter Ueberroth (with Richard Levin and Amy Quinn), Kingswood Press, 1986, pp.87–88. Ueberroth was appointed in March 1979.

4 Minutes of FISA congress in Bled, 4 September 1979.

5 Letter from Thomi to his friend Pablo Span dated 11 December 1979.

6 Minutes of FISA congress in Moscow, 19 July 1980.

7 *Made in America*, p.89; minutes of FISA congress in Garching, 31 August and 1 September 1981.

8 Interview with the author. The Games eventually produced a surplus of some $228 million.

9 "Bringing the Olympics Home" by Anna Sklar, *Los Angeles City Historical Society Newsletter*, vol.XLVI, issue 2 August 2013. Rene Henry told me via email that he and Thomi became good friends. He said he was subsequently approached by another timing company to represent them, but declined while advising them not to spend money on a bid owing to their lack of experience in sports timing. The *Official Report for Los Angeles 1984* confirms that requirements for timing and measurement services were handled by Swiss Timing. It states: "After soliciting bids from a number of potential timing sponsors, Swiss Timing was chosen and included in a sponsorship agreement with the [organising committee] in conjunction with Westinghouse."

10 Minutes of FISA congress in Moscow, 19 July 1980.

11 Interview with the author; minutes of FISA congress in Garching, 31 August and 1 September 1981.

12 Letter from Monique Berlioux, IOC director, to international Olympic sports federation presidents dated 24 October 1980.

13 Minutes of IOC tripartite commission meetings in Baden-Baden, 23 January 1981 and Lausanne, 3 June 1981.

14 "Unheralded Sports Exert a Pull, Too" by Ira Berkow, *New York Times*, 28 July 1981.

15 Turin.

16 *Running Scared: How athletics lost its innocence*, Steven Downes and Duncan Mackay, Mainstream, 1996, p.131.

20. DIVIDE AND RULE

1 *Olympic Revolution: The Olympic biography of Juan Antonio Samaranch*, David Miller, Pavilion Books, 1994, pp.21 and 27.
2 Flor Isava Fonseca from Venezuela and Pirjo Häggman from Finland.
3 *Olympic Revolution*, p.27.
4 Minutes of an ad hoc meeting of the Olympic summer and winter federations in the Salle du Ponant, Centre de Rencontres in Monte Carlo, 16 October 1981.
5 *ibid.*
6 Eulogy to Thomas Keller delivered by Peter Coni at St Peter's Church in Zurich, 6 October 1989.
7 Email exchange with the author.
8 Minutes of fifteenth GAISF general assembly at the Centre de Rencontres in Monte Carlo, 15–17 October 1981.
9 Telephone interview with the author. In 1981 Kasper was secretary-general of the International Ski Federation. He would go on to become president and to serve as an IOC member. In spite of the chasm between them, I think even Samaranch was sometimes awestruck at the depth of Thomi's dedication to his sport.
10 *Olympic Revolution*, pp.27–28.
11 Minutes of fifteenth GAISF general assembly, 15–17 October 1981.
12 *Olympic Revolution*, p.28.
13 *Olympic Revolution*, p.28.
14 President/secretary-general's report in minutes of sixteenth GAISF general assembly in Monte Carlo, 12–16 October 1982.
15 Minutes of GAISF extraordinary meeting in Monte Carlo, 13 October 1982.
16 *Olympic Revolution*, p.28.
17 President/secretary-general's report in minutes of 1982 GAISF general assembly.
18 *Olympic Revolution*, p.29.
19 Email exchange with the author.
20 Letter from Primo Nebiolo to Juan Antonio Samaranch dated 20 July 1983.
21 *Olympic Revolution*, p.29.
22 Summary of the constitutive meeting of the international summer Olympic federations at the Palace hotel in Lausanne, 30 May 1983.

23 Minutes of the meeting of ASOIF at the Palace hotel in Lausanne, 31 May 1983.

24 *The Official History of the Olympic Games and the IOC*, David Miller, Mainstream, 2012, p.238.

21. FOR WHOM THE BELL TOLLS

1   Minutes of FISA congress in Duisburg, 27 August 1983.

2   Email exchange with the author. Rothenbach-Seiler says that some months after Thomi's death she travelled to Argentina and saw the original Tronador – "a huge mountain covered in snow".

3   Face-to-face interview with the author. Way says the engineer who completed Tronador's engine was called Ken Woodham.

4   Face-to-face interview in Zurich with Irmgard Meister.

5   According to the Union of International Associations' *Open Yearbook*.

6   Minutes of fifteenth GAISF general assembly in Monte Carlo, 15–17 October 1981.

7   President's report in minutes of FISA congress in Duisburg, 27 August 1983.

8   President's report in minutes of FISA congress in Lucerne, 21 August 1982.

9   Face-to-face interview with the author.

10 Minutes of FISA congress in Duisburg, 27 August 1983.

11 Minutes of FISA congress in Lucerne, 21 August 1982.

12 Minutes of FISA congress in Duisburg, 27 August 1983.

13 *The Official History of the Olympic Games and the IOC*, David Miller, Mainstream, 2012, p.239.

14 Face-to-face interview with the author. According to the minutes of the June 1984 FISA congress in Lucerne, a SFr50,000 per annum post for co-operation and development was also provided for within the FISA budget.

15 *The Story of World Rowing*, Christopher Dodd, Stanley Paul, 1992, pp.133–34.

16 Minutes of FISA congress in Lucerne, 15 June 1984.

17 Minutes of FISA congress in Lucerne, 21 August 1982.

18 Christopher Davidge obituary, *The Times*, 9 January 2015.

19 Email exchange with the author.

20 Letter from Juan Antonio Samaranch to Thomi dated 31 July 1984.

21 Telephone interview with the author. Bakinowski says Hunt-Wesson Foods corporate officers were "thrilled" that their logo had been seen on television as cameras focused on the bows of the US boats during the first days of racing. Several photographs of US rowers posing as they removed the logos from their shells were distributed.

22 President's report in minutes of FISA congress in Antwerp, 26 August 1985.

22. LIGHTWEIGHTS, SANDWICH-MEN AND THE BEGINNING OF THE END

1   An account of events surrounding ISL's foundation in late-1982 can be found in *Pitch Invasion: Adidas, Puma and the Making of Modern Sport*, Barbara Smit, Penguin Books, 2007, pp.193ff. Dassler's *volte-face* affected Nally profoundly. "I was on a trajectory that was taking me to the moon in a very short period until 1982," he told me. "I became a pariah until the day ISL collapsed... For a whole period of my life, it was like I never existed. The only nice thing is I saw my kids grow up." ISL collapsed, amid controversy, in 2001. The IOC had severed its ties with the agency in 1996, nine years after Dassler's premature death aged fifty-one.

2   Letter to Thomi from ISL deputy managing director Jürgen Lenz dated 11 July 1984. Just over a year earlier, Dassler had submitted ideas on the development of an Olympic marketing programme in a video to the 1983 IOC session in New Delhi. As outlined by Michael Payne – the former West Nally and ISL executive who went on to become the first IOC marketing director – in his book *Olympic Turnaround* (2005), Dassler's message was: "You, the International Olympic Committee, own the most valuable and sought-after property in the world. Yet the Olympic rings are the most unexploited trademark in existence. No major corporation in the world would tolerate such a situation."

3   Hempel's comments are taken from an extended, two-part article on ISL by Christian Gerig, published in October 1985 by a German-language magazine called *Werbewoche*. I came across an English translation of this during research, as I recall in the FISA archive. Hempel also observed that "the people in Bienne were very uncooperative" regarding an athletics programme ISL was marketing. This was perhaps not altogether surprising, given that the head of world athletics was Primo Nebiolo, the Italian who was also president of ASOIF, the body whose foundation had enabled IOC president Juan Antonio Samaranch to emasculate GAISF and undermine Thomi.

4   *Olympic Turnaround*, Michael Payne, London Business Press, 2005, pp.83–84.

5   Email exchanges with the author.

6   A detailed account of these negotiations can be found in *Olympic Turnaround*, pp.24ff.

7   Minutes of extraordinary FISA congress at Parco dei Principi hotel in Rome, 10–18 January 1985.

8   Minutes of FISA congress in Nottingham, 16 August 1986.

9   *Guardian*, 12 and 14 July 1986.

10 Medical commission report in minutes of FISA congress in Antwerp, 26 August 1985.

11 Minutes of extraordinary FISA congress in Rome, 12 January 1985.

12 Letter from Juan Antonio Samaranch to Thomi dated 11 February 1985.

13 Minutes of FISA congress in Antwerp, 26 August 1985.

14 Minutes of FISA congress in Nottingham, 16 August 1986.

15 *FISA Centenary Book*, Jean-Louis Meuret, FISA, 1992, p.222.

16 Minutes of FISA congress in Antwerp, 26 August 1985.

17 Face-to-face interview with the author.

18 It seems Thomi continued to lead in his autocratic style right up to the end. The International Ski Federation's Gian Franco Kasper remembers getting a phone call from him in 1986 while in Finland. Thomi told him he had just made him a member of the GAISF council. "I knew what GAISF was, but that was all," Kasper told me. "He liked young people who were sports-minded; that was the only reason. I am still a member."

19 President's annual report included in FISA Bulletin 1988.

23. THE STATE OF DENMARK

1   Annual presidential reports in FISA Bulletins for 1987 and 1988.

2   Frank Keating wrote a vivid short portrait of Coni published in the *Guardian* under the headline "I am the ruler of the Queen's regatta" on 2 July 1988.

3   Interview with the author.

4   Annual presidential report in FISA Bulletin for 1988.

5   Letter to Thomi from William P. Breen, president of ISL Marketing USA, dated 4 August 1988.

6   Letter to Thomi from Paula Oyer dated 14 December 1987.

7   Minutes of FISA congress in Brøndby, 22 August 1987.

8   Letter to Thomi from Dan Bakinowski dated 10 January 1989.

9   English translation of 3M product list dated 25 May 1988.

10 Letter to Thomi from Dan Bakinowski dated 4 November 1988.

11 Telephone interview with the author. Oyer/Berezin came to rowing from synchronised swimming.

12 Interview with the author.

13 "British pair just miss golden double" by Christopher Dodd, *Guardian*, 31 August 1987.

14 Interview with the author.
15 *Guardian*, 31 August 1987.
16 Interview with the author.

24. WHEN I'M SIXTY-FIVE

1 Minutes of FISA congress in Brøndby, 22 August 1987.
2 Minutes of FISA congress in Lucerne, 15 June 1984.
3 Interview with John Coates, Australian IOC member, former coxswain and president from 1983–88 of the Australian Rowing Council. According to additional details supplied by John Boultbee, Thomi was returning from the rowing course, en route to a dinner in Devonport, when he saw a possum on the road. He apparently stopped and tried to pet the animal, with predictable consequences.
4 FISA Information 5/89, 15 October 1989.
5 Email exchanges and interview with the author.
6 Minutes of FISA congress in Bled, 2 September 1989.
7 Email exchanges and interview with the author.
8 Ingrid Dieterle kindly agreed to put some questions to Helga Hess, Claus's wife, on my behalf and to relay the answers. Helga said that Thomi had often asked her to persuade Claus to run for president but that he had declined. Hess felt that a Swiss national should continue to hold the position.
9 Minutes of FISA congress in Duisburg, 27 August 1983.
10 President's annual report published in FISA Bulletin 1990.
11 Secretary-general's annual report published in FISA Bulletin 1990.
12 Details provided by Helga Hess via Ingrid Dieterle. Helga organised provision of VIP food at the rowing venue, including lunch on the day of Princess Anne's visit.
13 Interview with the author.
14 Minutes of FISA extraordinary congress in Athens, 26–28 January 1989.
15 Minutes of FISA congress in Seoul, 16 September 1988.
16 Telephone interview with the author. Pratt also said that while the ARA leadership thought Oswald very efficient, there was concern that if Thomi stepped down East German council member Wilfried Hofmann might be pushed into power.
17 *The FISA Centenary Book*, Jean-Louis Meuret, FISA, 1992, p.247.
18 This is inexact: Schurter worked in such an office but did not manage it.
19 The memo is in a collection of research materials given by author Christopher Dodd to the River & Rowing Museum at Henley-on-Thames.
20 Telephone interview with the author.

21 Email exchange with the author. Boultbee first told Thomi of his interest in the position at the athletics stadium in Seoul, at a time when it looked like the role would go to another candidate.

25. CHECKMATE

1 President's annual report published in FISA Bulletin 1990. September 1989 was the month when constitutional amendments to introduce parliamentary democracy to Slovenia were passed. The first democratic election was held in April 1990.
2 President's annual report published in FISA Bulletin 1990.
3 Report of the Committee of Management, Henley Royal Regatta, 1989.
4 "Nebiolo is almost out for the count" by John Rodda, *Guardian*, 27 April 1989.
5 Minutes of FISA congress in Bled, 2 and 8 September 1989.
6 Email exchange with the author.
7 Telephone interview with Helga and Claus Hess conducted on the author's behalf by Ingrid Dieterle, former women's rowing commission member.
8 *ibid.*
9 Email exchange with the author.
10 Telephone interview with the author.
11 I found a copy of Thomi's telex, along with an official invitation, stamped by the Chinese Olympic Committee and referencing Thomi's passport number, 1701680, in FISA's archive in Lausanne.
12 Transcript of interview with Thomi Keller by Tina Fisher Cunningham, Fisher Forde Media, in Bled, Yugoslavia, 1989.

26. TOO EARLY

1 Interview with the author.
2 Email exchanges with Dominik Keller.
3 Eulogy for Thomi delivered by Peter Coni in St Peter's church in Zurich on 6 October 1989; also fax from Beatrice Rothenbach-Seiler, Thomi's personal assistant, to Christopher Dodd dated 21 September 1989.
4 Interview with the author.
5 *ibid.*
6 Email exchange with the author.
7 "Thomas Keller – battling for amateurism in Olympic sport", *The Times*, 3 October 1989.
8 Thomas Keller obituary, *Independent*, 2 October 1989.

9 Coni's eulogy.
10 FISA Information 5/89, 15 October 1989.
11 Email exchange with the author.
12 FISA Information 5/89, 15 October 1989.
13 The words "without" and "unfairness" are each underlined.
14 *The Story of World Rowing*, Christopher Dodd, Stanley Paul, 1992, p.ix.
15 Elsewhere in the newsletter, reference is made to a new contract with the Swiss agency Telesport. This "guarantees FISA and the organising committee SFr600,000 for the TV transmission rights of the world rowing championships in 1989 and 1990, and SFr700,000 in 1991 and 1993, as opposed to the [European Broadcasting Union]'s last payment of SFr250,000". (1992 was a Summer Olympic year.)

AFTERWORD

1 Email exchanges with Beatrice Rothenbach-Seiler, Thomi's personal assistant from April 1986.
2 Thomi's reply to an introductory letter from Reggie Alexander, an experienced IOC member from Kenya, dated 23 June 1986, encapsulates his dismay. "I am also deeply concerned as to where we are going," he writes. "Some of today's sportsleaders seem to be far more interested in promoting their own ego and their personal interests than working for the good of sports."
3 Grainger recently entered the realm of sports administration as chair of UK Sport.
4 *Olympic Revolution: The Olympic biography of Juan Antonio Samaranch*, David Miller, Pavilion Books, 1992, p.29.

Index

239